ELEMENTARY LITERACY LESSONS

CASES AND COMMENTARIES FROM THE FIELD

ELEMENTARY LITERACY LESSONS

CASES AND COMMENTARIES FROM THE FIELD

Janet C. Richards

University of Southern Mississippi

and

Joan P. Gipe

University of New Orleans (Professor Emerita)

California State University, Sacramento

LAWRENCE ERLBAUM ASSOCIATES, PUBLISHERS

2000   Mahwah, New Jersey   London

Copyright © 2000 by Lawrence Erlbaum Associates, Inc.

Lawrence Erlbaum Associates, Inc., Publishers
10 Industrial Avenue
Mahwah, NJ 07430

Cover design by Kathryn Houghtaling Lacey

Library of Congress Cataloging-in-Publication Data

Richards, Janet C.
Elementary literacy lessons : cases and commentaries from the field /
   Janet C. Richards, Joan P. Gipe.
      p. cm.
   Includes bibliographical references and index.
   ISBN 0-8058-2988-1 (paper : alk. paper).
   1. Language arts (Elementary)—United States Case studies.
      2. Student teachers—United States Case studies. I. Gipe, Joan P.
      II. Title.
   LB1576.R517 1999
   372.6'044 —dc21   99-30243
                                                                        CIP

Books published by Lawrence Erlbaum Associates are printed
on acid-free paper, and their bindings are chosen for strength and
durability.

Printed in the United States of America
10   9   8   7   6   5   4   3   2   1

To many wonderful people—my students; my husband, Paul; my sons and their wives, David and Allison, Matthew and Missy; and to my grandchildren, Elizabeth, Madeline, and Noah.

—JCR

To all of my former and current students who have taught me so much over the years. You always will be special to me.

—JPG

Contents

3   INDIVIDUAL AND GROUP MANAGEMENT CONCERNS   25

LITERACY CONCEPTS AND TERMS   25

OVERVIEW   25

4   SPEAKING AND LISTENING   47

LITERACY CONCEPTS AND TERMS   47

OVERVIEW   47

Contributors

CASE WRITERS

We are indebted to the following preservice teachers at the University of New Orleans and the University of Southern Mississippi. Their teaching cases serve as the nucleus of this text.

Julie Applewhite
Brandi Aquilo
Ashley Armington
Tashia Aroyo
Kathryn Blackwell
Kristen Boyce
Renee Breaux
Sharon Brown
Rebecca Clemens
Malinda Cooper
Kristine Denning
Heather Friloux
Amy Gex
Stacy Gorum
Linda Griggs
Christal Hammond
Ruth Hayes
Michael Jackson
Alicia Marx
Renee Mauffray
Lynne McDonald
Denise Nelon
Kim Anh T. Nguyen
Karyn Pennison
Rachel Reilly
Jennifer Schrable
Heather Stevens
Patricia Suter
Marie Turner
Wendy Van Belle
Colleen Vizzini
George West

COMMENTARY WRITERS

We also are grateful to the following commentary writers—a cadre of skilled classroom teachers and teacher educators who work in diverse educational settings throughout the United States and in Canada.

Terri Austin, Alaska

Mary Alice Barksdale-Ladd, Florida

John Barnitz, Louisiana

Camille Blachowicz, Illinois

Beverly Bruneau, Ohio

Kathryn Carr, Missouri

David Clarke, Louisiana

Lauren Combs, Mississippi

Connie Crichton, California

Janice DiVincenzo, Illinois

Martha Eshelman, Missouri

Bruce Fischman, Pennsylvania

Fredda Fischman, Pennsylvania

Mary Gobert, Mississippi

Margaret Genesio, Wisconsin

Suzanne Gespass, New Jersey

Bill Gilluly, Nevada

Dana Grisham, California

Karen Parker Guillot, Louisiana

Lynda Hagey, United States Department of Defense Schools

Shirley Howlette, Nevada

Miriam Jones, Mississippi

Susan Lensky, Illinois

Jill Lewis, New Jersey

A. J. Long, Arizona

Nancy Masztal, Mississippi

Mary McCroskey, Montana

Kathleen McKenna, Illinois

Marilyn McKinney, Nevada

Maria Meyerson, Nevada

Tom Nass, Iowa

Margaret Olson, Canada

Jennifer Opitz, Florida

Elaine Kane Owens, Illinois

Katherine Perez, California

Elizabeth Pickell, Missouri

Timothy Rasinski, Ohio

Darlene Sellers, Mississippi

Diane Sullivan, Illinois

Bonnie Stiles, Illinois

Karyn Wellhousen, Louisiana

Foreword

Working Together From Stories

Nel Noddings, Professor of Education
Stanford University, California

There was a time when most of human wisdom was passed from one generation to another in stories. Today, although most of us love a good story, we get our knowledge through direct instruction and planned courses of study. Often, we spend years absorbing information intended to prepare us for future needs. Much of what we painstakingly acquire turns out to be as irrelevant as we suspected it would be when we were students. Unfortunately, many preservice teachers share the young student's complaints. They assess their formal preparation for teaching as too theoretical or, at worst, totally useless. Yet, experienced teachers have tremendous reservoirs of knowledge—experientially acquired wisdom that could be used effectively in teacher education.

Both stories and formal instruction can be offered in two general ways. We can tell stories that we have chosen by whatever means we believe defensible. The stories need not have direct relevance to the listener's present needs; they become part of the curriculum because we think their message will some day be useful. This is the way most of the school curriculum is chosen. The difference between stories and other material selected in this fashion is that stories often have dramatic appeal. They are usually more exciting than the regular curriculum and, for that reason, they may be remembered longer. They may be useful when recalled. The second way is to offer stories (or indirect instruction) in response to the expressed needs of students. This way requires a large repertoire, mastery of the subject matter, and considerable artistry.

In learning to teach, most of us have profited from well-chosen stories. I think of *Goodbye Mr Chips* (Hilton, 1986), *To Sir With Love* (Braithwaite, 1990), *The Prime of Miss Jean Brodie* (Spark, 1989), *The Blackboard Jungle* (Hunter, 1994), *Out of the Dark* (Katz, 1996), *Good Morning Miss Dove* (Patton, 1954), *Hoosier Schoolmaster* (Eggleston, 1984), and many others. Some of these stories inspire us with examples we will strive to emulate; others appall us and elicit vows that we will never, never be "like that." But the really great stories come when a professor or teacher pauses in regular lessons and says, "Let me tell you what happened to me once." When the teacher is a fine one, these are wonderful moments. We are taken back to an earlier time when the aspiring young learned through the stories of their elders. Because these stories are told in response to an immediate problem, they are vital.

This volume blends the two basic approaches. It presents stories—short narratives of actual teaching problems selected because they have a high probability of relevance for beginning teachers. In response to the stories, teacher educators and experienced teachers comment. The result is a useful blend of theory and practice. Some recommendations come from theoretical perspectives, but these are almost always offered as "things to try." Other recommendations are based on the concrete experiences of master teachers. All are presented in the context of further questions to be asked and alternatives that might be available. They are presented lovingly, with the clear desire to help and support instead of admonish and correct.

Both the stories and the responses are convincingly real. Readers will find themselves arguing with some of the writers and generating their own solutions to the problems described so vividly. As I read the stories, I thought again and again how hard it is to teach young students who are compelled to attend classes, and how enormously difficult it is to teach well in certain circumstances. Students come to their early classes eager or fearful, ready or dismally unready, happy or sad, cooperative or angry, trusting or deeply distrustful, bright or slow, in tune or off tune. Each one needs a caring and competent teacher. For the past 25 years, I have taught, for the most part, graduate students who have chosen to study with me. Even then, teaching well is a challenge. To teach the young, for whom so much is at stake, is worthy of heroes. This practical, inspiring book will help.

Preface

No textbook can ever come close to describing the real-life scenarios we encounter out in the field. We've learned firsthand about group management techniques, the importance of thorough planning, how to motivate students, ways to present reading and language arts lessons, and the problems and concerns teachers face and try to solve daily—like how to help children who can't read or write, or what to say when a child says his father is in prison. Textbooks can never prepare us for all that we need to know.

(Preservice teacher's journal excerpt, December 1998)

INSPIRATIONS

We think this is a most unusual and practical methods textbook. Like the majority of elementary reading/language arts texts in the field, its purpose is to help prepare you to support the literacy learning needs of all students, including academically, linguistically, and culturally diverse students in Grades K–6. However, this book differs considerably from most conventional texts currently offered: It contains original teaching cases written by preservice teachers just like you, who work in field-based literacy courses. Their authentic cases candidly and poignantly describe each of their plans, problems, hopes, disappointments, dilemmas, and reflective thinking as they address the multilayered complexities and ambiguities associated with learning to teach reading and language arts in elementary classrooms.

Our work with preservice teachers in elementary schools served as an inspiration for the book, and their voices are a major part of the text. Writing in the first person, they describe their very early teaching experiences; the questions and dilemmas they encounter working with young literacy learners, special needs students, and those who are linguistically and culturally diverse; and their concerns about enhancing students' reading, writing, listening, and speaking abilities. They also confront family and environmental influences on students' literacy development, as well as individual and group management issues. Their teaching stories reveal glimpses of literacy instruction, and allow us to enter real classrooms and experience the wide varieties of situations that reading/language arts teachers encounter daily. Through their narratives we come to understand that we can neither oversimplify the intertwined processes of teaching and learning, nor overgeneralize solutions to instructional dilemmas. Moreover, most problematic teaching situations are connected to other underlying and related teaching concerns that must be identified, considered, studied, and resolved. In short, teaching is complex, fraught with ambiguities, and full of problematic situations.

OVERVIEW AND FEATURES

The text is organized into 12 chapters. Each chapter begins with a listing of critical or potentially new concepts and terms to alert you to what might be unfamiliar vocabulary. We strongly support the use of the International Reading Association's *The Literacy Dictionary* (Harris & Hodges, 1995) as an additional aid to help you understand the concepts and terms listed.

Chapter 1 provides practical information about the specific attributes of well-constructed cases. This chapter also offers guidelines for writing your own case narratives that can help you examine your own professional development or illuminate your professional expertise. For example, cases might be included in your teaching portfolio, or they can be shared and discussed in collegial peer conversation groups.

Chapters 2 through 12 focus on aspects of literacy instruction that we believe are essential for supporting elementary students' reading, writing, listening, speaking, and thinking abilities. Although many of the cases in these chapters involve primary-level classrooms (Grades 1–3), we believe that good instructional strategies are appropriate for any grade level. Likewise, many of the strategies discussed in the cases are equally successful for content areas (e.g., K-W-L), and for whole- or small-group instruction.

You also should note that although each chapter contains cases that are grouped according to specific dimensions of literacy theory and pedagogy, just as in real classrooms there are other potential issues woven throughout each case that can be discussed. Thus, it is possible to conduct cross-case analyses and discussions of similar teaching concerns that run throughout chapters, such as dealing with easily distracted or unmotivated students, or providing for academic diversity.

Each case is accompanied by commentaries written by experienced teacher educators and skilled classroom teachers. The commentaries provide scholarly, and sometimes contrasting, perspectives and approaches through which you might consider the issues presented in the cases (see L. Shulman, 1992). However, these commentaries represent only two perspectives on the case. You are encouraged to explore and consider as many perspectives and issues as possible regarding each case.

Each chapter contains consumable Applications and Reflections exercises that will help you take an active part in analyzing, documenting, and talking about the particular issues portrayed in the case narratives. The questions in the Applications and Reflections exercises also can be used to guide your own case writing initiatives. Annotated bibliographies of suggested readings are provided at the end of each chapter to help you construct more in-depth knowledge of the instructional strategies and activities discussed in the teaching cases and the holistic, constructivist framework undergirding the lessons contained within each chapter. Margin references direct you to correlated readings for the strategies and parallel concepts mentioned in the cases and commentaries.

SUGGESTIONS FOR USING THE CASEBOOK

The chapters and cases in this text (with the exception of chap. 1) are not meant to be read and discussed in any particular order. Users of the text should select cases for discussion based on their own personal needs and situations. However, we do recommend that chapter 1 be read first, especially by those who are unfamiliar with the concept of teaching cases. The topics presented in each chapter represent the most common issues that arose for our preservice teachers. As such, the content of this text shares authentic teaching experiences and preservice teachers' honest responses to those experiences. We think that our preservice teachers are not unlike other preservice teachers; thus, these teaching cases should have universal applicability.

Using the questions in the Applications and Reflections exercises as a guide, the cases and accompanying commentaries can be read and discussed as a whole-class activity, in small collaborative groups, or by individuals. Suggested readings can be discussed within the format of literacy study groups.

Not only have we included a separate chapter on classroom management, but there is also a pervasive discussion of classroom management issues throughout the text. This is the nature of teaching. Classroom management often is cited as the number one concern for preservice and novice teachers (Brock & Grady, 1996; Kiley & Thomas, 1994). Issues of thorough planning, anticipating student behaviors, establishing routines and procedures, and having a repertoire of behavior management techniques relate to the teaching of *any* content. All preservice teachers and novice teachers learn the value of classroom management as they interact with students in classrooms. Classroom management is a necessary consideration in any teaching event.

Experts and practitioners agree that it is impossible to provide one with all that he or she needs to know in order to teach effectively (see Harrington & Hodson, 1993). We think that the teaching episodes presented in this book offer glimpses of literacy instruction that provide considerable opportunities for novice teachers to discover what they need to know and how they need to think in order to teach reading and language arts successfully.

ACKNOWLEDGMENTS

We offer grateful thanks and appreciation to our preservice teachers, who help us learn every day. Their candid, compelling narratives allow us to experience their concerns and reflective thinking as they implement literacy instruction for students with widely diverse literacy learning proficiencies and requirements. We also are deeply indebted to the commentary writers—a robust, collegial network of teacher educators and skilled classroom teachers throughout the United States and in Canada. They willingly, enthusiastically, and skillfully responded to the dilemmas and situations portrayed in the preservice teachers' cases. When viewed as a collective body of knowledge, their suggestions, advice, ideas, and understanding of sound, current literacy theory substantiate the considerable wisdom comprised by literacy practitioners.

Heartfelt appreciation to Nel Noddings, who graciously agreed to write the foreword for this casebook. Her caring, insightful remarks and observations help to validate and clarify the use and benefits of authentic stories and case methods in teacher education.

We wish to recognize and applaud Maria Meyerson and Shirley Howlette in Nevada, for their commentary contributions in the early stages of this project.

We are also indebted to the reviewers of this text, Victoria Chou, University of Illinois at Chicago; Carolyn Eichenberger, Arkansas State University; and Deborah Nieding, Gonzaga University, Spokane, Washington; and to Lori Hawver and Sara Scudder, Erlbaum staff; Faye Brophy, librarian at the University of Southern Mississippi; and Ramona Moore at Western Washington Univeristy, for her careful reading of the text manual.

And, of course, we thank our wonderful editor, Naomi Silverman. She knows how to listen carefully and understands when and how to contribute thoughtful suggestions and advice. She is astute, kind, clever, humorous, sensible, and—above all—uniquely approachable.

CHAPTER 1

Introduction: Writing and Sharing Personal Teaching Cases

Concepts and Terms

-case methods
-narrative learning approach
-pragmatic cognitive approach
-reflective thinking

OVERVIEW

In the past few years, **case methods** have become increasingly important to the field of education (Merseth, 1991; J. Shulman, 1992). This chapter presents our rationale for preservice teacher use of case writing and analysis, and describes the particular attributes of well-written cases. The chapter also provides guidelines designed to help case authors write and assess their case writing efforts.

RATIONALE FOR USING CASE WRITING AND ANALYSIS

We take a combination of the **pragmatic cognitive approach** (Zeichner, 1983) and the **narrative learning approach** (Sykes & Bird, 1992) to using cases in teacher education. That is, we use case writing and case analysis and discussion to emphasize practice as a means to understand or construct theory (pragmatic cognitive approach), and also to explore "questions of human intention or the meaning of experience" (Sykes & Bird, 1992, p. 473—narrative learning approach). These two approaches emphasize that what happens in the classroom goes far beyond plans and procedures. For instance, the wonder and excitement of learning represent dimensions of teaching that are not easily ensured through theories, rules, or methods. However, delight and joy are crucial aspects of education that teachers need to learn how to foster. Thus, "the narrative mode of learning helps [preservice] teachers to focus on the meaning and intentionality of these dimensions of teaching and learning" (Munro, 1997, p. 5). The cases in this book are designed to serve as a format or vehicle for helping you construct knowledge about both the cognitive and the affective dimensions of teaching reading and language arts from particular, context-specific episodes.

Developing teaching cases requires that you identify, reflect on, and write about worrisome classroom dilemmas, concerns, or successes that affect your teaching. Our experiences show that focusing on authentic educational situations, pondering possible solutions to dilemmas, and interpreting teaching events enhance preservice teachers' professional growth early in their educational careers. Over the course of the semester, you will become more reflective in your practices and "more analytic about [your] work" (L. Shulman, 1992, p. 9).

Exploring and seeking solutions to teaching concerns will also help you recognize that there is no single right answer in teaching. Equally important, authoring cases will help you become a problem solver who is responsible for your own actions (Merseth, 1991). An added bonus is that your cases can serve as catalysts for class discussions and, thus, provide additional opportunities for fostering professional attitudes. Sharing cases with one another in a collaborative setting, asking clarifying questions, and seeking and discussing possible alternative actions and approaches to the dilemmas portrayed will help you construct and establish yourself as a teacher.

THE BENEFITS OF CASE WRITING FOR PRESERVICE TEACHERS

Recently, we asked preservice teachers in our classes to give us their thoughts and ideas about the benefits of writing personal teaching cases. Here are some of their responses:

Case writing does several things for me. It allows me to:
1. Isolate a teaching problem or series of related teaching problems.
2. Make a plan to solve the problem.
3. Initiate the plan.
4. Reflect on how the plan is working.
5. Rethink the problem and possible solutions to it, and adjust accordingly.
6. Show that I can think like a professional.

Case writing makes me:
1. Focus on students and situations that need help.
2. Reflect about my practices as a teacher.
3. Recognize that I am responsible for solving problems in the classroom.
4. Realize that even though I am a busy classroom teacher, I have to take time to notice and write down important observations about each of my students.

How does case writing help me? It:
1. Teaches me to be a problem solver.
2. Encourages me to reflect about my practices and professional decisions.
3. Helps me become aware of my strengths and shortcomings in the classroom.
4. Teaches me to ask these questions of myself: What did I do right? What did I do wrong? What do I need to change? What did I do that was helpful? What did I do that

was harmful? How did I contribute to events going well or poorly? What do I need to know about my students to be able to meet their needs?

ATTRIBUTES OF A WELL-WRITTEN CASE

"There is not yet a consensus among educators as to what [exactly] constitutes a good case" (Merseth, 1991, p. 7). However, scholars do agree that cases employed in teacher education are focused, engaging narratives varying in length from 1 to 30 pages (Sykes, 1992). They describe "a wide variety of situations, decisions, dilemmas, and difficulties that routinely confront teachers and teacher educators" (Sykes, 1992, p. ix). Usually written in the first person, cases may tell one main story, "but embedded in that story are other problems that can be discussed" (Shulman, 1993, p. 2). Like all good stories, cases portray characters that appear real, contain dialogue and rich detail, present a problem or a series of related problems that unfold over time, and are "contextualized in time and place" (L. Shulman, 1992, p. 21).

It is important to note that all stories of teaching are not cases. Besides describing a context-specific incident or a series of incidents, cases exemplify "an instance of a larger class [or category] of knowledge [such as multicultural issues, social promotions, instructional problems, or relational conflicts among teachers and students] and therefore merit more consideration than a simple anecdote or vignette" (L. Shulman, 1992, p. 17). For example, consider the following case excerpt written by a former preservice teacher during her first few weeks in the field. This case documents her confusions about encouraging first graders to use invented spelling. However, it also illustrates underlying classes or categories of abstract knowledge that are common to many university field-based initiatives (e.g., conflicts between a university supervisor's and a classroom teacher's literacy instructional orientation, and lack of communication).

CASE EXCERPT 1.1 INVENTED SPELLING

Stacy Gorum

Invernizzi, M., Abouzeid, M., & Gill, J. T. (1994). Using students' invented spellings as a guide for spelling instruction that emphasizes word study. *The Elementary School Journal, 95,* 155–167.

I had been working in my first-grade classroom for a few weeks when I began to realize that the classroom teacher's strategies and the strategies that I have been instructed to use were totally opposite. What made it apparent that we had conflicting strategies was when my students would write in their journals.

In a typical lesson, I write an entry to each of my students and my students respond to the entry. Often, they ask me to spell a word for them. But I always encourage them to spell the word the way they think it is spelled and not to worry about using standard spelling in their journals.

One day, I began my lesson by passing out the students' journals and walking around to help them respond to my entry. As usual, they asked me how to spell words. I told them, "Spell words however you think they are spelled because I can read anything you write."

The problem began when the students became irritated with my answer. They began to ask the classroom teacher how to spell words, and to my chagrin and frustration, she spelled them for her students. Was she correct or was I correct?

GUIDING PRESERVICE TEACHERS' CASE WRITING EFFORTS

In order to help you author cases, we have developed the following guidelines. The information also can be used to guide you as you evaluate your case writing efforts and to provide suggestions for collegial peer editing sessions.

Guidelines for Writing and Assessing Your Own Cases

As Wassermann (1994) noted, writing good case narratives takes considerable time and effort. The first step is to identify and consciously reflect about a worrisome classroom dilemma or a series of related problems that require your attention. Then, after some preliminary planning, begin writing the first draft of your case. Write in the first person. Identify who you are, the context for the case (e.g., an urban school or an overcrowded kindergarten classroom), and the dilemma or series of related problems that affect your teaching and your students' learning. If appropriate, provide some background information about your students, the curriculum, and yourself. Write as vivid an account as you can, and include some real-life dialogue. Your case will be more interesting to read if your "characters" seem real, you exclude most extraneous details, and you choose a topic about which you feel strongly and passionately. Your case may be as long as you wish, but should be a minimum of two pages. Remember, overly long narratives are tedious and sometimes confusing to read.

It is most important that, as you write, you examine the many sides of your teaching dilemma in a truthful way, considering all possible contributing factors. For example, a boy named Johnny who is in your second-grade class comes to school late every morning. He rarely has his homework, and he often acts overly tired and lethargic. You keep reminding Johnny to come to school on time and to bring his homework, but Johnny continues to be late. Is this Johnny's fault? Have you spoken with Johnny privately? Have you contacted the school social worker, nurse, or guidance counselor? Have you phoned or visited Johnny's parents to find out how they and their family situation or neighborhood environment might contribute to his tardiness? As Johnny's teacher, how might you be part of the problem? How can you become part of the solution?

After completing the first draft of your narrative, read it carefully. You may find the following questions helpful for evaluating the quality and depth of your writing. The questions also can serve to guide your case revisions:

1. Is it easy to identify the problems or issues in your case? What are the problems and issues?
2. Is this case interesting to read? Why or why not?
3. Is your case written in a formal or informal style? Document examples of the writing features in your case to support your opinion.
4. On a scale of 1 to 5 (5 being the highest score), rate the quality of your writing? Document examples of the writing features in your case to support your opinion.
5. What do you think might make your case better? For example, is there too little information? Does your case contain too much extraneous information? Have you included authentic dialogue?
6. Have you tried to brainstorm and come up with some alternatives to the situation(s) presented in your case?
7. Have you tried to research the issue presented in your case?
8. Have you titled your case?

After you have edited and reedited your case, you may find it worthwhile to have one of your peers read and critique your writing. We have found that using the following questions is helpful for peer reviewers:

1. What did you particularly notice about this case?
2. What is it a case of? Is more than one issue involved?
3. Was the case interesting for you to read? Why or why not?

4. What do you think might make this case better? For example, is there too much or too little information? Is there dialogue? Is the context clear? Is background information sufficient? Is the case vivid and moving? Are you drawn to the case? Is the writing style reader-friendly?
5. How would you attempt to solve the problem(s) or resolve/explore the issue(s) presented in this case, or what suggestions would you provide the teacher?
6. What aspects of literacy teaching are mentioned in this case? If few aspects of literacy instruction are mentioned, how do the issues presented in this case (e.g., students' behavior, home or neighborhood conditions) affect students' literacy achievements?

Continue to refine and improve your narrative until you are satisfied with the final product. Once your case is completed you might include it as part of your professional portfolio. You also could read and discuss your case with teaching colleagues. Your narrative might be of such high quality that it could be published in a professional casebook.[1]

SUMMARY

We believe case methods provide an approach for helping you to explore, in advance, the many teaching situations you will face as a classroom teacher. Discussing teaching cases readily reveals the complexities of teaching and encourages consideration of alternative methods, techniques, and instructional strategies. However, writing teaching cases does even more. Authoring cases promotes **reflective thinking** and thoughtful, analytical consideration of teaching. Case writing can serve as an evaluation tool for your professional development, and can raise new and important questions for you to address. We hope that reading, analyzing, and discussing our preservice teachers' literacy cases will encourage you to write and share your own teaching cases.

SUGGESTED READINGS

Shulman, J. (Ed.). (1992). *Case methods in teacher education.* New York: Teachers College Press.
   This book is not a methods text—its purpose is to show how to develop and use cases and to demonstrate the wide-ranging role of case-based teaching. Many of the chapters include actual cases and case commentaries. Readers learn about the inseparability of teachers' thoughts, feelings, and actions.

Wassermann, S. (1994). Using cases to study teaching. *Phi Delta Kappan, 75*(8), 602–611.
   This paper tells us that when teacher education students read cases, they learn about life in classrooms and discover that there are no trite, simplistic solutions to teaching problems. Real-life teacher education classroom scenarios are portrayed.

---

[1]To share teaching experiences and contribute to collegial dialogue, send cases for discussion and possible publication to Dr. Janet Richards, University of Southern Mississippi, 730 East Beach Blvd., Long Beach, MS 39560.

CHAPTER 2

Working With Young Literacy Learners

Literacy Concepts and Terms

- -cloze passages
- -dialogue journals
- -emergent literacy
- -guided reading
- -interest inventory
- -letter strings
- -literature logs

- -predictable books
- -prediction logs
- -prephonemic stage of spelling
- -readers theatre
- -shared reading
- -story mapping
- -visual

OVERVIEW

The cases and commentaries in this chapter target literacy lessons offered to young learners in kindergarten and first grade. Many children experience significant difficulties when they initially enter school. Some have not matured sufficiently to be able to sit still during story hour. Others have little knowledge about the joys and diverse purposes of reading and writing, because they come from homes where people do not engage in authentic literacy activities. Some children have not yet discovered what is expected of them in group learning situations, or perhaps their oral language and listening abilities are not commensurate with their age.

Developmentally appropriate practices and child-centered environments facilitate young students' active participation in literacy events, and promote student discovery and peer interactions. Appropriate learning environments also help to develop young children's independence and sense of responsibility. In addition, suitable learning atmospheres enhance children's sense of group cohesiveness, oral language [see Cases 4.1 and 4.2], and overall **emergent literacy** abilities.

McGill-Franzen, A. (1998). Early literacy: What does "developmentally appropriate" mean? In Richard Allington (Ed.), *Teaching struggling readers: Articles from The Reading Teacher* (pp. 31–34). Originally from the September, 1992 issue of *The Reading Teacher.* Newark, DE: International Reading Association.

CASE 2.1: MAGGIE

Alicia Marx

The first time I worked with my small group of first graders I started with an **interest inventory.** Each student reached into a bag covered with playing cards and pulled out an ace with a question on it. My attention immediately was drawn to Maggie. She sat patiently, waiting for her turn. When she finally did answer the question, "Who reads to you at home?" she whispered, "Nobody."

"Nobody reads to you?" I asked.

"Nope," she replied in a barely audible voice.

The next time we met I read *Uncle Jed's Barbershop* (Mitchell, 1993). Maggie sat and stared intensely at the pictures. When we did our **dialogue journals,** Maggie tried to copy the date that I had written in my entry to her. She got as far as the *J* in *January* and the rest of her entry was a hodgepodge of letters that had no meaning.

Another day, we read *In the Small, Small Pond* (Flemming, 1993), and I brought in five stuffed geese as a **visual.** Maggie was thrilled. For the first time, she began to speak and interact with the group, although her voice was still very low. I wondered if she was ever scolded at home for speaking out of turn or for being annoying.

When we did our journals the next day, I tried something new. I wrote the date for her with "hash marks" and had her trace it. Not only did she accomplish that, but when I tried to take her dictation in her journal entry to me, for the first time she answered right away, instead of staring blankly. "What do you want to be when you grow up?" I had written in her journal. When I read my entry to her she whispered, "A princess."

I wrote, "I want to be a princess," for her and then she did something I couldn't believe. She began to copy the question I had written to her better than she had ever written before. She even signed her letter to me. What an improvement!

The next day I had her trace the date and the heading once again and she was happy. When she saw the hash marks she said, "You want me to trace them. I can do that."

Wollman-Bonilla, J., & Werchadlo, B. (1995). Literature response journals in a first-grade classroom. *Language Arts, 72,* 562–570.

She even drew a picture in her journal. Then, when we did our **literature logs** for the day and I had my students write their opinions of *In the Small, Small Pond,* I helped Maggie write her answer: "I liked holding the gooses." She even copied part of it.

Maggie does not know any sounds that alphabet letters make, and she frequently has to ask me how to write alphabet letters. My question now is where do I go from here? I have not a clue as to what to do next or even if what I have done is appropriate. Maggie moves slower than the rest of my students, and that slows down our group accomplishments [see Cases 12.1 and 12.2]. In my opinion, what Maggie needs is more attention from her parents and her classroom teacher [see Case 11.1]. I know that she can succeed in school.

CASE 2.1: APPLICATIONS AND REFLECTIONS

What do you think is the purpose of this lesson or series of lessons?

_____

_____

_____

_____

How was the original teaching plan interrupted, or what surprised Alicia?

_____

_____

_____

What actions did Alicia take in response to the interruption/surprise?

_____

_____

_____

Examine the consequences of Alicia's actions. What alternative action(s)/procedures would you suggest?

_____

_____

_____

_____

Identify the resources (e.g., outside readings; conversations with peers, teachers, or other professionals) used by Alicia in this case. What other specific resources might you suggest (e.g., titles of related articles or books, community agencies, etc.)?

_____

_____

_____

_____

From whose perspective is the case written?

_____

_____

_____

What do you think is Maggie's perspective?

_____

_____

_____

_____

Who are the players in the case?

_____

_____

_____

_____

What seems to be working well in this case?

_____

_____

_____

_____

What needs to be improved?

_____

_____

_____

_____

Can you distinguish between the symptoms and the problems presented in this case?

_____

_____

_____

_____

Adapted from Morine-Dershimer, 1996; Shulman, 1996; Silverman & Welty, 1996.

COMMENTARY 2.1A: MAGGIE

Suzanne Gespass, Teacher Educator
Rider College, New Jersey

Hello Alicia,

Yes, you're right. Of course Maggie can succeed in school, and your job as her teacher is to make sure that she does succeed. Remember that all students come to school with different kinds of literacy experiences. Some students have been read to every day of their lives since birth, and others have had very limited exposure to hearing books read aloud to them. It sounds like Maggie is ready to learn and finds literate activities engaging. She is responding to literature and she is attempting to write. At this point she still seems very tentative but she is willing to try. It is important that she be allowed to take risks and that she feels supported in her attempts at reading and writing. I would agree that Maggie needs more attention and that she specifically needs someone to read to her and interact with her about books. Finding time during class can be difficult, but there are ways of ensuring that this will happen. One idea you might try is cross-age tutoring. This is when you have students from an older grade pair up and read with younger students. Cross-age tutoring has been very successful with both older and younger students in this kind of pairing. Another idea is to enlist the help of seniors in the community who are usually quite eager to volunteer in schools and spend time reading with young students [see Commentary 2.1B]. Often you can find senior citizens who are retired teachers—wonderful resources.

Leland, C., & Fitzpatrick, R. (1994). Cross-age interaction builds enthusiasm for reading-writing. *The Reading Teacher, 47,* 292–301.

Be sure to continue lots of **shared reading** experiences as well. Make sure that Maggie is able to see the print in books and understands that the print carries the message. Shared reading also will allow you and Maggie to work on the concepts of directionality, voice-print match, and concept of "word." Use books with very predictable language so that Maggie can gain confidence in her abilities to develop into a reader and writer. Encourage and invite her to participate, but be careful not to demand her participation. She needs to feel very safe.

Shared writing also will help Maggie hear the sounds of the letters as you and she write about her experiences. Remember that students at this age are very self-involved and their names are their identities. Start with the letter *M* for *Maggie* and have her search for other words that begin with the letter *M*. Help her see that your last name, *Marx*, starts with the same alphabet letter as *Maggie*.

One last suggestion I would recommend is to make sure that Maggie takes home a book every night. Reach out to her parents and see if there is someone at home who can spend about 15 minutes every day reading with her. If necessary, take the time to teach Maggie's parents how to read with her in a way that is supportive. A great source of inexpensive books on the emergent literacy level is KEEP books published by The Ohio University. The intent of these books is for young students to take them home to read and keep them in their personal library so that they can begin to establish a collection of books at home that they are able to read.

Saccardi, M. C. (1996). Predictable books: Gateways to a lifetime of reading. *The Reading Teacher, 49,* 588–590.

Ohio State University, KEEP BOOKS, 1929 Kenny Road, Suite 100, Columbus, OH 43210.

COMMENTARY 2.1B: MAGGIE

Fredda Fischman, Classroom Teacher
Allentown, Pennsylvania

It seems that Maggie responds very positively and actively to direct human interaction. Alicia might want to find an older student in the building who could work with Maggie to get her talking and writing more. This older student might be someone who needs reinforcement as a mentor, either for academic or social reasons. Thus, this pairing could benefit both pupils [see Commentary 2.1A]. If there are no older students available, perhaps there is a community volunteer, such as a business partner with the school or a PTA member, who could help Maggie and give her the personal attention she seems to crave and needs [see Commentary 3.1B]. There also might be a grandparenting program available anyone who could spend some extra time with Maggie, reading books, writing in journals, and so on, which would be helpful to Maggie's literacy development.

Maggie seems to lack awareness of how letters are formed. Working with a geoboard and rubber bands could help her become familiar with horizontal lines, vertical lines, circles, and diagonal lines. With just those few shapes mastered, Maggie should soon be able to construct (write) the entire alphabet.

If no one reads to Maggie at home, perhaps it is because her parents or caregivers do not know how to read meaningfully to a child, or perhaps there are no books in the home. It is important to see if Maggie has her own personal library or access to a public library. If not, then perhaps Alicia could send books home with her on a weekly basis, with simple guiding suggestions for home readers to key into as they read to Maggie. Are Maggie's parents amenable to visiting the school for a conference on how to work with her at home? If so, Alicia could gather simple work materials in resealable plastic bags and enclose easy-to-follow instructions. Maggie could take these materials and instructions home. The adults at home may not know where or how to begin teaching, and this easy school-made support would fill in that gap. Alicia needs to know if there are scissors, crayons, paper, and pencils available at home. If not, then perhaps they can be borrowed from the school. Alicia also needs to look at Maggie's chronological age and her developmental readiness to learn how to form alphabet letters and the sounds associated with alphabet letters. Perhaps Maggie needs some support skills before she is ready to learn these two advanced skills.

I wonder if Maggie's eyesight is okay? Are her fine motor skills appropriate for her age? If not, then adaptations need to be made to strengthen these problems.

And finally, Alicia needs to remember that young students need time ... not every student learns at the same pace. If it is only Maggie who is slowing the whole group down, 10 minutes might be taken from the small group so that Alicia can work with just Maggie in a one-on-one situation. [see Commentary 3.1B]. Even 10 minutes is an enormous amount of time to accomplish a great deal with one student, and the rest of the group can move ahead at its own pace. Then, no one is frustrated or made to feel either superior or inferior, and all students can feel good about their work.

CASE 2.2: EMPOWERING ALEXANDRA

Sharon Brown

Alexandra is a tiny first grader. When I first met her she would not say one word. For example, I handed out the journals and I asked the students, "What do you think about writing in journals?"

Most of the students seemed to know what journals were, and they said things like, "I'd like to write to you in my journal." But Alexandra didn't say anything. I thought, "Maybe she's not in a good mood today or maybe she's shy."

Another day, I was reading the story *The Princess and the Pea* (Anderson, 1985). We were using our **prediction logs** and I asked the students, "Would anyone like to make a guess about what is going to happen to the princess?"

Robert said, "I think that the princess will get married."

Bonnie yelled out, "This book is like the Cinderella story."

"Good for you," I said. So then, I decided that it might be a good time to have Alexandra make a prediction. I said, "Alexandra, what do you think will happen?" But, she just sat there and wouldn't open her mouth. She just nodded.

Another time, we were going over the different features in a story, using the find-the-features-and-connect-them reading comprehension strategy. I talked about the story characters, settings, problems, and solutions in *The Three Bears* story I was reading. I also used a chart that I made to help us list the story features in *The Three Bears* (Barton, 1991). I began calling on several students to tell me some of the characters, the settings, the problems, and the solutions. They all did fine, except for Alexandra. She just sat there. This has happened all semester.

Now that it is near the end of the first semester of school Alexandra is talking a little and she's trying to write to me in her journal, so she's learning and she's trying. But, she just writes **letter strings,** nothing else. Also, when we were reading *The Three Billy Goats Gruff* (Stevens, 1995) last week, to my surprise Alexandra asked me, "What's the troll going to do to the little billy goat?" I wanted to tell her but instead I asked the students, "What do you all think that the troll will do to the Billy Goat?"

Arian answered, "He's going to scare him away."

So, Alexandra didn't say anything. Well, I'll keep trying but I am at a loss as to what to do about her. What do you think?

Richards, J., Gipe, J., & Necaise, M. (1994). Find the features and connect them. *The Reading Teacher, 48,* 187–188.

CASE 2.2: APPLICATIONS AND REFLECTIONS

What do you think is the purpose of this lesson or series of lessons?

_____

_____

_____

_____

How was the original teaching plan interrupted, or what surprised Sharon?

_____

_____

_____

_____

What actions did Sharon take in response to the interruption/surprise?

_____

_____

_____

_____

Examine the consequences of Sharon's actions. What alternative action(s)/procedures would you suggest?

_____

_____

_____

_____

Identify the resources (e.g., outside readings; conversations with peers, teachers, or other professionals) used by Sharon in this case. What other specific resources might you suggest (e.g., titles of related articles or books, community agencies, etc.)?

_____

_____

_____

_____

From whose perspective is the case written?

_____

_____

_____

_____

What do you think is Alexandra's perspective?

_____

_____

_____

_____

Who are the players in the case?

_____

_____

_____

_____

What seems to be working well in this case?

_____

_____

_____

_____

What needs to be improved?

_____

_____

_____

_____

Can you distinguish between the symptoms and the problems presented in this case?

_____

_____

_____

_____

Adapted from Morine-Dershimer, 1996; Shulman, 1996; Silverman & Welty, 1996.

COMMENTARY 2.2A: EMPOWERING ALEXANDRA

Maria Meyerson, Teacher Educator,
University of Nevada, Las Vegas

Dear Sharon,

Alexandra appears to be a very shy child who is not comfortable talking in a group. She may be younger than the other children in her class, as indicated by her small stature and lack of writing maturity in comparison to what the other students can do. Before I offer my opinion in terms of teaching strategies, I suggest that some other observations be made. What does Alexandra do in noninstructional settings, such as on the playground and in the lunchroom? What is her other classwork like? What can you learn about Alexandra's interactions with adults and siblings at home?

I think you missed a great opportunity to help Alexandra when you asked the other children to answer the question she directly asked you. I would have treated the situation as a conversation between two readers: "I think that the troll will chase the Billy Goat. What do you think, Alexandra?"

It does appear that once Alexandra hears others' responses, she sees no reason to contribute. Many children are unaware that there can be more than one answer to a question. You may want to make this point explicit to your group of children.

Gentry, J. R. (1987). *Spel ... is a four letter word.* New York: Scholastic.

Are you aware that children go through developmental stages in writing and in spelling? Alexandra appears to be in the **prephonemic stage of spelling,** because she is writing letter strings. Does she know how to write her name? Can she write any words that demonstrate some understanding of the relationship between letter names and sounds? Concentrate on what Alexandra can do, and then plan your instruction.

COMMENTARY 2.2B: EMPOWERING ALEXANDRA

Shirley Howlette, Classroom Teacher
Las Vegas, Nevada

Based on the teacher's description, Alexandra is indeed a quiet child. I am reminded of a study done by Shirley Brice Heath (1983) in which she discussed middle-class teachers' methods of questioning.

The students in the study came from homes in predominantly African American neighborhoods in which the standard type of question was very different from the teachers' styles of questioning. Mothers in these homes only asked questions when they wanted to know the answers. The investigation found that the middle-class teachers in the study tended to ask questions to which they already knew the answers. The students in these teachers' classes seemed to understand that the teachers already knew the answers to the questions they asked. Therefore, the students didn't bother to answer the questions.

It appears that Alexandra may be suffering from academic low self-esteem. She is afraid to voice an opinion, seemingly worried that her views will not be accepted by her peers and her teacher. I would like to know more about Alexandra's economic status, home situation, and her social skills on the playground. Does she have friends or is she a loner? Does she live in cultural poverty? Is she allowed to speak and encouraged to ask questions at home?

When Alexandra would not or could not write in her journal, I wondered if she knew what a journal was. Is this her first experience with a journal? If so, the teacher should model journal writing. The strings of letters in her journal indicate that she currently is writing on a prephonemic or early phonemic level. This is very common for many kindergarten and first-grade students.

Alexandra appears to be struggling with reading as well. However, the first time Alexandra actually responds to a story by asking a question, the preservice teacher seems to have embarrassed her. Alexandra is very shy and needs positive reinforcement when she doesn't talk. When Alexandra asked, "What's the troll going to do to the little

Billy Goat?" a good response by the preservice teacher might have been, "That's a good question class, what do you think?" Instead, the teacher let Alexandra think that everyone in the class knew the answer but her.

Some activities that might prove beneficial are **predictable books, guided reading, story mapping, readers theatre,** and puppetry.

Forsythe, S. (1995). It worked! Readers theatre in second grade. *The Reading Teacher, 49,* 264–265.

Mc Master, J. (1998). "Doing" literature: Using drama to build literacy. *The Reading Teacher, 51,* 574–584.

CASE 2.3: PUSHING TOO FAR

Wendy Van Belle

Valmont, W. (1983). Cloze and maze instructional techniques. *Reading Psychology, 4,* 163–167.

I have been working with a group of four first-grade boys. One day we were filling in **cloze passages.** I thought this was a way that my students could see how a sentence is supposed to look and how it is constructed. It should have been a very easy, all-around successful lesson for everyone in the group. Well, it backfired on me with one of my students named Michael—not because of him, but because of me.

Michael can't read or spell on his own. He has great difficulty staying focused, and he isn't able to comprehend stories that I read to him. He also appears to have no confidence in anything that he does. Understandably, Michael really enjoys copying words that are around the room and on other students' papers, because this is something that he can do successfully.

The lesson started out beautifully. I had written the cloze passage on a dry erase board. The passage was about our homes and families and things of that sort. I gave directions orally and in written form on the dry erase board. Then I read the passage out loud, skipping over the blanks. The students all began copying the passage, filling in the blanks as they went along. I walked around, giving help when needed. They all were writing slowly. I had anticipated this, so I was not at all frustrated or concerned. Michael was slower than the other students, and I had also expected this. Because he did not know how to spell or read, it was understandable. I walked Michael through the first two sentences of the passage, step by step. I asked him, "Can you do the rest of the passage by yourself?"

He nodded his head and said, "Yes."

I went around to the other students to give assistance, and thought that Michael was doing fine. After about 15 minutes into the lesson I noticed Michael was doodling next to where the passage was supposed to go. I went over to him, pointed to what he had written, and asked, "Can you finish this passage?"

He replied "Yes," and began working on it again.

He wrote one more word and then he turned his paper over to the other side and began drawing again. After I had finished answering some questions from other students, I went back to Michael and turned over his paper. I knelt down by him and asked, "What's wrong?"

He shrugged his shoulders and sat slumped in the chair. Did I get a clue? Apparently not, because I continued to urge him to finish the passage. At this point Michael was upset and began to draw very hard with his pencil. He intentionally broke the point on the pencil. I sternly said, "This is not okay. You may not break the pencils."

He noticed that I had let Jordan, another student, go to the bathroom and asked if he could go. I said, "Wait 'til Jordan gets back."

I continued to try to get him to tell me what was wrong, even though I knew that he had lost interest and wanted to do something else. I leaned down and asked, "Did I lose you?" He took a deep breath and leaned back in his chair distressed as can be and so very sad (my heart sank to my stomach). He leaned up again and tossed his pencil on the desk and said, "Man, you lost me!"

I gave him a big hug and asked, "How can I get you back?"

He replied, "I don't know."

Jordan returned and then Michael asked if he could go to the bathroom. When he returned I asked, "Do you want to color your picture or a picture of your house?"

He said something under his breath that I couldn't hear. I asked him what he said and I got no reply. I handed him a box of crayons. He opened it and took his favorite red color out and began to color very hard. He was pressing as if he was trying to break it. I looked him in the eye and said "That is not okay! You may not break my crayons!"

At this point he was beyond bringing back to this activity and the end of our hour was near. I stopped the lesson, moved my group into a semicircle and read, "We Are All Alike … We Are All Different," a story created by some kindergarten students at another elementary school. Michael was listening but he became distracted when the rest of the class began moving back to their desks.

I know now that I pushed Michael into something he wasn't ready for—an extended lesson. He has a very short attention span and he needs to be active and change routines more often. I should have planned for this. If I would have changed to a different activity, possibly a manipulative activity, I would have spared both Michael and me a failure. This disregard that I had for Michael is inexcusable in my eyes. I knew better and, yet, I continued to press on. I know now that I'll remember this situation and not make the same mistake.

My questions are: How can I help the other students continue something they are doing well and at the same time help Michael? How can I help other students like Michael? How can I help Michael extend his attention span? Am I just being impatient or controlling when I put a child into this situation?

CASE 2.3: APPLICATIONS AND REFLECTIONS

What do you think is the purpose of this lesson or series of lessons?

_____

_____

_____

_____

How was the original teaching plan interrupted, or what surprised Wendy?

_____

_____

_____

_____

What actions did Wendy take in response to the interruption/surprise?

_____

_____

_____

_____

Examine the consequences of Wendy's actions. What alternative action(s)/procedures would you suggest?

_____

_____

_____

_____

Identify the resources (e.g., outside readings; conversations with peers, teachers, or other professionals) used by Wendy in this case. What other specific resources might you suggest (e.g., titles of related articles or books, community agencies, etc.)?

_____

_____

_____

_____

From whose perspective is the case written?

_____

_____

_____

_____

What do you think is Michael's perspective?

_____

_____

_____

_____

Who are the players in the case?

_____

_____

_____

What seems to be working well in this case?

_____

_____

_____

What needs to be improved?

_____

_____

_____

Can you distinguish between the symptoms and the problems presented in this case?

_____

_____

_____

Adapted from Morine-Dershimer, 1996; Shulman, 1996; Silverman & Welty, 1996.

COMMENTARY 2.3A: PUSHING TOO FAR

Susan Lensky, Teacher Educator
Illinois State University

In her case, Pushing Too Far, Wendy expresses a very real problem that teachers face—how to cope with students who have varying abilities [see Cases 12.1, 12.2, and 12.3]. She also had an important personal realization, that all teachers make mistakes. I believe that Wendy's example describes both an instructional dilemma and a terrific learning experience.

When a teacher is not successful teaching a lesson, it is a good idea to determine if a different approach might have caused more success. In Wendy's case, I think that there are some options that might be considered as she reflects about her lesson. First, for first-grade students, copying words from the board can be a frustrating experience. Second, I question the value of copying sentences for the purpose of learning to read and write. A better choice would have been for Wendy to duplicate the cloze passage or write the passage on a chart. Then Wendy and her students could have filled in the blanks in the cloze passage together, and Wendy could have modeled her thinking for her students.

Graves, M., Graves, B., & Braaten, S. (1996, February). Scaffolding reading experiences for inclusive classes. *Educational Leadership, 53*(5), 14–16.

When asking students of varying abilities to complete an activity, such as a cloze passage, teachers also have to think about ways to make the activity successful for students for whom the task may be difficult. In this case, Wendy could have given Michael a list of words that he could use to fill in the blanks in the cloze passage. The other three boys could have completed their cloze passages independently. Michael needed considerable scaffold support. Giving him a list of words to use might have made the task possible for him. In order to make decisions about what would be scaffold support for any individual student, teachers need to constantly be aware of students' ever-changing, expanding proficiencies.

I was impressed with Wendy's informal assessment of Michael's reading and spelling capacities. She recognized that Michael had difficulty reading and spelling independently. She understood that he could not stay focused, and she recognized that he lacked confidence. In addition, she drew many important conclusions about Michael's reading abilities. Knowing all of these facts provides the basis for Wendy to structure learning experiences for Michael so that he will have success, even though some of his assignments may be different from the other students' [see Commentaries 12.3A and 12.3B].

As Wendy makes decisions about each of her student's differing abilities and how best to instruct those students, she will learn from her mistakes. I can sense that she already has learned from her blunder with Michael. Therefore, her professional knowledge has become enhanced. No teacher will ever have all of the answers and make all of the right decisions, or always teach perfectly. Teaching is an ongoing, constructive activity. That's what makes teaching so exciting!

COMMENTARY 2.3B: PUSHING TOO FAR

Terri Austin, Classroom Teacher
Fairbanks, Alaska

How can I help students with diverse abilities when they are situated together in one group? [See chap. 12.] How can I develop hands-on learning activities for reading and writing tasks? How can I help students focus on challenging literacy tasks without getting them discouraged? Wendy's questions are ones that I ask myself frequently, because I also work with a diverse group of multi-age primary learners.

Wendy had some prior knowledge about Michael before she began the lesson. She knew that Michael had difficulties reading and writing, and she recognized that he understandably suffered from low self-esteem. But she disregarded Michael's problems. She started out well by helping Michael through the first few sentences of the cloze passage.

Then things fell apart when she left him. To extend support to Michael, Wendy could have paired her students together. Peer collaboration would have given Michael the necessary support he needed and enabled him to understand how his partner solved the problems of completing cloze passages. When Michael and his partner achieved their goal, Michael would have felt successful.

Another approach Wendy could have employed is to have met with Michael prior to this lesson. They could have reviewed the cloze passage together, and then Michael probably would have been more proficient in completing the passage independently. I find that struggling students often benefit from some short one-on-one student/teacher interactions before beginning independent literacy tasks.

A variety of words printed on small cards also might help Michael. From these cards, he could choose words appropriate for filling in the blanks of the cloze passage, pasting them onto the page. In this way, he could concentrate on completing the passage and not have to worry about spelling or writing.

A final consideration is to focus on one task at a time and not overload young students like Michael with multiple-level lessons. Was Wendy's lesson focused on writing or on the problem solving of cloze passages? I think that Wendy needed to be more straightforward with her students about the purpose of the lesson.

SUGGESTED READINGS

Gestwicki, C. (1995). *Developmentally appropriate practice: Curriculum and development in early childhood education.* Boston: Delmar.
Although this text is not a literacy text, it covers principles of developmentally appropriate practices that impact young students' learning, self-esteem, and confidence. A critical component of the book is the idea of individual appropriateness. No absolute standard meets the needs of all students.

Goodman, Y., Altwerger, B., & Marek, A. (1991). *Print awareness in pre-school children.* Tucson: University of Arizona.
In this book, three experts describe differences in young children's developmental awareness and progressions as readers and writers. Typically, some children in kindergarten and first grade cannot recognize letters, whereas others recognize words and complete sentences.

Strickland, D., & Morrow, L. (1989). *Emerging literacy: Young children learn to read and write.* Newark, DE: International Reading Association.
This noteworthy publication explains how young children develop at their own pace as they learn to read and write. It also discusses the importance of structuring student-centered classrooms. In student-centered classrooms, all learners' literacy efforts are deemed worthy as the students progress toward goals of being able to read and write different types of text.

3

Individual and Group Management Concerns

Literacy Concepts and Terms

-collaborative learning groups
-flexible grouping
-kinesthetic learner
-literature circles
-web

OVERVIEW

The cases and commentaries in this chapter examine individual and group management issues. Many beginning teachers experience difficulties with behavior management. One especially prevalent concern for new teachers is how to understand and guide unmotivated, disruptive, or easily distracted students so that effective literacy instruction can take place. Motivation and other patterns of behavior (e.g., attending to instruction) are learned and are "related to attitudes, incentives [students' home and neighborhood circumstances, and] developing personality" (Robeck & Wallace, 1990, p. 30).

An educational environment that encourages and supports readers and writers so that they can accomplish literacy tasks regardless of their individual abilities will help all students want to put forth effort. Additionally, when troubled students recognize the value of reading and writing, they gradually become more engaged in learning (Rhodes & Dudley-Marling, 1996).

Flexible grouping is one instructional approach that meets the needs of unmotivated and easily distracted literacy learners. In classrooms that honor students' diverse abilities and interests, learners can join any reading or writing group that suits their interests and ability levels. In addition, many student management problems are easily solved if teachers structure a variety of grouping arrangements, including whole-class interactions and small teacher-led interest and ability groups. Ad hoc meetings (i.e., groups formed to address students' specific instructional needs), **collaborative learning groups,** and individual learning sessions also are options.

Case 3.1: Restless First Graders

Kristine Denning

For the most part, my experiences teaching nine first-grade students have been very positive. However, I do have a great deal of difficulty with classroom management. My students will not listen to my repeated reminders or warnings concerning their behavior. This problem started on the first day of teaching and has not gotten much better. On some days, I feel that it is only getting worse. There are three children that usually start acting up, and the others follow their lead. I begin each day by handing out name tags and going over the rules. It has become increasingly more difficult to keep my students under control. For example, Delexis and Arrielle were upset the other day because their name tags were handed out last. "How come we got ours last? It's not fair!"

It still amazes me how important little things are to these children. I try to insist that they raise their hands before speaking in large-group situations. Yet, some days they don't even remember that it is one of our three rules. Arrielle seems to have the biggest problem when it comes to raising her hand. She will call out, "Miss Denning … Miss Denning."

I usually tell her that I cannot and will not talk to her unless she raises her hand first. She still calls out my name repeatedly. This usually happens when we journal. The students love their journals and they are always reluctant to give them up. I know that they really enjoy this time of our day. It is the only time that they really appear to be focused on what they are doing. They usually want to take turns picking up the journals and giving them to me. This only creates more problems. Once, Brandon hit Arrielle and said, "This is mine! You can't take my stuff!"

Once the dialogue journals are collected, I attempt to get the students' attention in order to read to them. This is always a problem. They are getting out of their chairs, falling out of their chairs, asking to go to the bathroom, talking to each other, and anything else that you can imagine. I have done everything that I can think of to stop this behavior. Some seem to completely disregard warnings. There are two children that I have to put out of the group almost every day during this time. I really don't want to do that, especially because they will miss the story. I feel that they already know exactly how far they can push before they are put out of the circle. I am probably not being firm enough. It really worries me that they are not able to pay attention while I am reading. I have to stop to correct someone on almost every page. The stories are not too long. They are quality children's literature with beautiful illustrations. I do not understand why the majority of the children either cannot or will not pay attention long enough to read a story. I have come to realize that the other groups of children in the room are quite a distraction. Sometimes my children want to listen to another story that is being read by one of the other preservice teachers in the room. I have become extremely frustrated with this situation.

My group always finds something to argue about. Delexis was crying the other day because of something that Ardelle said to her. "She said my picture was ugly! She did, she really did!"

When I asked Ardelle why she would say something like that, she replied, "Because it *is* ugly!"

During the first few days, I gave each child a stamp on their hand at the end of the lesson. They knew that they had to behave in order to receive a stamp. It seemed to work for the most part. However, the other preservice teachers in my room asked me to stop giving my kids the stamps. They said that their students were asking them for stamps and it was causing trouble. I offered to give them some of my stamps and they refused because it was too much trouble. So, I gave in. Now I am not so sure that I did what was best. My students don't understand why they no longer receive stamps for a job well done. I started putting stickers in their journals. However, they really miss the stamps. Did I do the right thing?

I realize that many preservice teachers have concerns or problems with behavior management. There are some days when I leave feeling that all I did was correct my students' behavior. Sometimes it is a relief to get out of there at the end of the hour. I don't like feeling happy to be leaving the classroom. This worries me. I wish that I could figure out how to get the children to listen to me and to respect me as a teacher. I have observed that the classroom teacher has a problem with their behavior as well. This only makes me feel better temporarily. At times, I feel that I will not be an effective teacher in the future because of the problems I am having now.

CASE 3.1: APPLICATIONS AND REFLECTIONS

What problems are Kristine and her students experiencing?

_____

_____

_____

_____

What questions did Kristine ask that might help illuminate solutions?

_____

_____

_____

_____

What actions did Kristine take in response to these problems?

_____

_____

_____

_____

Examine the consequences of Kristine's actions. What alternative action(s)/procedures would you suggest?

_____

_____

_____

_____

Identify the resources (e.g., outside readings; conversations with peers, teachers, or other professionals) used by Kristine in this case. What other specific resources might you suggest (e.g., titles of related articles or books, community agencies, etc.)?

_____

_____

_____

_____

From whose perspective is the case written?

_____

_____

_____

_____

What do you think are these first graders' perspectives?

_____

_____

_____

_____

Who are the players in the case?

_____

_____

_____

_____

What seems to be working well in this case?

_____

_____

_____

_____

What needs to be improved?

_____

_____

_____

_____

Can you distinguish between the symptoms and the problems presented in this case?

_____

_____

_____

_____

Adapted from Morine-Dershimer, 1996; Shulman, 1996; Silverman & Welty, 1996.

COMMENTARY 3.1A: RESTLESS FIRST GRADERS

A. J. Long, Classroom Teacher
Lake Havasu, Arizona

I want to address my suggestions directly to Miss Denning. Classroom management is an issue shared by all teachers. Each year we greet a new group of students and, generally speaking, the framework and philosophy undergirding our classroom management plan remain intact. However, we also know that we need to adapt to the needs of each year's learners. I hope that my feedback will bring you great success.

You mention how amazing it is that little things can matter so much to these young people. Yes, that is especially true for students who have very few possessions or receive little attention at home.

The three classroom rules you mentioned are adequate for students this age. I have found that young students become confused when the number of rules increases past three. Your students must clearly know what each rule means and the appropriate behavior expected of them. Review the rules often and encourage your students to model examples of appropriate behavior. You could begin each teaching session by going over the rules, or a student could volunteer to read them to the class.

Why don't you make a chart that designates who will give out the journals at each session? That way, your students will know that each of them will have a turn handing out journals and that problem will be solved.

Make sure that you support and uphold your class rules—be fair, firm, and consistent. Once your students know that you always reinforce the class rules, your life will be easier. It is appropriate for you to hold your students accountable for their behavior.

I like your idea of providing stamps for appropriate student behavior. If it works for you, I advocate using them and trying to encourage your professional peers to use them as well. Immediate rewards work best for young students. Remember to also offer verbal praise to reinforce your students' appropriate behavior. Here again, you could devise a chart showing the rewards each student has earned (e.g., a sticker or star). Be specific in telling a student what you liked about his or her behavior and, like a miracle, your other students will start to act just like the student being praised.

I also must tell you that you can't afford to let those who break the class rules interrupt other students' learning. Be fair, firm, and consistent, and employ time out for students who need to straighten up. In order to strengthen your students' abilities to listen and pay attention to you, you could do a "countdown" activity by saying, "One, two, three" and, by the time you say, "Three," all of your students should be looking at you and listening to you. As a reward, they could receive a star on a reward chart. Young students also like the "clapping activity" in which the teacher claps a short message to signal that students must pay attention and listen. Students then return the same message to the teacher to show that they are listening for further directions. You also could play a daily game of Simon Says to sharpen your students' listening abilities [see Cases 4.1 and 4.2].

Remember, the problems you are experiencing now are professional learning experiences. They will strengthen your abilities to structure effective classroom management in the future. One final word: Capable teachers establish and share a game plan with their students. They remain positive and consistent so that the players know what it takes to win.

COMMENTARY 3.1B: RESTLESS FIRST GRADERS

Karyn Wellhousen, Teacher Educator
University of New Orleans, Louisiana

One of our ultimate goals as teachers is to produce students who understand that they are responsible for their own behavior and who learn how to behave appropriately in a variety of situations. For many reasons, some students enter school knowing how to act. Others need considerable guidance in becoming responsible school citizens.

I think that the most common reason these first graders are disruptive is to gain attention. Their strong need for attention can stem from a variety of reasons. The important thing for teachers to remember is that one-on-one attention is exactly what disruptive students need.

Teachers have to work hard to find times to give one-on-one attention to disruptive students, but this individualized attention will produce positive results. For example, teachers can invite disruptive students to help prepare materials for a lesson, or these students can stay a few minutes after school to help the teacher "clean up." That's the perfect time for teachers to talk informally with disruptive students, showing genuine interest in what these students have to say. Assisting with small classroom tasks also will help students recognize that their presence makes a positive difference in the classroom. Another idea is to set aside time daily when other students are involved in work. Teachers can use this special time to communicate privately with students who are acting out in the classroom and vying for the teacher's attention.

However, there are situations when the best solution for attention-seeking students is to ignore their behavior, as in the case of students who make cruel statements to others, call out loudly, or complain loudly about minor incidents being unfair. By asking a student why they made a cruel remark, reminding students not to call out answers, and trying to explain why something isn't meant to be unfair, teachers reward students by giving them valuable, undivided attention [see Commentary 3.3B].

An alternative to asking students to raise their hands during discussions is to ask them to sit quietly until called on. This technique enables teachers to be in control of who will respond, and students will pay closer attention. Remember—ignore students who call out and only call on students who are quiet.

Young students respond especially well to routine. Therefore, Miss Denning needs to establish a system for returning journals and distributing work materials. An idea is to color code materials and to make color-coded baskets available to use for collecting materials.

Miss Denning also can take clues from successful activities. For example, her students become absorbed in journal writing and, therefore, behave appropriately during journal time. She could provide her students with art and writing materials and, when she reads a story, her students could draw and write about their favorite parts of the story.

Finally, it is not unusual for preservice and beginning teachers to feel pressured by their peers to change their teaching or management style. In Miss Denning's case, a stamp on her students' hands served as an effective, positive reinforcer of student behavior. The other preservice teachers did not have a sound rationale for requesting that Miss Denning discontinue a management technique that worked. Preservice and beginning teachers need to practice standing up for their convictions.

CASE 3.2: PROBLEMS WITH A "STAR" STUDENT

Linda Griggs

Mrs. Smith greeted us as we entered her third-grade classroom. She explained that she would divide the children up into groups for us and that we would each have one "star" child. We each received a list of the students assigned to our group. On each list was one starred student. The star was to indicate which child had behavior problems. My little star was named Joseph, or so I thought.

The children were generally warm and fun. Joseph was definitely a little rambunctious, but he seemed manageable. In fact, Brianna seemed to be the student I needed to watch. She was very independent and strong willed, and she wanted very much to be in charge. My fears about Brianna soon became a reality. We had just finished reading *Where the Wild Things Are* (Sendak, 1988), and I asked the students to illustrate a night that they had that was similar to Max's, the main character in the story. That's when the problems began. Brianna started complaining that she had never had a night like Max's and therefore didn't have anything to write. We brainstormed and came up with an experience that she remembered, so I instructed her to begin working. Then she said, "I can't work with this funky paper. I want my own paper."

I told her, "No, I want you to use the same materials as everyone else."

I don't know if that was the right move. I just felt that if I let her get different paper, then everyone else in the group would want new paper. Brianna was not pleased with my response and became huffy. I gave her a warning (phase one in the punishment sequence), and suggested she begin working. She refused to work and then lost her sticker (phase two of the punishment sequence). She got even huffier and started to do the shoulder-to-your-face routine. At that point, I sent her up to sign her name in the classroom teacher's book (phase three in the punishment sequence).

The following week the tension continued. We were doing a beginning/middle/end story **web** for *Where the Wild Things Are,* and Brianna decided she was bored and that the activity was stupid. She said, "I'm not going to do this stupid web because I don't even remember the stupid story."

I asked Brianna to come and sit beside me so that we could go over the web and the story together. The story had been read out loud in class by three students and we had done another activity based on the story, so I knew that she knew was familiar with it. She pouted and said, "I won't do it."

It was time for us to leave, so I instructed the other preservice teachers to go on without me. I explained to Brianna that I would be happy to sit with her until 2:30 in the afternoon if that's what it took for her to finish her web. She finished it in about 3 minutes and it was absolutely correct. I told Brianna that we needed to talk. I explained, "I know you are very smart and you could help the other students if you would participate in our activities." (I did this in an attempt to create an ally.)

I told her, "It's fine if you don't like me at times. However, I am not going to tolerate your inappropriate actions."

Afterwards, I spoke with the classroom teacher about Brianna's behavior and she said it was becoming a real problem for her too, and what bothered her most was that she wrote letters to Brianna's parents and they were ignored. She recommended that I ignore Brianna, but I don't think that will work. Somehow, ignoring students' disruptive behavior just doesn't seem right.

CASE 3.2: APPLICATIONS AND REFLECTIONS

What do you think is the purpose of this lesson or series of lessons?

_____

_____

_____

_____

How was the original teaching plan interrupted, or what surprised Linda?

_____

_____

_____

_____

What action did Linda take in response to the interruption/surprise?

_____

_____

_____

_____

Examine the consequences of Linda's actions. What alternative action(s)/procedures would you suggest?

_____

_____

_____

_____

Identify the resources (e.g., outside readings; conversations with peers, teachers, or other professionals) used by Linda in this case. What other specific resources might you suggest (e.g., titles of related articles or books, community agencies, etc.)?

_____

_____

_____

_____

From whose perspective is the case written?

_____

_____

_____

_____

What do you think is Brianna's perspective?

_____

_____

_____

_____

Who are the players in the case?

_____

_____

_____

_____

What seems to be working well in this case?

_____

_____

_____

_____

What needs to be improved?

_____

_____

_____

_____

Can you distinguish between the symptoms and the problems presented in this case?

_____

_____

_____

_____

Adapted from Morine-Dershimer, 1996; Shulman, 1996; Silverman & Welty, 1996.

COMMENTARY 3.2A: PROBLEMS WITH A "STAR" STUDENT

Lauren Combs, Classroom Teacher
Waveland, Mississippi

I, too, would find Brianna very challenging. This type of child has always fascinated me. Brianna seems very independent and strong willed—the type of child who marches to the tune of a different drummer. She has her own style of doing things. She is not the type of child who wants to please. I am usually drawn to this type of child, because I am interested in seeing what makes them tick. Because these types of children have a unique way of looking at things, they tend to think creatively. However, they sometimes seek more attention from the teacher, and this can leave a teacher drained and frustrated at the end of the day.

I would have taken Brianna aside sooner to talk to her. In fact, the first day when I noticed that the group management plan was not working for her, I would have tried to get to the root of the problem. I would have questioned Brianna about her behavior and asked her why she was acting inappropriately. Talking to her privately would take time from the whole group. However, if you ignore a child's inappropriate behavior and allow the behavior to continue, a bigger problem ensues down the road. My advice is to deal with classroom problems when they surface or the problems will only get bigger.

You also need to determine why Brianna's parents do not respond to the classroom teacher's notes. There may be a problem at home that is carried into the classroom. Because Brianna is seeking attention, I'd want to know the reason why, especially if this is not her usual character.

I do believe that Brianna has to follow the same rules as the other students. Try praising the students who do follow the rules. Give a reward, such as a sticker, to the appropriately behaved students, and see if that will motivate Brianna. However, be careful of the rewards you give; otherwise, your students will be looking for rewards all of the time [see Commentary 3.3B]. Another suggestion is to catch Brianna being good and immediately praise her. Furthermore, try planning some activities that match Brianna's learning styles and multiple intelligences [see Commentary 9.2B]. Students learn to read and write easier when instructional techniques match the students' individual ways of learning. All of these suggestions take a lot of planning and preparation. You must get to know your students and then plan accordingly. You will be amazed at the benefits.

COMMENTARY 3.2B: PROBLEMS WITH A "STAR" STUDENT

Mary McCroskey, Teacher Educator
Montana State University

First, and very important, this preservice teacher is right when she says that ignoring a student's inappropriate behavior "just doesn't seem right." When teachers ignore students' improper behaviors, usually the behavior and other inappropriate actions continue and escalate. Effective literacy instruction cannot take place until all students attend to lessons. Therefore, this preservice teacher needs to help Brianna learn how to act in appropriate ways.

The essential components of this case seem to be that (a) Brianna exhibits inappropriate behavior in the classroom, (b) the family has not responded to the classroom teacher's attempts to discuss Brianna's behavior, and (c) Brianna's inappropriate behavior has escalated. All factors considered, the information in the case leads me to believe that something is happening in the home that is affecting Brianna deeply.

By third grade, the majority of students understand the social skills and work behaviors associated with school. Brianna is exhibiting inappropriate behavior by demanding the total attention of the person working with her. Her refusal to work without this attention is an indication that she feels the need to be in total control and even to control this preservice teacher. The question is, *why?*

In order to determine why Brianna seeks to be in total control, I would check with her previous classroom teachers to see if they could give some insights. I would also observe how the other students treat Brianna. In addition, I would try to determine when Brianna's negative behaviors began. Therefore, I would visit Brianna's family in their home, immediately. I wonder if an event has occurred recently that has taken parental time and affection away from Brianna, such as a new baby? Perhaps there is an ill parent, grandparent, or sibling? Perhaps the family is abusive or uncaring to one another or there is a harsh, uncaring family member causing constant discord in the home?

Do not assume anything when you have a parent conference. Simply state Brianna's behaviors in school and ask if her behavior is similar at home. Project a sincere concern for Brianna and enlist the help of her parents. Do not get into a contest of wills with Brianna or excuse her behaviors as the result of school or family problems. The goal is to help Brianna become a student who is achieving her fullest potential. She is very smart, and she needs to learn how to use her wonderful cognitive abilities to do what is expected of her. Be fair, firm, and consistent.

One more observation: As a preservice teacher, you may need assurance that good teachers do not treat all students in the same way. Instead, good teachers treat all students fairly. That means that good teachers meet each individual student's needs equally. This is not an easy task. Equal, fair treatment does not mean the same treatment for each student; instead, it means that teachers expect students to act in appropriate ways and that teachers help students to reach their fullest potential according to each student's individual needs.

CASE 3.3: THE KIDS ARE TELLING ME WHAT TO DO!

Ruth Hayes

From Day One, I knew Christopher was going to be one of the biggest challenges in my group of second graders. He permanently displays a frown on his face. This breaks my heart every time I see him. I constantly try to give him extra attention and cheer him up. At our first session, I asked him, "Christopher, are you upset or ill?" He would not say anything. I then asked him if he wanted to go to another group. Christopher replied, "Nope, I'm fine."

I just placed this situation under "first day jitters." However, on the second day of teaching, I noticed Christopher picking on Cassondra. Christopher said, "Move over fat gorilla."

Cassondra replied, "You have an ugly face."

I said "That is enough! This is your warning. If you cannot behave then you will have to leave the group and your name will go to the bottom of the helper chart." This seemed to stop the bickering for the day.

Now comes day three—doom day! I had the two children separated. However, I made the mistake of placing their chairs across from one another. I thought their misbehavior was a one-day thing. I soon realized that I was wrong. Christopher was the helper for the day. He cooperated with me all the way up to the prediction logs. All of the sudden he had the pouting face on from Day One. I said, "Christopher, is something wrong? Do you feel well?"

He said, "I just don't feel like writing today."

I said, "O.K., maybe you can draw a picture about your prediction." His response was, "No."

I took a deep breath and said to myself, "Well, Ruth, just let him sit there and pout." So that is just what I did. I did not think that he was going to cause any more problems because he was upset. However, I was wrong again. Soon he found Cassondra right across from him. He started kicking her and made faces at her. She was playing with him as well. I noticed this misbehavior and corrected it by placing a warning in effect for the both of them. Halfway through reading our book for the day, they began to act up again, but I ignored them. Christopher kept taking Cassondra's pencil. The other students were so deeply involved with the book that I did not stop. However, one third through the book, Christopher and Cassondra were acting up even more.

Soreonne, another second-grade student said, "Miss Ruth, you should send them in the hall."

I said to myself, "Holy Cow Ruth, the kids are telling you what to do."

I soon realized that I had to take control, but that's easier said than done, isn't it? I said, "That is enough! Christopher and Cassondra go out in the hall. When I am ready for you to return, I will come and get you."

I felt so bad, but at the same time I felt relieved. I actually felt in control of the group. When those two left, the rest of the book went smoothly and we were able to begin an art project about the book's story characters. Halfway into the art project, I told Christopher and Cassondra that I was almost ready for them to rejoin us. However, they were misbehaving in the hall, so I brought them into the classroom. When I did this, the classroom teacher said not to put the students in the hall if they misbehaved. I just want to know is there an effective way of smoothly correcting within the classroom so the other students will not give their undivided attention to the troublemakers? Could I perhaps establish a "punish corner?" But what happens when more than one student misbehaves at the same time, as in this situation?

CASE 3.3: APPLICATIONS AND REFLECTIONS

What do you think is the purpose of this lesson or series of lessons?

_____

_____

_____

How was the original teaching plan interrupted, or what surprised Ruth?

_____

_____

_____

What actions did Ruth take in response to the interruption/surprise?

_____

_____

_____

Examine the consequences of Ruth's actions. What alternative action(s)/procedures would you suggest?

_____

_____

_____

Identify the resources (e.g., outside readings; conversations with peers, teachers, or other professionals) used by Ruth in this case. What other specific resources might you suggest (e.g., titles of related articles or books, community agencies, etc.)?

_____

_____

_____

_____

From whose perspective is the case written?

_____

_____

_____

_____

What do you think are these second graders' perspectives?

_____

_____

_____

_____

Who are the players in the case?

_____

_____

_____

_____

What seems to be working well in this case?

_____

_____

_____

_____

What needs to be improved?

_____

_____

_____

_____

Can you distinguish between the symptoms and the problems presented in this case?

_____

_____

_____

_____

Adapted from Morine-Dershimer, 1996; Shulman, 1996; Silverman & Welty, 1996.

COMMENTARY: 3.3A: THE KIDS ARE TELLING ME WHAT TO DO!

Lynda Hagey, Classroom Teacher
United States Department of Defense Schools

It is hard to start a new teaching situation. You enter the classroom with your highest hopes and want to touch each child in a positive way. Suddenly, you are there, in front of the class, wanting to share a great new beginning with your students, and a "Christopher" begins to creep into your path—a child that presents a challenge to you immediately. Each year that I have taught I have had at least one Christopher.

In Ruth's situation, Christopher did not act out on the first day, but he had a permanent frown on his face. Many children do not react well in new situations. The thought of having a new teacher with new expectations can cause children to have fears. Unless a child showed serious signs of distress the first day, I would probably not give extra attention. I would simply try to make my expectations clear in a positive, upbeat, but firm manner. If the frowns continued for several days without any display of disciplinary problems, I would then talk to him about his concerns. I would also contact the child's parents. Often a parent can provide the vital insight you need to deal with the situation.

Christopher began to display disciplinary problems during Ruth's second day. She was right to stop the behavior immediately and provide him with a clear, firm consequence if he did not stop the behavior. Sometimes taking a positive reward away, such as being a helper, will be enough, as it was for him that day.

Then came Day Three, Ruth's "doom day," and Christopher began to frown again as he had on the first day. In my opinion, this on-again, off-again pouting face was Christopher's attempt to sway attention to himself. When Ruth gave him that attention, he began to challenge her authority.

Teachers cannot make a student do anything, but they can keep him or her from disrupting the rest of the class. The moment Christopher began to bother another student I would have said to him, "Christopher, you have chosen not to participate in this activity but I will not allow you to keep others from learning. You have two options, complete the activity or go sit in the back of the room until you choose to be part of our class again."

If he chose to go to the back of the room, I would ignore any pouting or clownish actions from him unless they disrupted the class. In my experience, most students will rejoin the class within 5 to 10 minutes. But if he continued to challenge my authority, I would never ignore it. I would stop the lesson, deal with the problem immediately, and make a call home that very night. It is better to stop one or two lessons in the beginning than have a miserable year of disruptions.

If I had two students acting up while I was reading a book as Ruth was, I would first stop just long enough to motion or tell one of the students to please come sit next to me. This may be all that is needed. If it appeared to be a recurring problem between the same students, I would talk to them separately and then together to try to resolve any hostilities they may hold for one another. I have often explained to my third graders that even as adults there will be times when they must work with people they do not like.

I have not found it necessary to establish a "punish corner." I know of one class where some students made a game of going to such a corner. A student can be sent to any isolated area of the room if you feel he or she needs to be separated from the group. If more than one student is misbehaving, simply find separate isolated areas in the room. Sitting at the computer table, in the reading corner, or at a table off to the side can work well. I tell the students that their learning is too important to be interrupted and I stress that they should respect each others' right to learn.

One positive approach I have used with each grade level I have taught, first through fifth, has worked beautifully. It is a team approach. Using this approach, I develop teams or groups of students who help each other remain on task and follow the rules. I give points for everything from lining up quietly, being caught on task, or any positive thing that I see. This is not a competitive approach, because teams work for team rewards and for class rewards. When teams reach a certain level, they may get extra time in the reading corner or do an extra science experiment. When the class reaches a certain point level, we may have a popcorn party or we may go outside and sit under a tree and read. This approach has helped with those students who seem to place greater value on peer acceptance than they do on adult authority.

Whatever approach Ruth decides to use as a teacher, the first few days are always hard. Clear, firm, and consistent expectations need to be established. Ruth needs to be firm. Being firm is not being mean. She needs to develop her "teacher face" to let students know when they are stepping out of bounds [see Commentary 3.3B]. She needs to be empathic to students' feelings, but she also needs to be aware that some may try to use emotions to seek the wrong type of attention. She needs to talk to parents and learn all she can about each student. I always try to talk to each parent within the first 2 weeks of school. Most of all, Ruth needs to never give up. What she has to offer is too important!

COMMENTARY: 3.3B: THE KIDS ARE TELLING ME WHAT TO DO!

Darlene Sellers, Counselor Educator
University of Southern Mississippi

It does feel disconcerting when we are supposed to be in control as teachers but we aren't. Let me share some observations about Ruth's concerns with her classroom management skills. It seems to me that she wants her kids to know that she cares about their feelings. Nevertheless, and understandably, she wants them to respond to her expectations. So, how do you let your students know that you really care about them and their feelings and, at the same time, orchestrate an environment so that your students get their needs met and you maintain the control that you need in your classroom?

First, if teachers want a classroom that is an organized learning environment, they need to develop their students' self-discipline. Ruth needs to stop thinking about punishing students! The first place to look for this crucial atmosphere of self-discipline is in the mirror. Ruth needs to look at her own self! She needs to practice teacher behavior and verbalizations that are firm but kind, and she needs to be absolutely certain of the desirable behaviors that she expects from her students. She needs to practice how she will look and react when her kids are meeting her expectations and when they are not. She can reward them for good behavior with social approval (e.g., smiles, winks, hand shakes, back pats, specific compliments, encouraging words). She can also give some special rewards. But Ruth must remember not to do this all of the time or her students always will expect tangible rewards [see Commentary 3.2A]. She can give stickers, happy faces by the students' names on a behavior chart, stamps, erasers, pencils, and so forth. This will reinforce her students' school-appropriate behaviors and will serve to enhance their sense of self-worth. Ruth recognizes her students as individuals and as members of a cohesive group. Rewards will help to guarantee that her students' appropriate behaviors are repeated.

Now, when Ruth's expectations are not being met, Ruth and her students must know in advance what plan they will follow. She can scold, frown, withdraw her attention, and assign consequences to those students who require a penalty. I would use banishment from the group (i.e., time out), only for student behavior that is particularly harmful to others' learning and well-being such as "on-purpose" humming, harming others, mocking, cursing, and threatening other students so that they become terrified. I would not assign time out for less serious infractions, such as pouting, failing to follow directions, or being fearful or hesitant. Teachers need to ignore students who report others for misbehaving (e.g., "He hit me!") if they haven't observed those behaviors firsthand. I think that all future classroom teachers need to receive training in classroom management techniques, but they usually don't. Teachers need to understand that they must remain calm and firm when students are acting out. A nonaggressive "in control" manner is essential for teachers. Teachers should never stoop to their kids' level of emotionality. Instead, teachers need to help their students develop self-control and the ability to self-monitor their actions. This is an especially big task for new teachers. It takes careful planning, practice, and coming to the realization that behavior as a teacher is critical to students' success as functioning, kind, considerate human beings.

CASE 3.4: ONE, TWO, THREE, ALL EYES ON ME

Jennifer Shrable

Silver, H., Strong, R., & Perini, M. (1997). Integrating learning styles and multiple intelligences. *Educational Leadership, 55*(1), 22–27.

As an elementary education major, I have been fortunate to have had field experiences in different schools. This has helped me recognize that there always is a variety of learning styles and backgrounds among schoolchildren. At this school I teach four African American second-grade boys. I have been quite pleased with the work they have done so far. However, I sometimes find it beyond challenging to get them to follow my instructions and become fully engaged in my lessons.

When I begin my lessons, I try to find some aspect that will hold my students' attention for the duration of our class time. The group always responds to my opening comments, but I begin to lose them about 20 minutes into each lesson.

Charles seems to be a **kinesthetic learner.** He also jumps out of his chair so much that he continually distracts the others. Devin gazes around the room periodically. Chris constantly asks me to go look at his Lego house. Scotty seems to be the only one who pays attention consistently. The most common distractions are, "May I go to the bathroom?" "Can I show you my Lego house?" and "When can we draw?"

I do not want them to have an accident in the classroom, so I usually let them go to the bathroom, but it seems to be a pattern with them. I have tried to remember to ask them to go to the bathroom at 9:45 am before I begin the day's lesson, so there will be no interruptions. However, this still causes a delay of about 7 to 10 minutes. In addition to these disruptions, I have had to take away crayons or other objects from the boys so that they will pay attention to the book I am reading or the lesson I am teaching.

The boys love to illustrate stories they have written, and I do not mind that. But here, too, this type of work causes them to get distracted. They talk out and laugh, and grumble when I tell them to stop drawing.

Another problem is that if we do get started on an activity or a writing assignment, I cannot seem to explain the goals of the lesson in enough ways so all four boys will understand what they are to do. I do not feel that I am speaking over their heads or introducing something they have never seen before. The problem is that far too often I walk out of the room feeling as though nothing was accomplished and that no effort was made by my students. I strive to find interesting and relevant books for my group, such as books on the Komodo dragon (they told me they were interested in dragons). I also share books that portray realistic African American story characters. But it does not seem to work. Are they testing me? Are they bored and I do not know it? Am I really teaching over their heads? I am willing to try anything to get these boys to participate and make full use of my time and their time.

CASE 3.4: APPLICATIONS AND REFLECTIONS

What problems are Jennifer and her students experiencing?

_____

_____

_____

_____

What questions did Jennifer ask that might help illuminate solutions?

_____

_____

_____

_____

What actions did Jennifer take in response to these problems?

_____

_____

_____

_____

Examine the consequences of Jennifer's actions. What alternative action(s)/procedures would you suggest?

_____

_____

_____

_____

Identify the resources (e.g., outside readings; conversations with peers, teachers, or other professionals) used by Jennifer in this case. What other specific resources might you suggest (e.g., titles of related articles or books, community agencies, etc.)?

_____

_____

_____

_____

From whose perspective is the case written?

_____

_____

_____

_____

What do you think are these second graders' perspectives?

_____

_____

_____

_____

Who are the players in the case?

_____

_____

_____

_____

What seems to be working well in this case?

_____

_____

_____

_____

What needs to be improved?

_____

_____

_____

_____

Can you distinguish between the symptoms and the problems presented in this case?

_____

_____

_____

_____

Adapted from Morine-Dershimer, 1996; Shulman, 1996; Silverman & Welty, 1996.

COMMENTARY: 3.4A: ONE, TWO THREE, ALL EYES ON ME

Miriam Jones, Classroom Teacher
Ocean Springs, Mississippi

I've asked myself the same questions about my students and my teaching that you ask in your teaching case, Jennifer. It's good that you are trying to reflect on your own teaching practices and are not concentrating just on your students' behaviors to solve this problem. In this situation, the answers to your questions may be that yes, Charles, Devin, Chris, and Scotty are testing you. Yes, they probably are bored. And although you may not be teaching "over their heads," you may be expecting these second graders to sit still and attend to literacy tasks for too long.

Second-grade students, all students for that matter, need to be drawn into a lesson and engaged throughout. Continue to select books based on your students' interests and cultural heritage. Try using props, costumes, music, or puppets to set the stage for your literature readings [see Commentary 5.2A and Cases 9.1 and 9.2]. While reading, stop and engage the boys with thought-provoking questions. Ask for their predictions about what will happen next in a story. Lead a discussion about why a particular story event happened. Collaborate together on discovering the major themes of a story.

I also suggest that you not read the entire book and then do an activity. Because the boys enjoy drawing illustrations, stop at an appropriate place in a story and ask them to draw what they think will happen next. While they are working you can assess their abilities to appropriately predict story events and characters' actions. Ask the boys to share their work and then see if it matches the author's ideas as you continue reading. Draw the boys back into reading by continuing to engage your students in such activities as **literature circles,** in which they give their opinions and feelings about literature. Remember to break up reading lessons with arts activities to keep the boys' attention. This should eliminate unnecessary trips to the bathroom, and you can make better use of your time together.

COMMENTARY 3.4B: ONE, TWO THREE, ALL EYES ON ME

Susan Lenski, Teacher Educator
Illinois State University

Hello Jennifer,

The problems you identify—motivating students and keeping them engaged in a literacy activity—reflect one of the most challenging aspects of being a teacher. Keeping students engaged is a skill that effective teachers share. Most teachers face the same problems you describe no matter what ethnic or cultural group they teach. There are no easy answers, but having a few more strategies in your repertoire will help. I'm glad to see that you have tried many alternatives and are still willing to try new options.

You mention that the group always responds to your opening comments. That shows that your students do want to listen to you. However, you say that they become distracted after about 20 minutes. Actually, that's not too bad. If you can keep the attention of second-grade boys for 20 minutes, you are doing well. Consider that a triumph.

Because you have their attention for 20 minutes, capitalize on it. Make those 20 minutes as instructionally dense as you can. Quickly move from introduction or review to the main part of the lesson. Present as much new material as you can while you have their undivided attention. If you are assessing their reading, or if you want to hear them read, give them that opportunity before they lose interest.

After the first 20 minutes and the students' attention wavers, give them a short break to use the washroom, take a drink of water, or jog in place. It sounds as if these boys need to release some energy. A 3-minute break will help, and will make the rest of your lesson more effective. Then, proceed to the next part of the session.

The third part of your lesson could be some activity that is designed for active participation. You might try group discussions rather than individual work. Or you might play a learning game with the boys. Because you mention that Charles is a kinesthetic learner, you should design a learning activity that requires movement, even if it is writing on a chalkboard.

You also mentioned that you have difficulty giving directions so that all four boys understand. That can be frustrating. Try to give only one direction at a time. Say the direction, write the direction on the board, and then ask the boys to repeat it [see Commentary 8.2B]. Finally, make the boys accountable for listening to directions by refusing to repeat the direction you just stated.

I don't think that the boys are testing you or that they are necessarily bored. I think they are behaving like lively, second-grade boys. The job of a teacher is to encourage engagement in learning in ways that appeal to active students as well as to students who have no difficulty sitting and listening. This will be a challenge you will face for your entire teaching career. Teachers need to be flexible. So, even if something works for awhile, always keep on the lookout for new ideas. You will need them eventually.

SUGGESTED READINGS

Collins, J. (1994, April). *Dialogue and resistance in small group reading-writing instruction.* Paper presented at the Annual Meeting of the American Educational Research Association, New Orleans, LA. (ERIC Document Reproductive Service No. ED 371 306).

This work examines resistant students' interactive reading and writing practices within a participant framework. Data from observations, audiotapes, and transcripts of teacher-led discussions indicate that resistive students may be sufficiently competent, but choose to participate intermittently and to oppose lessons for a number of reasons.

Daniel, P. (1996). A celebration of literacy: Nine reluctant students and one determined teacher. *Language Arts, 73,* 420–428.

This very readable article describes a first-grade teacher's determination to help nonmotivated and reluctant readers in her classroom. The teacher worked energetically to convince her students that they were capable and could succeed. She used many motivating strategies, including celebrating students' literacy accomplishments, stressing students' interdependence, and providing her students with choices.

Ng, M., Guthrie, J., McCann, A., Van Meter, P., & Solomon, A. (1996). *How do classroom characteristics influence intrinsic motivations for literacy?* (Reading Research Report No. 56). Athens, GA: National Reading Research Center, Universities of Georgia and Maryland.

This report summarizes third- and fifth-grade students' motivations for participating in literacy tasks. Students were videotaped participating in normal classroom literacy activities. Then they were interviewed to determine their motivations for literacy tasks and their perceptions of the context. Grade 3 students reported more intrinsic motivations when they perceived the learning context to be socially supportive. Grade 5 students reported higher motivations when the learning context was perceived as being autonomy supportive.

4

Speaking and Listening

Literacy Concepts and Terms

-auding
-author's chair
-communicative competence
-K-W-L
-schemata

OVERVIEW

The cases and commentaries in this chapter highlight optimizing students' speaking and listening abilities. All teachers would agree that proficiency in speaking and listening correlates strongly with students' academic performances, especially in the areas of reading and writing. Teachers also recognize that students who have opportunities to talk and interact with both their teacher and their peers enhance their oral language, **communicative competence,** and active listening abilities (i.e., **auding**). Teachers are challenged to create classroom contexts that minimize too much "teacher talk" and maximize opportunities to nurture and encourage students' auding and oral communication efforts.

CASE 4.1: BASHFUL OR ASHAMED?

Brandi Aquilo

I try to get my third-grade students actively involved in lessons through group discussions and sharing of work. For example, when my students create stories, I usually ask them to share the stories with their peers. I believe oral language is an important aspect of developing total literacy in children.

There is one student named Alvin who never wants to share his work. Although he doesn't share his work, he does enjoy discussing the stories we read. For example, when I asked my students how the story of *The Three Little Pigs* (Kincaid, 1983) was different from the *The True Story of the Three Little Pigs* (Scieszka, 1989), Alvin eagerly raised his hand and said, "One is the pig's version and one is the wolf's version."

I think that Alvin's eagerness to answer questions about stories is a sign that he may not be shy and that his oral language is commensurate with his age and grade level. Alvin also seems to be an intelligent child. He comprehends everything I read and usually knows the meanings of words that other children choose for vocabulary words. But when I ask him to share his journal entries, Alvin declines.

When I asked him to share his letter to the President, Alvin also declined. So I decided to try something different, called the **author's chair.** First, my students and I created a story through a story impressions activity. Then, we drew pictures and practiced our stories. When I explained what we were going to do in our author's chair activity, Alvin asked, "Do I have to share my story?" He looked very uncomfortable and nervous.

I told Alvin I would like him to share his story but, if he didn't want to, it would be okay. I took his paper and quickly scanned through his story. When I handed it back to Alvin, I complimented him. I said, "Your story is wonderful!"

But Alvin still didn't want to share his story with the group. I would like Alvin to share his work. At the same time, I don't want to make him feel uncomfortable. How do I go about accomplishing both of these things? I thought about Alvin's self-esteem and wondered if that had anything to do with his reticence. I know Alvin is intelligent and I know I want to find a gentle way to help Alvin share his work. But where do I go from there? Is it even necessary for Alvin to share his work? Will it be more harmful if I push him when he really gets nervous about sharing his work? I guess my ultimate question is how do I make Alvin realize that his work is wonderful and just as good as his that of group members.

McGinley, W., & Denner, P. (1987). Story impressions: A prereading/writing activity. *Journal of Reading, 31,* 248–253.

CASE 4.1: APPLICATIONS AND REFLECTIONS

What do you think is the purpose of this lesson or series of lessons?

_____

_____

_____

_____

How was the original teaching plan interrupted, or what surprised Brandi?

_____

_____

_____

_____

What actions did Brandi take in response to the interruption/surprise?

_____

_____

_____

_____

Examine the consequences of Brandi's actions. What alternative action(s)/procedures would you suggest?

_____

_____

_____

_____

Identify the resources (e.g., outside readings; conversations with peers, teachers, or other professionals) used by Brandi in this case. What other specific resources might you suggest (e.g., titles of related articles or books, community agencies, etc.)?

_____

_____

_____

_____

From whose perspective is the case written?

_____

_____

_____

_____

What do you think is Alvin's perspective?

_____

_____

_____

_____

Who are the players in the case?

_____

_____

_____

_____

What seems to be working well in this case?

_____

_____

_____

_____

What needs to be improved?

_____

_____

_____

_____

Can you distinguish between the symptoms and the problems presented in this case?

_____

_____

_____

_____

Adapted from Morine-Dershimer, 1996; Shulman, 1996; Silverman & Welty, 1996.

COMMENTARY 4.1A: BASHFUL OR ASHAMED?

Kathryn Carr, Teacher Educator
Central Missouri State University

I think that Brandi was correct to not insist that Alvin share his writing. His lack of confidence and fear that classmates will laugh or criticize are not uncommon. Due to the personal nature of writing, anyone may find it quite threatening to submit work for the inspection of peers.

My suggestions for helping Alvin are threefold: establish a supportive classroom environment, allow plenty of time for Alvin to gain confidence, and provide some extra support for Alvin that I think he may only need temporarily. As to classroom structure, I think that the author's chair, although generally a good idea, focuses attention on the importance of writing and puts a spotlight on the author. This is the likely reason why it didn't work with Alvin. A less threatening approach would be a small-group writing conference. In this technique, four or five students and the teacher sit around a table to discuss their works in progress or their finished pieces. This kind, sharing, trust-building community takes awhile to create, and I would not expect Alvin to share for a long time.

I would recommend teaching students the PQP technique from the Bay Area National Writing Project (Noyce & Christie, 1989). The first *P* stands for praise after the author has shared (i.e., listeners tell something they liked about the piece). Then, *Q* questions are in order. The questions elicit clarification of something not understood as well as questions of general interest (e.g., "Where did you get the idea for the story?" or "How will your piece end?"). The final *P* stands for polish, when the group may offer suggestions for improvement. Of course, teacher modeling, both as a writer and a discussant using PQP, is an important aspect of building a sense of community and trust.

Cora Lee Five (1992) made a point about having patience during the extensive length of time required for some students to develop enough confidence to share their own work. She described the case of Angela, who eventually was willing to share her writing in a group conference after months of listening to other students in her group.

An additional thought—it may be that Alvin would be willing to have the teacher or another student read his writing to the group, perhaps standing next to the teacher until he develops more confidence [see Commentary 4.1B].

Lyons, B. (1981). The PQP method of responding to writing. *English Journal, 70*(3), 42–43.

COMMENTARY 4.1B: BASHFUL OR ASHAMED?

Martha Eshelman, Classroom Teacher
Knob Noster, Missouri

To share one's own created production is a very personal thing. It's a little like baring your soul to the world. Some students are far more sensitive than others about sharing work, and this sensitivity must be respected. To force students to share and talk in front of others before they are ready should be avoided. In fact, teachers usually don't need to give grades for sharing in front of others. Sharing personal thoughts is very different from participating in class discussions and answering questions about material read. Perhaps that could explain Alvin's willingness to talk about literature, and his reticence about not reading his own work.

No mention was made in this case about Alvin's reading ability. Perhaps his reticence to share his own writing stems from an insecurity about his reading fluency rather than from a lack of confidence about the excellence of his manuscript.

Getting Alvin to share his writing with others should be accomplished very gently. One approach is to inquire if Alvin would like someone else to read his work while he stands next to the reader. I have frequently dealt with such a situation over a several-month period. The young authors stood by me as I read their pieces, holding my arm around their shoulders, making it obvious to the audience that they were the authors of the pieces and deserved ownership and recognition.

As classmates respond positively to the various pieces of writing over several months, a writer's confidence and sense of being accepted is bolstered and, usually, he or she becomes willing to read his work aloud. I have yet to see a student go all year refusing to share writing assignments.

Gentle urging is the answer, along with emphasis on the positives about the reticent student's writing. Heavy pressure is not the way to go. It is almost a given that, in time, Alvin will be more willing to read his own writing to his peers.

CASE 4.2: BEYONKA

Rachel Reilly

My group of kindergartners are all very special. Many of them seem to be very interested in my lessons. However, I have one student who seems to be very easily distracted. She also seems to have trouble expressing herself, and she seems to have feelings of insecurity.

Last week I was reading a story and Beyonka was watching the other groups in the classroom. I thought I would ask Beyonka a question to capture her attention. I decided to try the yes/no and why reading comprehension strategy. I asked Beyonka, "Do you have a 'Yes' for this page of the story? A 'Yes' is something you really like or understand."

I waited a minute so Beyonka could gather her thoughts. I asked Beyonka, "What is your 'Yes,' and why?"

Beyonka just shrugged her shoulders. I asked her, "Can you point out your 'Yes' on the page and explain why it is your 'Yes'?"

Beyonka said, "Yeah."

She began telling me her answer but she was talking so softly that I couldn't understand her.

I said, "Beyonka can you say your answer a little louder so that I can hear your answer?"

Finally, one of the other students said, "Miss Reilly, I think she said she liked where the frog lived."

I asked Beyonka, "Is that what you were trying to tell me?" All she said was "Yeah."

Because of this incident, I thought it would help if she sat closer to me for our journal writing. When the other students were working on their journals I read my journal entry to Beyonka aloud to her. I asked her, "Would you like me to write your answer in your journal?"

Beyonka said, "Yeah."

I asked her, "What would you like to say?"

Beyonka replied, "I don't know."

I then said, "Why did you draw this picture and is that your answer to my message to you?"

She said, "I don't know."

Then, she put her hands in her mouth. I kept trying to get an answer from her and she kept looking at me, not saying anything. I was very patient, but she still did not speak. Because of all this I put her out of the group, but it didn't bother her one bit. I watched her and she exhibited the same noncommunicative behavior outside of the group when she was working with her classroom teacher.

I think that too much of my time is taken up by having to give extra help to some of the students like Beyonka. I really am worried about her because all she ever says is, "Yeah."

In my heart I know she has the potential to be a great reader, writer, and speaker, but she has very little self-confidence. I try to praise her when she does something good. I think she might have a really big problem. If you can give me any advice I would greatly appreciate it.

Richards, J., & Gipe, J. (1992). Activating background knowledge: Strategies for beginning and poor readers. *The Reading Teacher, 45,* 474–475.

CASE 4.2: APPLICATIONS AND REFLECTIONS

What do you think is the purpose of this lesson or series of lessons?

_____

_____

_____

_____

How was the original teaching plan interrupted, or what surprised Rachel?

_____

_____

_____

_____

What actions did Rachel take in response to the interruption/surprise?

_____

_____

_____

_____

Examine the consequences of Rachel's actions. What alternative action(s)/procedures would you suggest?

_____

_____

_____

_____

Identify the resources (e.g., outside readings; conversations with peers, teachers, or other professionals) used by Rachel in this case. What other specific resources might you suggest (e.g., titles of related articles or books, community agencies, etc.)?

_____

_____

_____

_____

From whose perspective is the case written?

_____

_____

_____

_____

What do you think is Beyonka's perspective?

_____

_____

_____

_____

Who are the players in the case?

_____

_____

_____

_____

What seems to be working well in this case?

_____

_____

_____

_____

What needs to be improved?

_____

_____

_____

_____

Can you distinguish between the symptoms and the problems presented in this case?

_____

_____

_____

_____

Adapted from Morine-Dershimer, 1996; Shulman, 1996; Silverman & Welty, 1996.

COMMENTARY 4.2A: BEYONKA

Karyn Wellhousen, Teacher Educator
University of New Orleans, Louisiana

At times, students who are shy and noncommunicative can be as frustrating to teachers as those who are loud and boisterous. Initially, Rachel's reactions to Beyonka's introverted behaviors were right on target. She called Beyonka's name when she wasn't paying attention, and she invited Beyonka to respond to a question. Rachel also allowed Beyonka's classmate to repeat Beyonka's inaudible answer. Then, Rachel moved Beyonka into close physical proximity. Furthermore, Rachel assisted Beyonka with her journal writing and praised her attempts to respond to a written message. These teacher actions showed Beyonka that Rachel was patient and caring.

Unfortunately, Beyonka received a very different message when Rachel removed her from the group. I think that Beyonka's behavior did not warrant banishment from her peers. Teachers should save time-out punishment for students who commit more serious rule infractions, such as hitting other students or having temper tantrums [see Commentary 3.3B].

Students who do not answer questions usually are not trying to act inappropriately. Rather, they may be intimidated, or they may not know the answers to the questions the teacher asks. Perhaps Beyonka has limited oral language and has difficulty speaking in complete sentences.

When deciding how much time should be devoted to students like Beyonka, teachers need to recognize that individual attention from the teacher may be exactly what quiet, shy, reticent students need to help them feel comfortable in group situations. Beyonka needs time to get used to school. After all, she is just a kindergarten student.

My advice is to remember that when new teachers reach a point of frustration with reserved, unsure students, they should resist imposing a punishment for students' failures to respond. This only reinforces students' feelings of distrust. Instead, teachers can conclude attempts to get students involved by giving an encouraging message, such as, "I know you can do this," and moving on to the next student. Another suggestion is to speak privately with noncommunicative students, such as on the playground, in the lunchroom, or on a field trip. Teachers also might ask quiet, shy students to be helpers in handing out or collecting work materials.

If preservice teachers are seriously concerned that a student may be exhibiting atypical behavior, they can record brief, anecdotal records describing the students' behaviors and the conditions under which the behaviors occur. Sharing these observations with the classroom teacher or with teacher colleagues to determine if the behavior is typical for the student or for students of the same age can prove very helpful.

COMMENTARY 4.2B: BEYONKA

Mary Gobert, Classroom Teacher
Hancock County, Mississippi

Hello Rachel,

First of all, Beyonka needs some "spit and polish" on her self-confidence. Start looking for Beyonka's gifts. Every child has special gifts; it's just that some students' abilities and talents are easier to spot than others'. Maybe Beyonka can jump rope well, sing, run, paint, or grasp math concepts quickly.

It's your job as the teacher to find an outlet of self-expression that will bring her into the mainstream of the class. Now, what else can you do? Find out as much as possible about Beyonka's background and family situation. I recommend a simple interest inventory and a parent conference.

For the nitty gritty on Beyonka's language development, which is closely related to success in reading and writing, look at picture books together and ask her to name the objects she sees. This will give you a gauge on her vocabulary and world knowledge. Assess her understanding of language structure and syntax by asking her to construct sentences about what she sees in books.

Besides apparent problems in language, perhaps Beyonka's background knowledge is not sufficiently developed for language related activities—another important dimension of literacy success. Begin to take more time to expand and enhance Beyonka's **schemata.** Read, read, read to her, and have someone else do it too. An assistant, older child, or more able reader all could be reading helpers [see Commentary 2.1A]. Beyonka also should be given the opportunity to work actively with her peers (e.g., collaborating on a group mural, participating in reading comprehension and writing strategies, whatever), so that she is not singled out as being different from the other students, and she has additional avenues to build her self-confidence as a learner.

Send a tape recorder and tapes of books home for Beyonka. Enlist help from home, if possible. It is so beneficial when parents read and write with their children. Find videos or picture books about subjects that interest her and make them available to her in the classroom. Plan coordinated field trips. Continue to journal with her, one-on-one, gradually enlisting another student to join your dialogue journaling. The student should be one who has interests similar to Beyonka's. Assign Beyonka small roles in group leadership positions as she becomes a more able communicator. In short, do whatever it takes to open up Beyonka's world more. It is important that you remain nonjudgmental throughout this long process. Beyonka must have total confidence in your acceptance of her and her ideas. You also could have a talent show and let Beyonka display her artwork and creative books, or she could give a short talk about her favorite author. Take a video and photographs of the production. Afterward, show the video to the class and put pictures from the show on the bulletin board. Invite the class to journal or create books about the fun. I truly believe that if you offer Beyonka all of these literacy learning opportunities, she will begin to blossom!

CASE 4.3: ACTIVE LISTENING

Wendy Van Belle

Ogle, D. (1986). K-W-L: A teaching model that develops active reading of expository text. *The Reading Teacher, 39,* 564–570.

I've been working with a small group of first-grade boys with varying interests and levels of abilities in reading and writing. Because of this I try to select materials and activities they all will enjoy and have success doing. In one of my first lessons, I gave them a choice of reading material, either squirrels or ladybugs. Jordan yelled out, "Squirrels!"

The others happily agreed and I chose the book *Squirrels* by Brian Wildsmith (1975). Before we began reading about squirrels, we began a modified version of **K-W-L.** The boys really liked doing this strategy very much. Trevor was the first to volunteer what he knew about squirrels. He said, "They live in trees."

Jordan immediately jumped in with, "They eat nuts."

Kody was very frustrated, because the other two boys had come up with some great ideas before he had a chance to respond. He's a bit slower than the other two and he likes to talk all the time. So, I looked at him and asked, "Kody, what do you know about squirrels?"

He thought about it for a minute (meanwhile, the other two boys kept waving their hands). Kody said, "They climb on trees." Trevor then said, "They walk on wires."

This first part of K-W-L (the *K* part) went very well, and helped the boys activate their background knowledge about squirrels. The second part of the K-W-L lesson (the *W* part) got very silly. Jordan had trouble sitting still, but he was able to participate in the conversation and it didn't seem to bother the others in the group. Thus, I let his behavior slide. Kody came up with the first question—"How do squirrels eat?"

Jordan interrupted with, "How do they go to the bathroom?"

Naturally, they all laughed. However, we were able to get back on track, because I took the question seriously. Trevor was getting very excited about getting to the book at this point. He asked, "Can we hear the story now?" I told him in just a few moments. Then he asked, "Where do squirrels sleep?"

Of course, wouldn't you know, Jordan brought up the bathroom thing again and they all got silly. I played it down by saying, "Well, why don't we see if it says something about this topic in the book."

I took out the book, we looked at the cover, and I had the boys read the title and the author of the book. Then, we discussed the type of art the author used to illustrate the book. The boys were very interested in this part of the lesson. Fortunately, none of them had heard the story before, and we were able to get something new out of this lesson. At various points throughout the book we stopped and discussed the similarities between the squirrels represented in the book and the squirrels that live near our homes. Everyone in my group wanted to share their ideas. Kody especially wanted to talk about how squirrels hold onto trees. Trevor was excited about everything in the book. Jordan wanted to read the book by himself. He was particularly interested in the way squirrels sleep and the ways they store food for winter. Because there are so many squirrels around our homes and in our parks, the boys were able to relate easily to the concepts in the book. Once we finished reading the book, we completed the last portion of the K-W-L (the *L* part). The boys were able to list almost everything we read in the book and everything we talked about. Each time one of them would come up with an idea or fact, another would follow with more information. It was like electricity. They fed off of each other. With every answer given, they each got more excited. Being able to participate in this shared reading activity through speaking and listening to each other definitely helped them to be motivated and to retain more information.

When we finished our K-W-L strategy, I did a comprehension assessment. I put the lists we had generated on our K-W-L chart away and handed them a sheet of blank paper. I then asked them to draw a squirrel doing one of the things we read about in the story, and to list four things about squirrels. The boys loved being able to show their knowledge this way (i.e., linking the creative arts and written language) [see Commentary 5.2A and Case 9.2]. They couldn't wait to show their papers to their classmates. My questions are: Is there a way I can go through a lesson faster and still keep my students actively engaged in listening and speaking to one another so that they do not get bored? Also, what do you do when a student brings up inappropriate topics in group discussions, like the squirrel bathroom thing? Finally, how much active listening is too much? I kind of got the idea that the classroom teacher thought we should have been quieter and that there was too much talking going on in our group.

CASE 4.3: APPLICATIONS AND REFLECTIONS

What do you think is the purpose of this lesson or series of lessons?

_____

_____

_____

_____

How was the original teaching plan interrupted, or what surprised Wendy?

_____

_____

_____

_____

What actions did Wendy take in response to the interruption/surprise?

_____

_____

_____

_____

Examine the consequences of Wendy's actions. What alternative action(s)/procedures would you suggest?

_____

_____

_____

_____

Identify the resources (e.g., outside readings; conversations with peers, teachers, or other professionals) used by Wendy in this case. What other specific resources might you suggest (e.g., titles of related articles or books, community agencies, etc.)?

_____

_____

_____

_____

From whose perspective is the case written?

_____

_____

_____

_____

What do you think are these first graders' perspectives?

_____

_____

_____

_____

Who are the players in the case?

_____

_____

_____

_____

What seems to be working well in this case?

_____

_____

_____

_____

What needs to be improved?

_____

_____

_____

_____

Can you distinguish between the symptoms and the problems presented in this case?

_____

_____

_____

_____

Adapted from Morine-Dershimer, 1996; Shulman, 1996; Silverman & Welty, 1996.

COMMENTARY 4.3A: ACTIVE LISTENING

Susan Lenski, Teacher Educator
Illinois State University

This case illustrates the magic of teaching. When students are engaged and learning, teachers feel the electricity! It sounds as if Wendy has a natural ability to succeed in a difficult part of teaching—engaging students.

Engaging students, although important, is not the only quality of successful literacy lessons. Students must be engaged, but they also must think and process text. Wendy's questions about keeping the pace of the lesson moving and how to respond to inappropriate student questions are good ones that will add to her ability to engage students.

Wendy's use of the K-W-L strategy is certainly appropriate for her lesson. As she moves through the K-W-L stages, she might try using "think-pair-share" to facilitate the group. With this technique, students think first about what they know about a given topic. Then, they share their thoughts with another student. Finally, they share their ideas with the entire group. Asking students to think carefully before answering provides time for slower students like Kody to gather ideas. Giving students opportunities to share with another student provides opportunities for each member of the group to express their ideas. Finally, when students share with the entire group, teachers can be sure that every student will have an appropriate answer. Wendy also might try calling on students in a random fashion to prevent the impulsiveness of students raising their hands and yelling out the answers.

Sometimes students offer inappropriate responses to teachers' questions, as Jordan did in this case. If a teacher believes that a student is asking a legitimate question (albeit inappropriate), she can say, "Let's find out the answer to this question later today."

In Wendy's case, however, she implied that Jordan's question about squirrels and their bathroom habits was motivated by silliness. When students try to get the group off task by asking silly questions, I recommend that teachers say, "We don't need to discuss that topic," and then move briskly forward. Students need to know that some issues are not appropriate for school discussions. They should not be allowed to sabotage good lessons by asking inappropriate questions.

One last point—when students are excited about learning, they can be noisy. Excitement and noise are wonderful, but Wendy needs to make sure that her noisy learning group does not disturb others when they are reading. She is on the right track with her reflections and questions.

COMMENTARY 4.3B: ACTIVE LISTENING

Bonnie Stiles, Classroom Teacher
East Peoria, Illinois

The enthusiasm created in this K-W-L lesson was outstanding! Many times, generating student enthusiasm and excitement is the most difficult part of teachers' work. Wendy did an excellent job of selecting a topic that interested her students; that's what helped to generate their excitement and influenced their many responses. Offering a reading topic that is familiar to students allows them to draw on their background knowledge.

Just like all good teachers, Wendy reflected on her teaching and recognized that there may have been a more effective way to ensure that her lesson ran smoothly. I commend her on her willingness and insight to look carefully at the strong and weak points of her lesson in order to figure out the best approaches to help her students achieve success.

I think all Wendy needs to do is refine her teaching through practice. One such refinement could be her classroom management skills. Students need to have rules and expectations modeled for them, and they need to practice those rules and be constantly reminded of what behavior is acceptable and what is not appropriate.

Wendy's K-W-L lesson needed some ground rules set first, followed by teacher modeling and student practice. The lesson would then have been more effective and satisfying. Perhaps she might limit the boys' responses to one fact per turn during the *K* (What do I know?) portion of the lesson. She also might ask the boys to raise their hands before they are called on. Then, she could call on Kody first, addressing the boys' differing abilities [see Cases 12.1 and 12.2].

Setting ground rules for the questions the boys asked during the *W* (What do I want to know?) section of the lesson and modeling appropriate questions might have avoided the inappropriate "squirrel bathroom question." If the boys continued to make inappropriate comments, stopping their remarks immediately is the best approach. Even first graders usually know what topics are okay and not okay in school.

Finally, maintaining student involvement is the key to a teacher's success. This allows the entire group to stay focused on a topic. Remember, teacher modeling and having students practice what will be expected of them in a forthcoming lesson promotes better group dynamics, helps to provide for students' differing ability levels, allows all students to contribute, and makes them feel that they are important members of a wonderful learning group.

SUGGESTED READINGS

Cullinan, B. (1993). *Children's voices: Talk in the classroom.* Newark, DE: International Reading Association.
This collection of essays offers teachers ways to help students develop their speaking and listening abilities. Activities include storytelling, drama, small group discussions, and literature circles, as well as especially appealing and creative group activities.

Jalongo, M. (1995). Promoting active listening in the classroom. *Childhood Education, 72,* 13–18.
Educators assert the importance of listening skills but receive little training in how to help students develop their active listening abilities. This paper offers tips for promoting students' auding skills. Developmentally appropriate practices include teachers being good listeners themselves. Students also should play a major role in formulating questions during literacy lessons and should spend as much time listening to one another as to the teacher.

Paratore, J., & McCormick, R. (1998). *Peer talk in the classroom.* Newark, DE. International Reading Association.
This reader-friendly text provides ideas and activities that teachers have found helpful for promoting students' talk and interactions in the classroom. Research undergirding the suggestions is also included, as well as explanations about how to implement the ideas offered (e.g., book clubs, cross-aged talks, and peer-led literature discussions).

Popp, M. (1996). *Teaching language and literature in elementary classrooms: A resource book for professional development.* Mahwah, NJ: Lawrence Erlbaum Associates.
Chapter 7 explains why listening and speaking activities enhance students' reading and writing abilities. This text also offers guidelines for promoting students' speaking and listening abilities, such as shared-pair reading, creative drama, readers theatre, puppet shows, and Friday afternoon sharing time (FAST).

5

Reading Instruction

Literacy Concepts and Terms

-DRTA
-letter/sound relationships
-K-W-L
-metacomprehension
-literature-based approach
-multiple story themes
-onsets
-phonemic awareness
-phonics
-print conventions
-prior knowledge
-reading instructional levels

-rimes
-running record
-schemata
-semantic map
-shared reading
-sound/symbol relationships
-storyboard
-text sets
-word identification
-word recognition
-word sorts

OVERVIEW

The cases and commentaries in this section focus on reading instruction. Effective teachers know that reading is an active, complex, cognitive task. As longtime literacy teachers, we believe that comprehension should be the focus of reading, and that reading is, essentially, thinking. Particular words used by an author are a stimulus for readers' thinking and will activate certain aspects of readers' **prior knowledge,** or **schemata.** The amount of prior knowledge a reader has for a particular text determines how well the reader will understand the text. In turn, prior knowledge can also influence how well a reader can decode unfamiliar words.

We also support a **literature-based approach** to reading instruction, so that readers are exposed to **print conventions,** uses of language, and a wide range of vocabulary, as well as enjoyable text. We encourage reading to students in order to draw attention to conventions of print, unusual vocabulary, or **sound/symbol relationships** (phonics) during this shared reading time. Although comprehension always is the focus, learners do need explicit instruction in recognizing common letter patterns found in printed text. There is a great deal of predictability that exists in the **letter/sound relationships** (phonics) in our language, and it is readily available in children's literature. An effective teacher recognizes opportunities within text for teaching phonics and sight words, but also reminds learners to use what they already know about the topic of the text to help them predict words unknown in print. Thus, it is comprehension that precedes and assists readers' **word identification.**

Stauffer, R. (1975). Directing the reading–thinking process. New York: Harper & Row.

Richards, J., & Gipe, J. (1996). I wonder...? A strategy to help children listen actively to stories. *The Whole Idea, 7*(1), 10–11.

Richards, J., & Gipe, J. (1993). Getting to know my character: A strategy to help young and at-risk children respond to story characters. *The Reading Teacher, 47*, 78–79.

Richards, J. C., & Gipe, J. P. (1998). Developing young students' awareness of story themes in literature-based reading programs. *The Reading Instruction Journal, 40*(2), 5–8.

Scheuermann, B., Jacobs, W., McCall, C., & Knies, W. (1994). The personal spelling dictionary: An adaptive approach to reducing the spelling hurdle in written language. *Intervention in School and Clinic, 29*(5), 292–299.

CASE 5.1: DON'T ASSUME AND SLOW DOWN!

Heather Friloux

I teach eight fifth-grade students for 1 hour twice a week. Having worked with elementary students last semester, I feel more comfortable and confident in the classroom this semester. I know more about managing students' behaviors. Therefore, my focus this semester is to become more familiar with reading comprehension strategies that help students become independent readers.

My fifth graders have become quite good at using reading strategies, and we have read a good deal of quality children's literature. We have used the following reading strategies thus far: I wonder?, **DRTA, K-W-L,** find the features and connect them, yes/no and why, and getting to know my character. I would like my students to become comfortable using these strategies before moving on to the more difficult strategy of what's the theme?

My students seem to understand the strategies that we have used and they have made some excellent inferences using the getting to know my character strategy. With everything going so smoothly, my mother asked me, "What could possibly be a problem worth writing about in a teaching case?"

Therefore, I began to ponder this question and could not think of a single thing to write. That was when I decided to listen to the cassette that I recorded of my teaching experiences last week. I made the tape when I read *I Can Hear the Sun* (Polacco, 1996), and we used the getting to know my character strategy. When I listened to the cassette, I discovered that I had weaknesses while teaching reading comprehension strategies!

One teaching flaw I have is that I tend to assume that students have the same background knowledge and vocabulary as I do. I have difficulty remembering that I am working with fifth-grade students, not adults. For example, I read a sentence from the the story that said, "Fondo had become such a familiar face there at the lake that even Mae Marie had taken up a great fondness for him." I said, "Isn't it interesting how the author chose to call the boy Fondo, and Mae Marie had a fondness for him? Even the other characters in the story, including the blind goose, were fond of Fondo."

I was hoping for some comments, but nobody in the group said anything. I continued reading the story and then I realized that perhaps they did not know what the word *fondness* meant. I asked, "What did the author mean when she said that Mae Marie had a fondness for Fondo?"

A few of the students shrugged their shoulders. Finally, one student said, "We don't know. We never heard of that word before."

Of course, I explained what the word meant. I used it in a meaningful sentence and then we entered it in our personal dictionaries.

Although I caught myself this time, I heard myself make this same mistake a few more times. I assumed that students knew what I was talking about. For example, I said, "It is good that we are able to compare the book *Hawk Hill* (Gilbert, 1996) with the story *I Can Hear the Sun* (Polacco, 1996) to see the similarities and differences between the two."

One student began to give examples of how the stories were similar and different. But the other students looked confused and probably did not have an understanding of the word *similarities*. I could have helped to clarify the term by using words such as *alike* or *same* along with the word *similarities*.

Another teaching flaw I discovered is that I do not give students enough time to respond to questions I ask that pertain to a story. Some students are quick to respond, but other students need more time to think. I need to slow down to ensure that all of my students have the opportunity to share their thoughts.

I also have a tendency to rush through the story by giving answers or hints to speed up in order to finish the story. I was horrified when I heard myself on the cassette tell a student, "Just a second on your question. We need to finish this story. But thanks for raising your hand."

I should have encouraged this student to make his comment. I do not want to worry about the amount of material covered. Rather, I want to focus on the quality of the time that we spend learning. It is very easy to forget that the quality is more important than the quantity. How does a teacher know when students are not getting the concepts presented? How does a teacher slow down so some students are not left behind?

CASE 5.1: APPLICATIONS AND REFLECTIONS

What do you think is the purpose of this lesson or series of lessons?

_____

_____

_____

_____

How was the original teaching plan interrupted, or what surprised Heather?

_____

_____

_____

What actions did Heather take in response to the interruption/surprise?

_____

_____

_____

Examine the consequences of Heather's actions. What alternative action(s)/procedures would you suggest?

_____

_____

_____

Identify the resources (e.g., outside readings; conversations with peers, teachers, or other professionals) used by Heather in this case. What other specific resources might you suggest (e.g., titles of related articles or books, community agencies, etc.)?

_____

_____

_____

From whose perspective is the case written?

_____

_____

_____

_____

What do you think are these fifth graders' perspectives?

_____

_____

_____

_____

Who are the players in the case?

_____

_____

_____

_____

What seems to be working well in this case?

_____

_____

_____

_____

What needs to be improved?

_____

_____

_____

_____

Can you distinguish between the symptoms and the problems presented in this case?

_____

_____

_____

_____

Adapted from Morine-Dershimer, 1996; Shulman, 1996; Silverman & Welty, 1996.

COMMENTARY 5.1A: DON'T ASSUME AND SLOW DOWN!

Janice DiVincenzo, Classroom Teacher
Barrington, Illinois

The points raised in this case are insightful reflections of some areas that may need to be addressed in this classroom. Heather noted the need to clarify background knowledge of specific vocabulary words for her students, and the need to provide time for students to reflect on a story and respond. In addition to these areas, I read into her comments that a repertoire of strategies for quick assessment of what her students know before initiating a story and what they have learned after completing stories also is needed [see Commentary 12.1A]. Finally, without knowing the nature of her classroom organization, I would also like to reflect on the amounts and types of learning opportunities that could be beneficial in discovering more about her students' proficiencies in their literacy development.

Regarding the question of students' knowledge of vocabulary, a few considerations come to mind. First, the difficulty level of the materials should be taken into consideration. Students may have difficulty with comprehension of materials that they cannot decode with at least 95% accuracy. The use of a **running record** to check for fluency may be beneficial before selecting instructional-level materials.

Second, the familiarity of a reading topic should be considered. Students who have sufficient background knowledge about a topic can generally comprehend materials that are above the level of other materials for which they do not have sufficient knowledge. For example, I can more fluently read and understand articles in *The Reading Teacher* than I can articles in the *Illinois Bar Journal*.

Checking for students' background knowledge pertinent to a particular text may be achieved through strategies such as K-W-L, anticipation guides, and story impressions activities. When students are lacking necessary background knowledge, teachers should plan introductory activities to help bridge the existing gaps in their knowledge.

Regarding comprehension, it seems that the use of DRTA and other guided reading strategies would be beneficial to learn more about how students are processing and understanding the story as they are reading it. Using think alouds is a very effective strategy for encouraging **metacomprehension** awareness and strengthening overall comprehension abilities.

With the use of think alouds, teachers must provide students with opportunities to practice strategies in small and large groups, to independently practice strategies, and to periodically self-evaluate the strategies they use during reading. In the initial stages of strategy instruction, students seem most comfortable with strategies that help them make connections to prior experiences or prior readings, make predictions about what will occur next in a text, and summarize what they have read. In a nutshell, all of those steps require time—time for students to acquire understanding of the strategies; time for students to practice in large groups, small groups, and independently; and time for students to evaluate their own use of the strategies. Devoting a daily 30-minute period over the course of 5 to 6 weeks to modeling, practicing, and evaluating strategy use would not be unreasonable to ensure student success.

As students become more comfortable with think alouds, they will begin to notice both when they are not comprehending and why they are not comprehending. They will note if the vocabulary is an obstacle or if they need to slow down, reread, visualize the content, or review their predictions.

My final suggestion is to offer students considerable opportunities for whole-group, small-group, and partner interactions [see Overview to chap. 3]. By balancing these organizational patterns, teachers will have multiple opportunities to observe if a student can perform in a large group, with lots of peer interaction and support; in a small group, where more direct responsibility for use of new skills and strategies is required; or independently, where the teacher and student can periodically assess individual performances, confer to set goals, and nurture a strong and healthy motivation to continuously learn.

Clay, M. (1979). *The early detection of reading difficulties* (3rd ed.). Portsmouth, NH: Heinemann.

Johnston, F. (1993). Improving student response in DR-TAs and DL-TAs. *The Reading Teacher, 46,* 448–449.

Carr, E., & Ogle, D. (1987). K-W-L plus: A strategy for comprehension and summarization. *Journal of Reading, 30,* 626–631.

Merkley, D. (1996/1997). Modified anticipation guide. *The Reading Teacher, 50,* 365–368.

Davey, B. (1983). Think alouds—modeling the cognitive process of reading comprehension. *Journal of Reading, 27,* 44–47.

Baumann, J., Jones, L., & Seifert-Kessell, N. (1993). Using think alouds to enhance children's comprehension monitoring abilities. *The Reading Teacher, 47,* 184–193.

COMMENTARY 5.1B: DON'T ASSUME AND SLOW DOWN!

Timothy Rasinski, Teacher Educator
Kent State University, Ohio

One of the things we have learned over the past 2 decades about successful reading experiences has been the absolute need of the reader to have sufficient background knowledge for the text he or she is reading. If background knowledge is missing, it is up to the teacher to provide that background knowledge as efficiently and thoroughly as possible.

Pressing against this need to provide students with sufficient background knowledge for the text they read is the likelihood that teachers will spend too much time away from actual reading in order to provide students with necessary background knowledge, go over vocabulary, or make explanations concerning the content of the text. This can contribute to unsatisfactory reading experiences for students.

It seems to me that there are several considerations we need to make in our choices of texts for students. First, texts that students read should be at their **reading instructional levels**—they should be challenging but not overwhelming in terms of content or **word recognition** difficulty. Teachers also need to be aware of their students' interests. In the case just presented, the story about Fondo as well as *Hawk Hill* and *I Can Hear the Sun* may simply have been above the students' reading level. Second, teachers often have no choice in the texts that are provided for their students to read. In these cases, teachers need to ensure that sufficient background knowledge is provided and generated for students. I have found that one way to do this is to introduce students to a set of related readings. These related readings will certainly build students' general knowledge about a topic and will most likely increase students' enthusiasm for the topic to be studied.

Providing wait time for students to respond to questions is an important part of asking for student response. However, for most of us, it is a goal that is easier said than accomplished. Knowing about the importance of wait time is the first step in giving students time to think. Continue to remind yourself about the importance of wait time and, eventually, you will become more relaxed in your discussions with students and you will make wait time an integral part of your teaching.

Last, the notion of awareness and assessment of our own teaching is an important characteristic of good teaching. Heather's self-awareness of her teaching performance is certainly praiseworthy. Her case makes me think about teacher characteristics that are critical to good literacy teaching. In my opinion, the most important characteristic of successful literacy teaching is passion for reading and for teaching. Beyond mastering instructional strategies and employing appropriate wait time in her discussions with students, Heather is demonstrating for her students her own love and value of reading. When teachers or parents demonstrate their own passion for reading, students surely will follow.

Opitz, M. (1998). Text sets: One way to flex your grouping—in first grade too! *The Reading Teacher, 51,* 622–624.

CASE 5.2: IDENTIFYING STORY THEMES

Michael Jackson

Richards, J. C., & Gipe, J. (1998). Developing young students' awareness of story themes in literature-based reading programs. *The Reading Instruction Journal, 40*(2), 5–8.

I have a great group of fifth-grade students. They are eager to learn and love to read. They really seem to work well together and like to explore reading strategies. We began the semester by exploring several reading strategies such as the DRTA, K-W-L, I wonder, and yes/no and why. The students accomplished these reading strategies easily.

Next, I decided to address a more difficult reading strategy, what's the theme? To begin the activity, I quickly gave a definition of a story theme. I said, "Story themes are messages that authors give to readers. Themes tell us about life."

To help my students understand the concept of **multiple story themes,** I modeled how to identify themes, using *Goldilocks and the Three Bears* (Brett, 1987). I said, "In the story of *Goldilocks and the Three Bears,* one theme is, 'Never go into someone's home uninvited.'"

I then asked my students if they understood what the theme of the story was. Ray inappropriately responded, "Yes, I think that Goldilocks was very rude."

Next, we explored the first five pages of the book *Young Guinevere* (San Souci, 1996), looking for evidences of story themes. In this first section, the underlying theme is Guinevere's love of nature. However, David expressed the theme as, "Guinevere should obey her father." David's idea did not accurately express the theme of the introduction to the story.

I asked David why he thought that obeying was the theme of the story. David stated, "I thought that Guinevere's dad didn't like her to go into the woods and she did anyway."

I couldn't understand his confusion, and wasn't sure whether I should correct his idea or give story themes another try. I decided to go on, so I encouraged my group to listen as I read the next section of the book. Once again, I asked them to try to figure out the special messages that the author was trying to express. The story unfolds as follows. Guinevere happens on a wolf eating a rabbit. She shoots the wolf with her bow and arrow. Later, she finds a young boy in the woods with an injured leg and an arrow sticking out of the wound.

Ray quickly figured out that the wolf shot by Guinevere represented the boy. Ray said, "Oh, I get it. The wolf and the little boy are the same person."

I praised Ray for discovering this and I asked him, "How did you know that the boy and the wolf were one and the same?"

Ray explained, "I saw this same story on a show last week."

I asked David to help Ray put the author's meaning into words. However, constructing the theme was a little too difficult for David to express in his own words. David finally stated, "Don't shoot animals."

I then modeled my thinking by showing how this concept could be expanded to include the idea that animals have feelings like people when they are hurt. I said, "I think the author is trying to get readers to understand that animals have feelings just like people."

Ray slowly began to grasp the idea that stories may have more than one theme. He said, "The author is trying to tell us how it feels to be a wolf that gets shot by an arrow. I sure wouldn't like it!"

David stated, "All creatures have feelings."

I think that the boys' uncertainties about themes could have been avoided if I had spent more time developing the idea of themes and modeling more examples of my thinking for them. I also think that I should reshape this activity using a simpler book with more easily discernible themes. How else can I help my students learn how to discover multiple story themes?

CASE 5.2: APPLICATIONS AND REFLECTIONS

What do you think is the purpose of this lesson or series of lessons?

_____

_____

_____

_____

How was the original teaching plan interrupted, or what surprised Michael?

_____

_____

_____

_____

What actions did Michael take in response to the interruption/surprise?

_____

_____

_____

_____

Examine the consequences of Michael's actions. What alternative action(s)/procedures would you suggest?

_____

_____

_____

_____

Identify the resources (e.g., outside readings; conversations with peers, teachers, or other professionals) used by Michael in this case. What other specific resources might you suggest (e.g., titles of related articles or books, community agencies, etc.)?

_____

_____

_____

_____

From whose perspective is the case written?

_____

_____

_____

_____

What do you think are these fifth graders' perspectives?

_____

_____

_____

_____

Who are the players in the case?

_____

_____

_____

_____

What seems to be working well in this case?

_____

_____

_____

_____

What needs to be improved?

_____

_____

_____

_____

Can you distinguish between the symptoms and the problems presented in this case?

_____

_____

_____

_____

Adapted from Morine-Dershimer, 1996; Shulman, 1996; Silverman & Welty, 1996.

COMMENTARY 5.2A: IDENTIFYING STORY THEMES

Bill Gilluly, Classroom Teacher
Las Vegas, Nevada

I would have modeled more examples of what story themes are before I ever attempted to ask my students to discover multiple themes in a story. One aspect of the lesson that stands out is that David seems to be missing the themes in *Young Guinivere* (San Souci, 1996) because he interprets the passage in a literal sense. Talking about themes to include possible morals in a story encourages students to search for themes. Furthermore, by defining themes as universally accepted characteristics of human behavior, Michael's students probably would have been better able to grasp the notion that the author is showing us examples of appropriate human behavior, such as kindness, respect, and goodness overcoming evil.

I think that a **storyboard** activity or a spontaneous skit might have helped Michael's students understand the section of the story about the boy and the wolf. When story actions repeat themselves and characters' emotions and thoughts are similar to those portrayed previously in a story, it often helps students to recognize and understand these similar aspects of a story if they can place figures of story characters on a storyboard. Then they can emote and role play characters' actions, thinking, and feelings, and relate these dimensions to possible themes in the story. Turning to the performing arts, such as skits or a readers theatre, also helps students construct and visualize story themes. Additionally, arts activities are especially helpful to special or kinesthetic learners [see Commentary 3.4A], and those who are particularly artistically talented [see Cases 9.1, 9.2, and 9.3].

Peck, R., & Rankin, B. (1996). Connecting books and the arts. *Book Links, 6*(1), 37–41.

Watson, D. (1997). Rain forest dance residency. *Primary Voices K-6, 5*(2), 6–11.

COMMENTARY 5.2B: IDENTIFYING STORY THEMES

Marilyn McKinney, Teacher Educator
University of Nevada, Las Vegas

This case provides wonderful insights into the importance of learning to listen to students as a way of knowing if they understand a lesson. Learning to identify themes in literature is *not* an easy strategy to teach, especially because themes are both explicitly and implicitly expressed by authors. The fact that most stories have multiple themes further complicates and, of course, enriches our reading of stories. In addition, themes are often not easily expressed in one or two words.

I agree that more discussion and teacher modeling would have been helpful in developing the idea of themes. I suggest that rather than jumping so quickly from trying to identify one theme to identifying multiple story themes, it would be helpful to first work with multiple examples of fairly explicit, singular themes in familiar stories, picture books, or chapter books. Finding ways to help students visually organize this information is important. For example, you could develop a classroom chart comparing and contrasting themes from five or six chapter books that students are reading. List titles and authors across the top, and note themes generated underneath, perhaps on sticky notes so that they can be lined up and reorganized through ongoing discussions. Let students discover that there are some universal themes, along with multiple dimensions of themes. Another visual organizer that links literacy activities with the creative arts is a story quilt. Students design quilt squares that can be arranged into a full-size quilt, either paper or cloth. The individual squares include text (the themes) and illustrations. This activity could be used as the culmination of a thematic unit centered around **text sets** on a particular theme (e.g., homelessness, change, or challenges).

Because many stories contain multiple themes, it seems important to have ongoing conversations concerning what students believe authors are revealing about a story theme or themes. Often, a theme isn't evident in the first few pages of a story. Being able to provide evidence to support ideas about themes also is crucial. Modeling for students and then asking them to supply proof with statements or illustrations from the text reinforces students' learning. This type of rigorous, interpretive work also engages students in critical thinking. In closing, I would suggest that you help students recognize why discussions of themes are important. Not only are themes used by authors as a literary element to tie characters, plots, and settings together—discussing story themes helps us discover and rediscover commonalities that bind us together as human beings.

CASE 5.3: IS SKIPPING WORDS REALLY OKAY?

George West

My individual group consists of six highly energized third-grade students. I designed a lesson today to give my students more exposure to fables and hopefully to help those who were missing the point of fables. We started the lesson by drawing a **semantic map** depicting our knowledge of fables. Then I had each child read a fable aloud. I was happy to see that all of my students read aloud pretty well. However, I noticed that they were quick to give up on long or difficult words. The result was, "Mr. West, what's this word?"

Sometimes my students skipped the words they didn't know and just kept on reading. When this happened, I usually told them, "Sound it out."

But sometimes I just told them the words in order to keep the lesson flowing. I noticed that, in a few instances, the students did go back and try to figure out unknown words by rereading and using context clues. But the majority of the time, the students just skipped words or stopped and asked me to tell them the word. My worry was that when my students skipped words they were losing meaning.

I had a written assignment to go along with the lesson. I instructed each student to rewrite in his or her own words one of the fables that we had read as a group. Because they did not all choose the fable we had just read, I did not get clear insight about whether the skipped words affected their understanding of the story, or if their understanding was diminished by the passage of time. After talking with my peers, I realized that by having the students read aloud I was placing them in a performance mode. The students may have seen the goal as finishing without making any mistakes and risking being made fun of, rather than reading for comprehension. A good suggestion was to let them rehearse the reading prior to their oral reading. Through my own brainstorming, I have also come up with an idea to assess whether comprehension is being compromised when the students skip words. I have selected one fable from the books I have gathered, and I will make copies for each group member. I am going to have the kids read the fable to themselves and then rewrite the story in their own words. This should indicate whether the words skipped are hurting their comprehension. If the "trouble" words are not affecting their understanding of the story, then there is no reason to dwell on the issue. However, the question then becomes this: If comprehension is being compromised, how do I get students to read the words without taking too much time and attention away from the context of the story? Another nagging question is: Why do I want my students to read aloud all of the time? Is it because I subconsciously think that they should read every word in the text correctly?

Case 5.3: Applications and Reflections

What do you think is the purpose of this lesson or series of lessons?

_____

_____

_____

_____

How was the original teaching plan interrupted, or what surprised George?

_____

_____

_____

_____

What actions did George take in response to the interruption/surprise?

_____

_____

_____

_____

Examine the consequences of George's actions. What alternative action(s)/procedures would you suggest?

_____

_____

_____

_____

Identify the resources (e.g., outside readings; conversations with peers, teachers, or other professionals) used by George in this case. What other specific resources might you suggest (e.g., titles of related articles or books, community agencies, etc.)?

_____

_____

_____

_____

From whose perspective is the case written?

_____

_____

_____

_____

What do you think are these third graders' perspectives?

_____

_____

_____

_____

Who are the players in the case?

_____

_____

_____

_____

What seems to be working well in this case?

_____

_____

_____

_____

What needs to be improved?

_____

_____

_____

_____

Can you distinguish between the symptoms and the problems presented in this case?

_____

_____

_____

_____

Adapted from Morine-Dershimer, 1996; Shulman, 1996; Silverman & Welty, 1996.

COMMENTARY 5.3A: IS SKIPPING WORDS REALLY OKAY?

Eileen Kane Owens, Reading Specialist
Vernon Hills, Illinois

Third grade can be a difficult time for some young readers. During this time, the focus of reading changes from learning to read to reading to learn. Therefore, students may read material that contains unfamiliar vocabulary terms. Telling students unknown words as they read aloud is a viable option. It alleviates students' anxieties and maintains comprehension through fluent reading. However, if you find yourself telling a student too many words, the reading material is obviously beyond the student's reading instructional level. Rehearsal prior to reading might help. Another suggestion is choral reading, in which the entire group reads aloud rather than individual students taking turns. I have to ask you two important questions: Why are you having individual students read aloud? What is your purpose?

You noted that your students were quick to give up on long or difficult words and were simply skipping them. Occasionally, skipping words is a valid strategy, but there are many other strategies you can offer your students to help them decode and figure out unknown words:

1. Skip the word and read to the end of the sentence. Then go back and reread the sentence.
2. Think of a word that makes sense in the sentence and begins with the first letter of the skipped word.
3. Look at any illustrations, graphs, or charts that are near the text. These visuals give clues.
4. Make a good guess.
5. Look up the unknown word in the dictionary.
6. When all else fails, ask someone for help.

To help your students remember these strategies, post them on a classroom wall and then make individual student bookmarks with the strategies printed on them. After your students are familiar with these strategies, you can introduce one of my favorite teacher modeling techniques—a version of a think aloud. This strategy lets students "look" inside your head to see what you do when you don't know a word in text. Make a copy of one of the fables for your overhead projector, or put the fable on a chalkboard. Begin reading the fable aloud and then pretend that you have come across an unknown word. Try to sound it out unsuccessfully. Then say, "I can't sound this word out. When this happens I think of what other strategies I know that I can use here to solve my problem."

Then, try the other strategies that you already have introduced until one of them works. Continue reading, again pretend that you encounter another difficult word, and repeat the process of using strategies. Remember that it is not enough to just model the strategy—modeling strategies for decoding is good, but modeling what you are thinking as you try to decode a word is much more effective. You are making your students think about their thinking (i.e., metacomprehension).

Because the words that your students are having the most problems with are multisyllabic words, you may want to use strategies Patricia Cunningham offered in her book *Making Words: Multilevel Hands-on Developmentally Appropriate Spelling and Phonics Activities* (1994b). This is a word activity that you can do daily or a few times per week to help your readers become more skillful at decoding words. There is a version for third to sixth grade called *Making Big Words: Multilevel Hands-on Spelling and Phonics Activities* (Cunningham, 1994a) that is available through most bookstores.

Finally, I want to address your last question. You seem concerned (rightly so) that there is so much content to cover and there is never enough time, especially if you must also find time to teach reading. This is a common problem in all grades. Finding a balance between teaching reading comprehension and teaching content is your challenge. Hopefully, by helping your students develop decoding skills early on, you will have more time for helping them with content learning.

COMMENTARY 5.3B: IS SKIPPING WORDS REALLY OKAY?

Camille Blachowicz, Teacher Educator
National–Louis University, Illinois

This question of "Is skipping words really okay?" looks like a simple one, but it is really quite sophisticated. Asking it means that you are making progress as a reflective teacher who observes and uses problems to learn more about the teaching of reading. As so often is the case, the answer to this question is, "It depends." What determines the appropriate response has to do with materials, purpose, and strategies.

First of all, think about your materials. Ask yourself if your students are skipping a lot of words because you have them reading text that is too difficult for them [see Commentary 5.1B]. We know that readers learn best when they read text on their instructional level, a level on which they won't have trouble with more than about 5 words out of every 100. Listen to your students read and do a running record, tallying the number of words they skip or the number of words that give then difficulty. If they aren't in the 95% accuracy ballpark, they are probably doing a lot of skipping because they are reading text that is above their developmental reading level. Back up a bit—choose text on your students' instructional levels.

If you are relatively sure that your students are reading from an appropriate-leveled text, then you may want to try radio reading, in which one good reader reads aloud and a less successful reader listens as the text is being read, or reads the text silently.

The most important consideration about whether or not skipping words is okay has to do with your students' repertoire of reading strategies. All readers need to know what to do when they come to a word they don't know. Skipping a word can often be strategic; that is, students can skip a word and continue reading. Usually, the meaning of the text isn't lost if only a few words are skipped. Many teachers emphasize a metacomprehension strategy to help students deal with unknown words: (a) stop and look at the print and the context; (b) see if you know a word that matches the print and fits the context; (c) test the word you come up with, and assess if it makes sense in context; (d) if you can't determine the word, skip it and try to come back to it later. Teachers need to model this strategy until students can utilize it on their own. Teachers also can model how to decode unknown words through analogy (e.g., "If I know the word *hat* and this word ends the same way as the word *hat* but begins with a *c,* this new word must be *cat.*"). So, as you can tell, it's okay for students to skip some words in text as long as the text isn't too difficult for them. It's also very helpful when teachers supply their students with strategies to help them decode and figure out unknown words.

CASE 5.4: USING ONSETS AND RIMES TO TEACH READING

Amy Gex

Fry, E. (1998). The most common phonograms. *The Reading Teacher, 51,* 620–622.

Gunning, T. (1995). Word building: A strategic approach to the teaching of phonics. *The Reading Teacher, 48,* 484–488.

I have been teaching 11 first graders, focusing on reading and writing instruction. Some approaches I have tried include reading to my students at every meeting, posting new words on a word wall, and corresponding with my students in journals. I still think that I need to give my students some type of information that will help them recognize and spell new words. **Onsets** and **rimes** seemed like a logical choice, because my students were very good at recognizing rhyming words. Because they recognized rhyming words, I thought that if I pointed out the rimes of the words, it would help them make connections among words that would help them read and spell new words. Thus, I set out to make a lesson to illustrate onset and rime.

To start the lesson, I read them a story titled *Alphabet Soup* (Banks, 1988). The story is about a little boy who makes words out of letters. I chose this story because I wanted my students to see how putting letters together makes words. When we completed the story, I did a mini-lesson using a pocket chart to manipulate many different words with the rime *at.* Then I handed my students onset and rime tiles and gave them their own *Alphabet Soup* bowls to fill with words.

At the time, it was hard to tell if the experience was sinking in, especially because some of my students just copied examples from the book *Alphabet Soup.* So I re-explained everything, and had my students start all over again. Most of the students made some great words with the *at, et,* and *all* rimes. They created words such as *hat, net, bet,* and *fall.* Some of the students asked, "Is this a word?"

I answered them, "Does it sound like a word?" One of the most exciting parts of this lesson was that the students thought up words that I hadn't even considered. My problem is that some of my students created nonwords, such as *nall* and *sall,* which made me realize that they still needed work with onsets and rimes. Therefore, I am trying to think of more activities to give my students a better understanding of onsets and rimes. Even though my students still need more practice, I think that the lesson was a success. Just the other day, I was working with one student and he was having difficulty spelling two words that rhymed. He had chosen the words *cat* and *mat* to write in his poem. I asked him to write these two words for me. "I can't spell them," he said.

"Can you spell *cat?*" I asked.

He quickly wrote *cat.* Then, I said, "Listen to the word *mat.* It ends just like *cat* but the first letter is different."

I then slowly enunciated the word *mat.* "Can you spell it now?" I asked.

I can't tell you how exciting it was to see him write the word *mat.* Then, he wrote the word *that.* That's when I knew that my lesson was working! But how does a lesson on onsets and rimes fit in with using quality children's literature and adhering to a holistic philosophy for teaching reading?

CASE 5.4: APPLICATIONS AND REFLECTIONS

What do you think is the purpose of this lesson or series of lessons?

_____

_____

_____

_____

How was the original teaching plan interrupted, or what surprised Amy?

_____

_____

_____

_____

What actions did Amy take in response to the interruption/surprise?

_____

_____

_____

_____

Examine the consequences of Amy's actions. What alternative action(s)/procedures would you suggest?

_____

_____

_____

_____

Identify the resources (e.g., outside readings; conversations with peers, teachers, or other professionals) used by Amy in this case. What other specific resources might you suggest (e.g., titles of related articles or books, community agencies, etc.)?

_____

_____

_____

_____

From whose perspective is the case written?

_____

_____

_____

_____

What do you think are these first graders' perspectives?

_____

_____

_____

_____

Who are the players in the case?

_____

_____

_____

_____

What seems to be working well in this case?

_____

_____

_____

_____

What needs to be improved?

_____

_____

_____

_____

Can you distinguish between the symptoms and the problems presented in this case?

_____

_____

_____

_____

Adapted from Morine-Dershimer, 1996; Shulman, 1996; Silverman & Welty, 1996.

COMMENTARY 5.4A: USING ONSETS AND RIMES TO TEACH READING

Diane Sullivan, Classroom Teacher
Downer's Grove, Illinois

Hello Amy,

The questions implicit in this case seem to be "Was I right to use onsets and rimes to teach reading to first graders? It seems to be working. This is how I've done it. What do you think?"

Your decision to offer a lesson on onsets and rimes based on your assessment of your students' strengths and instructional needs is a good example of teachers' reflective thinking. Your choice demonstrates appropriate instructional decision making to help move your students further along on the literacy instructional continuum. But, as you discovered, this lesson was harder than you anticipated.

The effectiveness of using onsets and rimes to help students learn how to read and write new/unfamiliar words has received much attention in the reading professional literature. Instruction in onsets and rimes is an excellent choice for beginning reading instruction when it is accompanied by shared book reading; guided reading in authentic, instructional-level texts (i.e., quality children's literature); and writing/composing text. And, certainly, holistically oriented teachers provide specific literacy lessons based on their students' reading and writing instructional needs.

First of all, you recognize that your students heard and identified rhyming words by sound, an important indication of **phonemic awareness.** By analyzing your students' use of developmental spelling, you also can determine your students' growing knowledge of sound/symbol relationships. In addition, asking your students to read back their writing can help you to appraise which sight words they recognize. You also can check your students' recognition of sight words by having them read words that are posted on a word wall, which you already have set up.

Teaching students to separate the onset (i.e., beginning consonant sounds) from the the rest of the word (i.e., the rime such as, *ie, at,* and *an*), and to substitute other onsets to form new words, can be accomplished in several ways. As you discovered, lack of experience with written language can cause students to run amuck with this process by forming nonwords and misspellings. For this reason, I think it is important for teachers to control the instructional process by selecting the onsets and rimes prior to the lesson, and providing sufficient practice for students to make the appropriate connections between the onsets and rimes. Students need to hear the onsets and rimes, and they also need to see what is alike and different in each of the words selected for the lesson.

It is crucial for teachers to model their thinking for students (e.g., "First, I identify the initial letter or letter patterns and the sounds that these letters make. Then, I add the final letters/sounds to the beginning letters. Finally, I test out my new word by sounding it out to see if it really is a word in our language").

Having your students create words with tiles was an excellent idea. You actively engaged your students in manipulating the letters/sounds to create words. Remember—to avoid the pitfalls of students creating nonwords, you can control the process by previously selecting words (i.e., the appropriate onsets and rimes) for the lesson.

Another approach to help students recognize and use onsets and rimes is to put words on cards and help them sort the words into patterns. Darrell Morris developed a word sort activity that uses onsets and rimes (1982). Using words that students know as exemplars, the teacher models using the visual patterns and the rime to quickly read and place each word, grouping words with similar spelling patterns. Limiting the number of words and patterns used at one time provides opportunities for all students to take turns and speeds up the pace of the lesson. After students read all of the words they write them in meaningful sentences, which adds a reading/writing connection to the lesson.

My sense is that you are right—your lesson was successful as an important first step in what should be a sequence of lessons that provides practice for (a) students to learn to read and write by recognizing common spelling patterns, and (b) using words they know, to assist them in learning new words.

Let me describe an instructional sequence that I use for teaching onsets and rimes:

1. Start with words that students recognize.
2. Help students hear and segment the onset and the rime in the known words.
3. Proceed to unfamiliar words. Choose words with common rimes for your students to make, read, and write.
4. Give students practice in reading, sorting and writing words using no more than four onset and rime patterns at a time.
5. Assess your students' progress, and the need for more practice with onsets and rimes, by noting their speed and accuracy in reading and writing words with targeted patterns.

In closing, your decision to add regular word study instruction with onsets and rimes to your holistic reading and writing program is appropriate. All effective whole-language teachers balance beginning reading instruction through integrated activities such as reading quality children's literature with their students, corresponding in journals with their students, and offering specific literacy lessons based on their students' instructional needs.

COMMENTARY 5.4B: USING ONSETS AND RIMES TO TEACH READING

Camille Blachowicz, Teacher Educator
National–Louis University, Illinois

Hi Amy,

This narrative snapshot of your students' learning is really rich. You have captured a lot of information about helping students learn to decode, about how they learn, and about how teachers assess their students' learning. Let's start with the first one and take these one by one.

Helping students learn to deal with the code—the way letters represent the sounds and words of language—is a critical part of beginning reading instruction. Some teachers use synthetic **phonics,** teaching the sounds associated with different letters and helping students blend these into words. For example, teachers might teach a synthetic phonics lesson by presenting the hard *c* sound associated with the letter *c* and having students connect it with the short *a* sound and the *t* sound to produce the word *cat.* This is a highly abstract process, and the blending process is quite difficult for some students. They say, "*c-a-t,*" but never associate it with the furry little pet so many of them have. Sometimes students overuse this strategy, resulting in nonproductive and sometimes nonsensical decoding, such as *tee* followed by *he* for the word *the.*

Other teachers approach the decoding task as an analytical one, and start with known words, having students substitute and blend new letters. For example, teachers might take the word *pin* and vary the first letter to make *fin, sin, tin,* and so forth.

Your approach also makes use of "decoding by analogy"—calling up a word you know to help you decode a new one. If you know *fan* you can figure out *man.* If you know *hat* and *her,* you can figure out the word *flatter.* Thus, you've chosen a productive approach.

In your first trials, your students have reminded you of something very important about instruction—kids usually do not get it the first time! This is something every teacher learns over time. Your idea that you need more activities is a good one. I'd like to elaborate it to more of a system. In our clinic and classrooms, we have a four-step model that we use for each lesson in our **word sorts,** which is another name for the type of lesson you are doing. First, we have the lesson where students sort two or more rime sets of words, such as one set of *hat, mat, fat, cat* and another set of *pan, man, fan, can.* After students see and verbalize the principle, the second set is individual sorts and writing. We have each student sort a set and write the words under the correct column headings on a paper. The third stage is fun—we play memory games with sets of word cards. Finally, we do assessment through dictation. We see if students can write words from

Fox, B. (1996). *Strategies for word identification: Phonics from a new perspective.* Englewood Cliffs, NJ: Prentice Hall.

Fresch, M., & Wheaton, A. (1997). Sort, search, and discover: Spelling in the child-centered classroom. *The Reading Teacher, 51,* 20–31.

particular families. This is the acid test. Your observation of your students in action is another way to see if the lesson has stuck.

Just remember the final, humbling lesson—sometimes teachers' lessons unstick. Kids don't move ahead in a smooth line in anything. They sometimes regress and need review and reminding. But their general progress should be forward. I hope you have many more "aha" moments like you wrote about at the end of your case. They are the rewards of teaching.

SUGGESTED READINGS

National Council of Teachers of English and Whole Language Umbrella. (Eds.). (1997). *Teacher inquiry: Reading matters* (Elementary Section). Urbana, IL.
This is a wonderful collection of 35 short articles published previously by noted scholars in the field of literacy. Topics include whole language and children's literature, selecting multicultural children's literature, and exploring classroom literature through drama [see Case 9.1].

Padgett, R. (1997). *Creative reading: What it is, how to do it, and why.* Urbana, IL: National Council of Teachers of English.
This book questions many current reading instructional practices, including placing too much emphasis on reading tests and spending too much student time on meaningless skill and drill workbook and ditto sheet exercises. The text enlarges our understanding of reading by demonstrating how to make reading more exciting, imaginative, and creative. The book's underlying assumption is that reading and writing are supportive, similar processes.

Tompkins, G. (1998). *Language arts: Content and teaching strategies.* Upper Saddle River, NJ: Prentice Hall.
Tompkins believes that, as we enter the 21st century, language arts instruction must expand "to reflect the greater oral, written, and visual communication needs [of students]" (p. 23). She includes many practical reading comprehension and writing strategies.

CHAPTER 6

Guiding Students' Spelling and Decoding Development

Literacy Concepts and Terms

-conventional spelling
-invented spellings
-phonemic awareness
-word patterns
-word wall

OVERVIEW

This chapter presents cases and commentaries that target developing students' proficiencies in spelling and word decoding [see Case 5.4]. In recent years, our knowledge of the ways children learn how to spell has expanded considerably (Wilde, 1992). Spelling ability no longer is equated with memorizing and mastering lists of words, we now recognize that children's spelling development is related to their exposure to words, understanding of **word patterns,** cognitive development, and willingness to take risks and attempt to spell unknown words. Therefore, teachers encourage students to construct their own spelling approximations, if necessary, in first drafts of compositions, dialogue journals, and other personal writing. At the same time, teachers teach students to value and focus on the standard or **conventional spelling** of words. Teachers also supply strategies for students to help them think about and generate appropriate spellings. When teachers examine students' spelling they also learn what their students know about letter–sound relationships.

CASE 6.1: SPELLING—WHY IS IT SUCH A PROBLEM?

Ashley Armington

Bromley, K. (1993). *Journaling: Engagements in reading, writing, and thinking.* New York: Scholastic.

Spelling is a major concern with my group of third-grade children. They are not willing to take risks. They are too concerned with the conventional spelling of words. Every day we write in our journals, which I hope will help my students to become writers. But the kids want everything they write to be spelled correctly. I am amazed that so many of my children cannot spell certain basic words. I also question why are they so concerned with the conventional spellings of words. Has someone belittled these children for not spelling words correctly? Do other students make fun of their **invented spellings?**

We start class each day by writing in our journals for 10 minutes. The children really seem to enjoy this time. I used to give the children topics of interest about which to write. But, after a few lessons, I decided that they would have to decide on topics themselves. I felt that I was hindering their creativity by telling them what to write.

On some days, my students ask, "Can we have a few more minutes?"

I always agree to this. However, Christopher constantly asks me, "How do you spell *baseball?*" "How do you spell *movies?*" "How do you spell *birthday?*"

I tell him, "Sound it out the best you can and write it the best way you know how. Spell it like it sounds in your head."

None of these ideas work. He does not like this.

Once in awhile, Mohammed will speak up. "This is how you spell it, Christopher," he says, as he spells the word that Christopher wants.

Deborah, who has a hard time concentrating, asks the same questions about her spelling. Janice also struggles with spelling. By the time we finish these conversations about spelling, the 10 minutes have passed and no time has been spent writing in journals. Being afraid to take risks in spelling is hindering the children's time to participate in other activities.

On a more positive note, in my students' journals I can sometimes see how they use their knowledge of phonics to attempt to spell words. Sometimes I find that, because of language variances, they pronounce words in nonstandard ways. Therefore, their appropriate use of phonics is incorrectly leading them to misspell words. When they do try to sound out words, it is very interesting to me to see these invented spellings and how they figure out how words sound.

I cannot justify spelling the words for them, but I feel that they are becoming frustrated. I realize that I must come up with a strategy for their spelling problems before I hinder their abilities. Through reading the book *Spelling in Use* (Laminack & Wood, 1996), I have become aware of many different strategies to help students with their spelling.

I have decided to try an alphabet spelling book. This is a 26-page booklet with one letter of the alphabet (*A* to *Z*) printed on each page. Students can ask me for help with spelling, and I will record the words that they want to spell in their alphabet spelling book. Hopefully, this will alleviate some of the problems that the kids are having with spelling words. At this point I will try anything!

CASE 6.1: APPLICATIONS AND REFLECTIONS

What do you think is the purpose of this lesson or series of lessons?

_____

_____

_____

_____

How was the original teaching plan interrupted, or what surprised Ashley?

_____

_____

_____

_____

What actions did Ashley take in response to the interruption/surprise?

_____

_____

_____

_____

Examine the consequences of Ashley's actions. What alternative action(s)/procedures would you suggest?

_____

_____

_____

_____

Identify the resources (e.g., outside readings; conversations with peers, teachers, or other professionals) used by Ashley in this case. What other specific resources might you suggest (e.g., titles of related articles or books, community agencies, etc.)?

_____

_____

_____

_____

From whose perspective is the case written?

_____

_____

_____

_____

What do you think are these third graders' perspectives?

_____

_____

_____

Who are the players in the case?

_____

_____

_____

What seems to be working well in this case?

_____

_____

_____

What needs to be improved?

_____

_____

_____

Can you distinguish between the symptoms and the problems presented in this case?

_____

_____

_____

Adapted from Morine-Dershimer, 1996; Shulman, 1996; Silverman & Welty, 1996.

COMMENTARY 6.1A: SPELLING—WHY IS IT SUCH A PROBLEM?

Jill Lewis, Teacher Educator
Jersey City State College, New Jersey

Hello Ashley,

Your students' concern for spelling gives you much to celebrate! As students become more widely read and increase their **phonemic awareness,** they also become more sensitive to sound/symbol relationships and will begin to recognize misspelled words. Now it is up to you to carefully guide them toward independent spelling behaviors.

There are several factors that will influence the extent to which your students will be concerned with their spelling and take spelling risks. One factor is their need for perfection, which they are expressing now. Model for them how you proceed unhesitatingly with your writing, later returning to uncertain spellings to edit them. This will show students that writers do not have to interrupt the flow of their writing because of spelling issues. Also, demonstrate how you perfect your spelling for your final draft. This will teach students about the options they have for handling their spelling concerns.

Parents' comments about the importance of correct spelling also can influence your students' spelling development. Many parents are concerned that youngsters who make spelling errors at an early age will continue to make them throughout life. These parents tend to equate spelling ability of emergent or novice readers with later reading and writing achievement. When children bring written work home, some parents criticize the spelling (and the teacher for not correcting it), and do not give praise for the content of the work. It is important for you to discuss your expectations for spelling with parents, and to demonstrate the methods you use to help children become better spellers.

The atmosphere you create about spelling in your classroom also will influence the students' own attitudes. You can take several steps to help students understand that there are tools to help them with their spelling, and that using these tools is an important part of being a good writer. You might have a **word wall** in your classroom [see Case 5.4]. This can be used for direct instruction on spelling patterns from which students are able to draw conclusions about spelling that will carry over to decoding. Students can be paired to assist each other. There should be many read-along books in the classroom in which students can see how words are spelled. Students might do word sorts and categorize words that have common features, using words they have placed in their spelling boxes or personal dictionaries. They can engage in cloze passages [see Commentaries 2.3A and 2.3B] and language experience activities to help draw their attention to particular spelling patterns of words. With cloze passages, you might provide only beginning and ending word cues and let the children supply the rest of the word. After language experience stories have been written and enjoyed, they can be revisited for spelling mini-lessons. Two other things that would be beneficial are instruction on how to use a dictionary, and having children become spelling buddies with a friend to help each other spell.

Your children will need many opportunities to engage in ungraded written work, and they need praise when they make new spelling discoveries. They also will need a vehicle that can help them identify their own spelling growth, such as a rubric through which they rate improvements they notice in their increased awareness of sound/symbol relationships and spelling patterns, recognition and correction of misspelled words, interest in trying out new words, and abilities to use tools for spelling assistance.

We also know that wide reading experiences make significant contributions to spelling development. A classroom that has a powerful literacy-centered environment is fertile ground for spelling achievement.

Heald-Taylor, B. G. (1998). Three paradigms of spelling instruction in grades 3 to 6. *The Reading Teacher, 51,* 404–413.

COMMENTARY 6.1B: SPELLING—WHY IS IT SUCH A PROBLEM?

Terri Austin, Classroom Teacher
Fairbanks, Alaska

Parry, J., & Hornsby, D. (1998). *Write-on: A conference approach to writing.* Portsmouth, NH: Heinemann. Also see Routman, R. (1991). *Invitations.* Portsmouth, NH: Heinemann.

I've been frustrated with my students' spelling problems, just like Ashley. There are so many issues at work here, aren't there? There's Ashley's concern that her students are misspelling basic words, there's her students' unwillingness to try their own constructions of spelling, and there's a concern about finding appropriate strategies to help Ashley's students spell fluently. I have two suggestions. The first involves changing the overall classroom approach to spelling in general, and the second involves providing spelling strategies.

I've found that it's very important for me to model the type of attitudes I desire from my students when they are writing first drafts of compositions or stories. Thus, when I write in front of my class, I am honest and model my thought processes when I am struggling to spell a particular word. I'm not a super speller, so this comes up frequently. If I'm not sure about how to spell a word, I do the best I can and then I put a question mark above the word in doubt. I tell my students, "We'll go on from here and then we'll figure this word out later after we have completed what we want to say."

I sometimes try several different ways of spelling the word and I share my thinking with my students about each spelling I use (e.g., "That just doesn't look quite right," or "This looks pretty accurate to me. I'll check later to make sure that I did spell this word correctly."). What I try to do is show my students that spelling doesn't have to hinder authors' thinking and writing. I also emphasize process writing. My students know that the editing process begins when their first draft is completed, so they seem willing to suspend their spelling concerns until that step in the editing process.

Have-a-go spelling at website: http://www.edbydesign.com/sp_haveago.html

Students do need help in spelling. I think it is important that teachers get students to do more of the thinking rather than have us, as teachers, do it all for them. Like Ashley, my students have personal spelling dictionaries, but I don't print the words they need in their dictionaries. Instead, we talk about various ways to find out how to spell words. I think it's important to move beyond the single "sound it out" strategy. That doesn't work for some students, because they haven't developed the necessary grapheme/phoneme awareness that is crucial to sounding out words. Equally important, a large amount of our English words are not spelled the way they sound. Thus, we talk about resources that we can use to find the spelling of a needed word, such as in a book, calendar, word wall, another student, and so on. My students also use a "have-a-go sheet." This is a piece of paper folded four times. In the first two columns, students try to spell a word that they need in two different ways. Then, they ask me to write the word for them in the third column. This provides an individualized spelling mini-lesson. As final steps, my students copy the standard spelling of the word in the fourth column of their have-a-go sheet. Then, they add that word into their personal dictionaries. Just a reminder—students need to understand that learning to spell is an ongoing process. In fact, learning to spell can be an adventure!

CASE 6.2: IS INVENTED SPELLING FOR EVERYONE?

Tashia Aroyo

Alexandria is a sweet first grader. She is very soft spoken, and the other students in my group often make fun of her. She comes to school very dirty. Her white shirt looks like it has not been washed for weeks. She is always very tired. In fact, one day she fell asleep while I was reading a story. I spoke to her teacher about Alexandria and she said, "Her mama keeps her out to 3:00 or 4:00 every morning and Alexandria doesn't get much sleep at home. Her mama never reads to her and I'm sure there is little writing going on in her home." When I heard this it made me realize why Alexandria is not able to stay on task and is always tired.

Alexandria enjoys drawing and listening to the stories that I read. She also enjoys journal time. But Alexandria always has me read the entries I write to her in her journal. After I have read what I have written to her, she always blurts out something that she wants to tell me. She usually looks at my entry and copies the date and my name. The problem is that when she starts to write what she wants to say to me, she just writes miscellaneous letters on the page. She isn't even using invented spelling. I think that she is just writing random letters so that I will be excited that she wrote something. I usually can't make it out to be anything.

Clarke, M. (1996). Learning from teacher-research. Journal writing with kindergarten children. *The Language and Literacy Spectrum, 6,* 70–74.

One day, in my entry to Alexandria, I asked her, "What are your favorite things to do?"

She said, "My favorite thing to do is my work."

I replied, "That's great! Write that down in your journal."

She then wrote the following letters: "Teknvolyahunftsg togo isimotkir etnki."

The only spaces that she left were the ones that I show after the *g,* before the *i,* and before the *e.* Then I said, "Alexandria, read me the sentence that you wrote me."

She replied, "You read it to me."

I tried to sound out the letters but they didn't make any sense to me, so I said, "Alexandria, I need a little help reading the sentence you wrote me."

When I said that, she got upset and said, "You can't read it cause I can't write right."

I replied, "You can write wonderfully. Maybe you just need a little help. What were you trying to say?"

She replied, "My favorite thing to do is my work."

That statement was the same one that she had said earlier when I originally read her letter to her. This made me think that she was really trying to write what she had said. At that point, I wrote the sentence in her journal directly underneath the random letters that she had written. I read the sentence aloud and then we both read the sentence together. Alexandria then said, "Now we have both write the sentence down."

I replied, "Right, and we both did a great job."

After I said that to her I kept thinking that I was encouraging Alexandria to write incorrectly. After all, she really did not write a sentence. But then I thought, "No, I am encouraging Alexandria to use invented spelling."

Since that day, Alexandria has not written in her journal, and she doesn't even give me dictation. I ask her what she wants to say and she always replies, "I don't know."

I don't know what I did or said wrong to discourage Alexandria from sharing her thoughts with me. I know that we are not supposed to teach isolated phonics lessons. But what Alexandria wrote down did not make any sense. Therefore, when I went to read the sentence, it didn't make any sense. I am a firm believer in promoting invented spelling, but does it work for every student? Also, how can you encourage students to use invented spelling if they don't know the first thing about spelling words?

CASE 6.2: APPLICATIONS AND REFLECTIONS

What do you think is the purpose of this lesson or series of lessons?

_____

_____

_____

_____

How was the original teaching plan interrupted, or what surprised Tashia?

_____

_____

_____

What actions did Tashia take in response to the interruption/surprise?

_____

_____

_____

Examine the consequences of Tashia's actions. What alternative action(s)/procedures would you suggest?

_____

_____

_____

Identify the resources (e.g., outside readings; conversations with peers, teachers, or other professionals) used by Tashia in this case. What other specific resources might you suggest (e.g., titles of related articles or books, community agencies, etc.)?

_____

_____

_____

_____

From whose perspective is the case written?

_____

_____

_____

_____

What do you think is Alexandria's perspective?

_____

_____

_____

_____

Who are the players in the case?

_____

_____

_____

_____

What seems to be working well in this case?

_____

_____

_____

_____

What needs to be improved?

_____

_____

_____

_____

Can you distinguish between the symptoms and the problems presented in this case?

_____

_____

_____

_____

Adapted from Morine-Dershimer, 1996; Shulman, 1996; Silverman & Welty, 1996.

COMMENTARY 6.2A: IS INVENTED SPELLING FOR EVERYONE?

Mary Alice Barksdale-Ladd, Teacher Educator
University of South Florida

Tashia brought up two important teaching issues in her case. First, she questioned the usefulness of invented spelling for all children. Second, she poignantly described the experience of losing a relationship with a student. I'll respond to each of these issues separately.

In her work with Alexandria in writing, Tashia did exactly what she'd been taught to do in her reading and language arts courses—she made a solid effort to engage a child in using invented spelling to express her thoughts in a written sentence. The result? Alexandria wrote a string of letters that in no way resembled the sentence she wanted to write and believed she had written. Every teacher who has had this experience with a child has faced a dilemma. Would it be helpful to write the sentence correctly for the child and read it, using a dictated story strategy? Would it be best to exclaim that Alexandria had made a marvelous attempt at writing her sentence? Would it be a good idea to start teaching this child the letter/sound relationships? Tashia took the first of these options, and it didn't work out. Why not?

Alexandria provided Tashia with a great deal of information. Alexandria showed that she knew that letters made up words, and she demonstrated that she had the ability to write strings of letters. She also confirmed that she knew sentences should have a few spaces in them, and maybe a dot here and there (a period). From a developmental perspective, this indicates that Alexandria is ready to learn about sound/symbol relationships. Invention of spelling requires that children understand that alphabet letters are usually representative of specific sounds, and that certain combinations of letters consistently spell specific words. Asking a child who has not yet developed these understandings to try to invent spellings would be about the same as asking me to launch the space shuttle!

Alexandria had already been to kindergarten for a year, and this incident happened during first grade. We can assume that Alexandria already had experienced quite a few failures trying to write letters, words, and sentences. We also can assume that Alexandria knew that there were things she was expected to be able to do with letters and writing and she had a strong sense that she couldn't do them, although other children could.

Let's say I've already worked at NASA for a year and a half, and I've been trained in launching the space shuttle, I've already failed many times, and I'm embarrassed. I'm also worried about my inability to do what I'm supposed to be able to do when I've observed that the other trainees in my class have been successful and have made the teacher happy. One day, a nice young preservice teacher in my NASA class, Tashia, asks me to go to the Cape and launch the space shuttle for her. I badly want to please her, so I give it a try, pushing buttons randomly (as usual). The Shuttle just pops and sputters a few times and doesn't move an inch. Now, Tashia tells me, "Mary Alice, I need a little help in understanding your launching procedure."

She asks me a few questions, that I'm unable to answer. I'm feeling more and more humiliated. Tashia now launches it for me, going right through the steps, and says, "This is the right way to do it."

It is clear from her successful launch that I did nothing right—more humiliation! The next week, Tashia asks me to try it again. Do you think I'm going to try?

Alexandria didn't give it another try. My guess is that she was not willing to risk another humiliation. This doesn't mean that using invented spelling won't work with Alexandria. There's a good chance that it will work when Alexandria is developmentally ready.

Now why didn't Tashia recognize that Alexandria wasn't yet ready for invented spelling? When she encountered this dilemma, what Tashia had listened to in lectures and observed in demonstration lessons conducted by her professors didn't pop right back into her mind. It's a normal aspect of the process of learning to teach, and an example of why teacher educators should work hard at integrating course learning experiences (i.e., theory) with field experiences (i.e., the practical).

The second issue Tashia brought up in her case was that of losing a good working relationship with a child. After her attempt to use invented spelling in teaching Alexandria, Tashia was bothered about the fact that Alexandria no longer would attempt invented spellings and wouldn't provide dictation for dictated stories. Every teacher has lost a child, and been upset by it. From my perspective, the big challenge at this point is to put the blame on myself, discover what I did wrong, and make every effort to turn the situation around. If I blame it on the child and her previous experiences (or lack thereof), or if I decide that my method failed and I need to throw out the old method and get a new one, I'm probably in trouble. In engaging in this kind of critical analysis of the experience, I hope I would do some reading, and ask some questions. What went wrong? Why didn't invented spelling work for Alexandria? It was only natural that Alexandria no longer wanted to participate with Tashia on writing sentences. She'd been asked to do something for which she wasn't developmentally ready.

Now, Tashia is faced with the task of regaining Alexandria's trust [see Commentary 8.5B]. My recommendation would not be to go after letter/sound relationships, word spelling, or sentence dictation with Alexandria. Instead, go after something different—something that Alexandria likes and with which she can be successful. Maybe it will be drawing or finger painting, maybe reciting familiar nursery rhymes with her peers. Once Alexandria's trust is regained, and a strong rapport has been redeveloped, the next goal will be to provide her with successful literacy experiences at her developmental level.

Commentary 6.2B: Is Invented Spelling for Everyone?

Lauren Combs, Classroom Teacher
Waveland, Mississippi

Hi Tashia,

My heart goes out to Alexandria. It appears that her problems go much deeper than learning to spell. Let's consider Alexandria's home environment. According to what the classroom teacher said, Alexandria does not have any opportunities to read and write at home. Therefore, if at all possible, it is imperative that you help Alexandria's mother become aware of the importance and benefits of parent–child literacy interactions. Alexandria's school environment also must be very supportive of her writing efforts.

I do encourage my first graders to use invented spelling, because research shows that students who are willing to take risks and construct their own developmentally appropriate spellings write more creative stories and more interesting journal entries than will students who only write words that they can spell correctly. Of course, the majority of my students come from print-rich environments. Their homes are filled with books, magazines, and newspapers. They visit public libraries and they are read to at home. Their oral language is well developed. So, there is a big difference between Alexandria's home and neighborhood environments and the home and neighborhood environments of my students [see Case 11.2].

Alexandria wants to please. Therefore, I think that it would be easy to encourage her to write and to demonstrate how pleased you are with her efforts. In addition, it is most important that you model the writing process for Alexandria. As you write, let her watch as you form letters, words, and sentences. Model your thought processes, and use invented spelling yourself, when appropriate.

You ask, "How can you encourage students to use invented spelling if they don't know the first thing about spelling?" Well, one answer is to model your thought processes as you write with your students (I call this "thinking aloud").

When you asked Alexandria to read the sentence she wrote and then you tried to read it aloud, you created a problem. By trying to sound out what appeared to be randomly written alphabet letters that you already knew did not make sense, you put yourself in a no-win situation and you hurt Alexandria's feelings. I would have approached this problem differently. I would have repeated what Alexandria had said earlier, (i.e., "My favor-

Cunningham, P., & Cunningham, J. (1992). Making words: Enhancing the invented spelling-decoding connection. *The Reading Teacher, 46,* 106–115.

ite thing is to do work"), or I would have reminded her that the activity called for her to read what she had written. I would have made a little game out of it so that she wasn't intimidated.

Because Alexandria has not given you dictation or written in her journal in quite awhile, you need to talk to her and try to find out what the problem is. There may be underlying reasons that have nothing to do with invented spelling. You need to try really hard to get Alexandria to share her thoughts with you.

CASE 6.3: IS THERE A PROBLEM?
Renee Breaux

I am concerned about one of my third-grade students. Nathan seems to be unable to get past the phonetic stage of spelling.

During this semester, I collected many samples of Nathan's writing. I noted that although Nathan misspelled a high percentage of words, he rarely asked for any help. The few times he did ask me how to spell a word, I had him try to spell it on his own in his spelling log. If he was unsuccessful, I spelled it correctly for him. I usually have no problems deciphering Nathan's constructed spellings of words, because he writes most of the words phonetically.

I realize that it is normal for students in third grade to still be in transition between phonetic and conventional spelling. However, there are a few things regarding Nathan's constructed spellings that concern me. My first concern is the high number of words that Nathan consistently misspells. Here is an excerpt from a story Nathan recently wrote: "Wons I terned into a bike areely fast bike but there was one problem there was no won to ride if my mom rode me I wod brake my dad can't ride me because his legs are to log sow I stade in the storeg closet for a log time and all of a soded the dor swog open."

A few things about this example interest me. First of all, Nathan spells the word *once* as *wons* at the beginning of his story. He understands that *once* is similar to the word *one* in *no one,* so he spells it *no won.* However, on the first line of his story he correctly spells the word *one* because he is talking about a number. Shouldn't a third grader know that these words are similar? He also spells the word *so* as *sow.* These are common words that Nathan should be exposed to fairly regularly. Why, then, is he misspelling them?

I stated earlier that Nathan does not often ask how to spell most words. I have thought that this may have been because he was embarrassed. However, after our class last week, I wondered if there is more to this. My group is currently writing a play using the book *The Elephant's Wrestling Match* by Judy Sierra (1992). I provided two copies of the book so that my students could share. Many of the words my students are using in their drama production are in this book. For example, the word *monkey* is practically on every page. Nathan is aware of this and he had the book right in front of him. Yet, when I read his play, I saw that he consistently spelled the word *monkey* as *mocky.*

My question is whether or not I should be worried about Nathan's spelling. I do believe that Nathan is a good writer. His stories are very interesting to read, and a lot of that has to do with the fact that he is willing to take risks and he uses words in his stories that he may not know how to spell.

What steps should I take to help Nathan with his spelling? For now I refuse to do spelling activities with my group, because Nathan is so far behind the rest of the students that I don't want to risk embarrassing him or making him feel that his risk taking in spelling is wrong. In the text *Spelling in Use,* Laminack and Wood (1996) discussed how to determine a student's "index of control" in spelling. This index is helpful for determining whether a writer is "controlling convention or is being controlled by it" (Laminack & Wood, 1996, p. 47). I thought that determining Nathan's index of control might provide me with some insight. Therefore, I looked at a story that Nathan had recently written. According to the index of control formula, Nathan is slightly above average, with an index of control of 69.6%. In other words, out of 69 different words he used in his story, he only used constructed spellings for 21 words. The rest were spelled conventionally. Does this mean that I shouldn't worry about Nathan's spelling or not try to intervene? I am not so easily convinced.

I still think that many of the words Nathan misspells are on a first- or second-grade level. Should I try to work with Nathan separately on the words he continually misspells in his writing? How could I do this without risk of embarrassing or frustrating him? I fear that too much spelling instruction will turn Nathan off to risk taking when he writes creative stories. However, despite my apprehension, I still think that Nathan needs extra help in spelling. Nathan is a fragile student who gets easily frustrated. He gives up when he is faced with a direct challenge. In order to prevent the loss of any valuable ground I have made with Nathan, I cannot implement any plan of action without careful consideration.

Case 6.3: Applications and Reflections

What do you think is the purpose of this lesson or series of lessons?

_____

_____

_____

_____

How was the original teaching plan interrupted, or what surprised Renee?

_____

_____

_____

_____

What actions did Renee take in response to the interruption/surprise?

_____

_____

_____

_____

Examine the consequences of Renee's actions. What alternative action(s)/procedures would you suggest?

_____

_____

_____

_____

Identify the resources (e.g., outside readings; conversations with peers, teachers, or other professionals) used by Renee in this case. What other specific resources might you suggest (e.g., titles of related articles or books, community agencies, etc.)?

_____

_____

_____

_____

From whose perspective is the case written?

_____

_____

_____

_____

What do you think is Nathan's perspective?

_____

_____

_____

_____

Who are the players in the case?

_____

_____

_____

_____

What seems to be working well in this case?

_____

_____

_____

_____

What needs to be improved?

_____

_____

_____

_____

Can you distinguish between the symptoms and the problems presented in this case?

_____

_____

_____

_____

Adapted from Morine-Dershimer, 1996; Shulman, 1996; Silverman & Welty, 1996.

COMMENTARY 6.3A: IS THERE A PROBLEM?

Kathryn Carr, Teacher Educator
Central Missouri State University

Hello Renee,

There are many "Nathans" in third-grade classrooms, so I would consider Nathan's stage of spelling development within the normal range. Nevertheless, with some help, Nathan can make more progress in developing concepts of spelling and other conventions of writing. Although I will address my recommendations to Nathan's spelling, they pertain to an individualized "process writing/spelling" program that I would recommend for the whole class.

First, Nathan needs to understand that the purpose for conventional spelling and writing is to communicate his ideas effectively with others. The philosophy of process writing is to get students' ideas written in the first draft, without worrying about writing mechanics so that these concerns will not interfere with composing. Then, through consultation with peers and the teacher, students revise the content in subsequent drafts. In order for the audience to fully appreciate students' work, we fix problems with spelling and punctuation in the final draft. It is helpful if something special occurs with the final draft, such as publishing it in a booklet to place in the school or class library.

I would not expect Nathan to correct all of his spelling or mechanics errors. Instead, I would help Nathan select only a few target concepts. Vygotsky's zone of proximal development (ZPD) [see Moll, 1993; and Commentary 8.3A] is a useful guide in identifying skill concepts that a student is ready to learn. This involves analyzing a student's work in depth to determine what he or she knows and almost knows, and is ready to learn.

You have begun the process of ascertaining what Nathan knows about spelling by identifying that he is in the phonetic stage of spelling. Further analysis of his writing reveals that, of the 69-word sample, he spelled all but about a dozen or so words correctly. The second step is to find the words he almost knows—look for those words that are only one letter away from the conventional spelling. Target these words for study. In the sample you provided, they are *turned, long, so,* and *door.*

Write these words on index cards and, in a brief conference during the final drafting stage, ask Nathan to compare the words on the cards letter by letter with the way he spelled them. Ask him to note the differences on spelling and then instruct him to correct his paper. Have Nathan file the words on the cards in his spelling file box for future reference and word study.

Fresch, M., & Wheaton, A. (1997). Sort, search, and discover: Spelling in the child-centered classroom. *The Reading Teacher, 51,* 20–31.

Word study includes tracing the words, making a mental picture of each word, and writing the words from memory. Using word-sorting activities, Nathan could learn other words that follow the same pattern and he could develop other spelling generalizations [see Commentary 5.4B]. For example, in a mini-lesson with a small group of students, you could point out that if Nathan can spell the word *turned,* he can spell the word *burned.* However, remember that in some words the /er/ sound may be spelled by /ir/ as in *third,* /er/ as in *fern,* or /ear/ as in *earned* or *learned.*

Although you are correct to be sensitive to Nathan's feelings, he will not feel singled out because all students will have personal spelling file boxes. Also, by keeping his list of target words small, he will not feel overwhelmed. Rather, he will feel encouraged as his box of words grows.

I think that Nathan has a lot going for him as a writer. He has creative ideas and a sense of composition, he is a risk taker, and he already uses conventional spelling for many words. An observant and tactful teacher can guide him in developing additional spelling concepts without dampening his spirits. I would like to supply a few references on spelling for you:

Atwell, N. (1998). *In the middle* (2nd ed.). Portsmouth, NH: Heinemann.
Cunningham, P. (1995). *Phonics they use* (2nd ed.). New York: HarperCollins.
Wilde, S. (1992). *You kan red this!* Portsmouth, NH: Heinemann.

Martha Eshelman, Classroom Teacher
Knob Noster, Missouri

There are a number of positives already in Ms. Breaux's approach with Nathan. She is sensitive to his sense of self-worth (perhaps too much so, but more on that later). She is aware of Nathan's strengths in terms of phonetic spelling and his knowledge of sound/symbol relationships when he forms words during his spontaneous composing, and she is having him keep a spelling log. She also observes that he is a "good writer" and she can see past his spelling errors.

Third graders are moving as quickly as possible on their own volition to standard English spelling. Nathan's plateauing in a mostly phonetic stage suggests that developmentally Nathan is showing some immaturity that will partly correct itself with some more months of growing up. Spelling is as much a visual sequential memory task as it is application of phoneme knowledge. In many ways, spelling ability seems to be associated with brain development.

Nathan might be helped by drill practice in spelling some of the very basic, frequently used words that Ms. Breaux says are his most frequently misspelled words. Take four or five words per week, build a word card file, and have Nathan practice spelling these words until he can spell them correctly and use them correctly in his spontaneously generated compositions. To meet his tactile learning needs, you could also encourage him to practice spelling by writing the words with finger paint. Another suggestion is to enlist the aid of a peer tutor for Nathan.

I have a bit of a problem with Ms. Breaux's refusal to do spelling activities with the whole group in deference to Nathan's possible embarrassment. Third graders all need some spelling program to bring them along into using standard English spelling. Each student needs some spelling instruction, and third graders understand that teachers help individual students according to their spelling levels and needs.

The sample paragraph of Nathan's writing reveals that he also lacks understanding of conventional punctuation, such as periods at the end of sentences and capital letters at the beginning of sentences. This, too, suggests an immature level of writing development. No mention has been made of Nathan's reading abilities. At times, a spelling problem is associated with reading difficulties. This needs to be checked out. Ms. Breaux is on the right track, but Nathan could surely profit from some direct instruction in spelling.

SUGGESTED READINGS

Bolton, F., & Snowball, D. (1996). *Teaching spelling: A practical resource.* Portsmouth, NH: Heinemann.
An important premise of this book is that although writing provides the purpose for learning how to spell, students will not necessarily become competent spellers just by writing frequently. Students need to form hypotheses about the ways words are spelled, try out their ideas about how to spell words, receive feedback from teachers, and refine their hypotheses accordingly.

Gill, C., & Scharer, P. (1996). Why do they get it on Friday and misspell it on Monday?: Teachers inquiring about their students as spellers. *Language Arts, 73*(2), 89–96.
This article discusses the results of a project that surveyed and interviewed 15 teachers regarding their questions about spelling instruction. During the project, the teachers also examined their students' spelling patterns and errors, and made changes in their instructional strategies based on their findings.

Laminack, L., & Wood, K. (1996). *Spelling in use: Looking closely at spelling in whole language classrooms.* Urbana, IL: National Council of Teachers of English.

This text asserts that an informed, attentive teacher can create a powerful effective writing curriculum in which spelling develops from students' own explorations with it as they write.

Rhodes, L., & Dudley-Marling, C. (1996). *Readers and writers with a difference: A holistic approach to teaching struggling readers and writers* (2nd ed.). Portsmouth, NH: Heinemann.

Chapter 12—"Transcription: Choices and Instruction"—provides comprehensive information about spelling as a cognitive, developmental process. Specific instruction is offered for prephonemic, phonemic, letter name, and transitional spellers. The test suggests that poor spellers tend to sound out words phoneme by phoneme, whereas good spellers use a wide range of strategies to spell words.

7

Teaching and Promoting Writing

Literacy Concepts and Terms

-creative books
-editing process
-multiple intelligences
-scaffolding

OVERVIEW

The cases and commentaries in this chapter focus on promoting students' motivations and competencies in writing. Scholars whose work emphasizes the process of writing frequently discuss the importance of teachers developing their own writing abilities so that they understand the writing process and can support and nurture their students' writing initiatives. Teachers who model the writing process, demonstrate enthusiasm for writing, and create a safe classroom environment that promotes and values students' writing efforts, inspire students to become successful writers (see Bratcher, 1997; Norton, 1997; Popp, 1996). Teachers, students, and writing experts can exchange useful ideas and publish their writing through such Internet resources as Ink Spot at http://www.inkspot.com or KidPub at http://www.kidpub.org/kidpub.intro.html.

CASE 7.1: HOW CAN I HELP HIM?

Julie Applewhite

I am working with third graders and I have a student who has a serious writing problem. I noticed John's problem right away, but it wasn't until recently that I discovered what was really wrong.

During the first few weeks of the semester, I noticed that John was turning in his journal and literature log, but he had made no entries in them. At first, I thought that I had not given the group sufficient time to complete their entries, so I began to remind the group, "Make sure that you read the question I asked you in your journals."

I also modeled, using one of the student's journals as an example. I pointed out, "See how Jasmine did her entry? This is how your entries should look."

During subsequent sessions I paid particular attention to John's work. I wrote in his journal, "You forgot to answer my question. Don't you have a favorite book?"

During class I stood near John while he was supposed to be writing in his journal. I noticed that he got easily distracted and had trouble focusing on the task. He looked around the room. He daydreamed. He looked at other students as they worked. Many times I had to get his attention by pointing to his journal and saying, "You should be writing in your journal."

He would respond by saying, "I don't have a favorite book," or "I don't like to do anything when I'm not in school."

Occasionally, he would write, "I don't know." He never used a salutation or a closing in his entry, even though at every session I reminded the students how the entries should be written.

During the past few weeks, I have found out what the underlying problem is with John and his journal writing. When I finally got him focused on what he was writing, I was really surprised. The majority of his entries are illegible! They are terribly misspelled and I can't make out one word. Now I know the reason for his apprehension about journaling with me—he can't form letters or spell words. I just don't know what to do about this. Lately I have been taking his dictation, but he continues to resist and makes comments like, "Man, I hate writing. I don't know what to write."

I also found out that he turned in a written assignment to his classroom teacher and she knew immediately that John didn't write it—another classmate did—so she punished him. I want to help John, but I feel helpless. Does anyone have experience with this type of problem?

CASE 7.1: APPLICATIONS AND REFLECTIONS

What do you think is the purpose of this lesson or series of lessons?

_____

_____

_____

_____

How was the original teaching plan interrupted, or what surprised Julie?

_____

_____

_____

_____

What actions did Julie take in response to the interruption/surprise?

_____

_____

_____

_____

Examine the consequences of Julie's actions. What alternative action(s)/procedures would you suggest?

_____

_____

_____

_____

Identify the resources (e.g., outside readings; conversations with peers, teachers, or other professionals) used by Julie in this case. What other specific resources might you suggest (e.g., titles of related articles or books, community agencies, etc.)?

_____

_____

_____

_____

From whose perspective is the case written?

_____

_____

_____

_____

What do you think is John's perspective?

_____

_____

_____

_____

Who are the players in the case?

_____

_____

_____

_____

What seems to be working well in this case?

_____

_____

_____

_____

What needs to be improved?

_____

_____

_____

_____

Can you distinguish between the symptoms and the problems presented in this case?

_____

_____

_____

_____

Adapted from Morine-Dershimer, 1996; Shulman, 1996; Silverman & Welty, 1996.

COMMENTARY 7.1A: HOW CAN I HELP HIM?

David Clarke, Classroom Teacher
New Orleans, Louisiana

I am really concerned about John. He is in third grade and Julie has discovered that he can't write personal thoughts in his journal or his literacy log. Clearly, John's writing abilities are considerably below the norm for third graders. I have two immediate questions. Can John write his name? That's one good place to start beginning writing instruction. Also, can he read at all [see Commentary 7.1B]? That's another place to begin planning and offering interventions to help John achieve literacy success. Once John can independently write or copy his name, Julie can devise writing activities for him that will enable John to see the connections between his name and other words (e.g., words that begin with the letter *j* or words that end with the letter, *n*). Another suggestion is that Julie can help John make a personal dictionary in which they enter only words that begin with *j*. John can illustrate each word in his dictionary. He also can learn to read, write, and illustrate simple sentences that contain his name, such as, "John is in third grade," "John is 8 years old," and "John has a bike."

Julie also can help John develop **creative books.** He can draw his ideas and then Julie can take his dictation. His books can be shared with his peers and with younger students. For example, John could have a standing arrangement to read his newest book to a kindergarten or first-grade class every Friday afternoon. John also can make murals and design posters and drawings that portray his thoughts. Here again, Julie can take John's dictation. In addition, John can create mobiles and dioramas, design puppets, take photographs, and engage in drama productions that portray his thoughts.

All of these activities draw on Howard Gardner's ideas concerning **multiple intelligences** (1983) [see Overview to chap. 9]. Engaging in these types of authentic activities will allow John to become an esteemed member of his class. In addition, his own self-regard will soar. Equally important, John will be using his special talents productively rather than planning how he will turn in writing assignments if he can't write. (No wonder he turned in a classmate's work—he recognized that he could not complete the assignment. That surely is a cry for help!)

Other ideas to help John are to provide him with a buddy who can sit by him and help him with writing activities; perhaps class writing activities could be structured so that all students occasionally work with a buddy. Students also could periodically participate in small, collaborative writing groups. Writing with a peer or in small groups could help John observe and learn how to form alphabet letters, words, and sentences. Additionally, he could begin to understand the writing process.

John certainly needs support from an after-school tutoring program. The successful program in my school meets three times weekly. Julie also needs to contact John's parents to determine what's going on at home and to ask them what they believe is contributing to John's inabilities to write. I suspect that he has a learning disability. Therefore, John's classroom teacher needs to initiate appropriate procedures to get John evaluated. In the meantime, Julie needs to work especially hard with John to enhance his writing abilities and to structure literacy learning activities that will enable John to achieve success. Above all, Julie needs patience. I've found that just when you think a student never will respond, he or she surprises you.

COMMENTARY 7.1B: HOW CAN I HELP HIM?

Dana Grisham, Teacher Educator
San Diego State University

Hi Julie,

Young, reluctant writers are often reluctant for very good reasons. It sounds as if John is a student with underdeveloped literacy skills who has learned to protect his academic self-concept by refusing to write. Thus far, he's been able to avoid writing. However, the instance in which he was caught turning in someone else's writing instead of his own work is pretty revealing. John wants to learn and to contribute to class activities. I think this is a good sign.

If John were my student, I'd begin by finding out everything I could about him. You don't mention whether John is a native English speaker. If he's not, then my course of action would be different from the one I'm suggesting here. You also don't mention John's ethnicity, socioeconomic status, or level of parental support. These are important issues with regard to John's literacy development. Where is John with regard to his emerging literacy? Is it only writing that gives him problems, or does he have trouble with reading? How is his verbal literacy? Thus, the first thing I would do is consult John's records, talk to his previous teachers, and observe John closely in his classroom interactions. If the home situation is good, I'd talk to John's parents.

I imagine that John is afraid of risking his self-concept when he writes. He is worried that he may be highly criticized, which is a frightening prospect for anyone. After he was punished for attempting to participate in a writing activity (however misguided he was to turn in another student's work), John probably sees the problem as a personal one. He may feel like a bad or stupid person because he is unable to write conventionally. John needs to know that you, as his teacher, recognize that his writing skills need to be developed, but that you still respect him as a person. In addition, he needs to recognize that you are willing to work with him to improve his writing skills. You may need to tell him that you do not blame him for his underdeveloped writing abilities. At the same time, John needs to understand that you are certain he can make progress in writing if he is willing to work with you.

Once you win John's trust, then you need to decide how you will initiate an instructional plan. Here's a suggested course of action for John as an individual student:

1. Determine John's level of phonemic awareness. If John has difficulty hearing the sounds in language, he probably isn't ready for phonics. Invented spelling in his journals should be encouraged as he participates in phonemic awareness activities. If direct instruction is indicated, an after-school program could help, if one is available.

2. John needs to learn the alphabet. A cross-age tutor who can relate to John and play instructional games with him might be able to make good progress here [see Commentary 2.1A]. An alternative is for his parents to work with him on this, if they are interested. John can learn the alphabet through sand tracing, finger painting, and games.

3. During journal time and literature log activities, John should write at his own level. He should always read back what he writes, and, as his teacher, you should spend time in direct instruction on one or two elements of his writing. For example, if you are working on writing certain alphabet letters, then you should show John how to form those letters so he can make the changes in his journal. Praise whatever efforts he makes, focus on any strengths he demonstrates, and then instruct on one or two issues that arise from the writing.

4. When John comments on how he dislikes writing, you should remind him that once we get better at a skill we don't hate it anymore, and that he will get better at writing if he keeps on trying and working with you. Keep a record of his progress over time, and when he gets discouraged, take out his progress chart and show him how much improvement he is making.

5. Try letting John select his own topics for journaling. When students self-select a writing topic, they become more motivated to write. On days when John is very discouraged, let him copy from a sentence frame, filling in only the words of which he feels sure.

Be patient, and treat John as an individual who needs your support and encouragement with his writing. In the meantime, find ways to emphasize John's other strengths so that he feels he is a capable student.

CASE 7.2: PEER EDITING

Brandi Aquilo

When my third-grade students chose to write to the President of the United States, I helped them participate in peer editing their writing. Before I made that decision, I reviewed the personalities of my students. These students did not interact very well as a group. They did not work well in pairs either. However, I still decided to let them participate in peer editing because I thought that it would help enhance each student's writing abilities and offer opportunities for them learn to help each other. I provided an editing checklist and instructed the students to edit according to the checklist.

While my students were editing each other's papers, I made myself available for their questions by walking around the table. That's when I heard some comments that really disturbed me. One student said, "Oh, you're circling all kinds of words on my paper so I'm going to circle a whole bunch on yours."

Griffiths, K. (1997). Know your value. *Primary Voices K–6,* 5(4), 18–23.

Then I noticed that my students started to look around to see what other students were writing on their papers. I found myself in a situation where I didn't know what to do. I decided to ask my students to stop what they were doing and listen to me. I tried to explain that they were helping each other by giving advice. I wanted them to understand that editing was a positive process instead of a negative one.

When I went home and read my students' editing suggestions, I became more discouraged. Some students had circled words that were correct and didn't circle incorrect items. I started to wonder, "Was peer editing pointless?"

I would like to try peer editing with my students again. I think that it is beneficial and should be used by writers of all ages. But I don't want my students to get upset when someone writes or circles items on their papers. How should I go about using peer editing with my group of students again? Should I just avoid using this strategy, because my students feel uncomfortable with it? I guess my ultimate question is, "How can I make my students understand that peer editing is helpful?" If I can accomplish this, then they may become comfortable when utilizing this strategy.

I tried to solve my dilemma by doing some research. After reading an article about peer editing that I found on the Internet, I felt better about the problem I was having with my students. The article encouraged me to want to try peer editing with my students again. The author of this article suggested that students will be motivated to edit their own papers if they are first taught how to edit. One way students can learn the **editing process** is through peer editing activities. This article also made me realize that teachers may have to provide a few lessons on peer editing before students understand how to do it. The author of the article suggested putting a code name on students' papers to provide student anonymity. I think I will try peer editing this way with my students. I also think they will improve each time we use this strategy.

CASE 7.2: APPLICATIONS AND REFLECTIONS

What do you think is the purpose of this lesson or series of lessons?

_____

_____

_____

_____

How was the original teaching plan interrupted, or what surprised Brandi?

_____

_____

_____

_____

What actions did Brandi take in response to the interruption/surprise?

_____

_____

_____

_____

Examine the consequences of Brandi's actions. What alternative action(s)/procedures would you suggest?

_____

_____

_____

_____

Identify the resources (e.g., outside readings; conversations with peers, teachers, or other professionals) used by Brandi in this case. What other specific resources might you suggest (e.g., titles of related articles or books, community agencies, etc.)?

_____

_____

_____

_____

From whose perspective is the case written?

_____

_____

_____

_____

What do you think are these third graders' perspectives?

_____

_____

_____

_____

Who are the players in the case?

_____

_____

_____

_____

What seems to be working well in this case?

_____

_____

_____

_____

What needs to be improved?

_____

_____

_____

_____

Can you distinguish between the symptoms and the problems presented in this case?

_____

_____

_____

_____

Adapted from Morine-Dershimer, 1996; Shulman, 1996; Silverman & Welty, 1996.

COMMENTARY 7.2A: PEER EDITING

Terri Austin, Classroom Teacher
Fairbanks, Alaska

I believe that peer editing is a very valuable experience for students, but I've found that teachers have to establish some very stable foundation work first. Before I place my students in a peer editing situation, my students and I participate in cooperative activities that encourage each student to have positive working relationships with other students. I wholeheartedly suggest that you read *Designing Group Work* by Elizabeth Cohen (1994) and *Tribes: A Process for Social Development and Cooperative Learning* by Jeanne Gibbs (1987). These two books will help you set the appropriate tone in your classroom that will enable students to work together.

As for the editing process, when I begin this with my students I spend at least a week modeling the entire editing process. I bring in my own writing to use as an example. I use an overhead projector to display my work, and my students and I work together, to edit my writing. Through these types of directed lessons, I can share my expectations and the editing procedure with my students. One thing I stress is that it is important for editors to be able to explain each editing mark they make. This seems to cut down on students putting random or inappropriate marks on their peers' papers.

I begin with simple tasks, such as punctuation and spelling. I have my students use small sticky-tab notes rather than writing directly on someone else's paper. There's something very discouraging about having someone write all over your paper. For example, students place a sticky note next to a misspelled word with the symbol "sp" written on it. I also ask each editor to sign the bottom of the paper they edit. Later, as I look over my students' papers, if I find that many editing problems have been overlooked, I have a mini-conference with the editor. As we work together, reediting the paper, the student editor recognizes that I'm serious about editors doing a good editing job. I also can help these student editors learn how to edit someone else's work. Ultimately, these little mini-conferences assist the editors with their own writing.

COMMENTARY 7.2B: PEER EDITING

Mary Alice Barksdale-Ladd, Teacher Educator
University of South Florida

Brandi has described an amazing peer editing disaster. I was almost expecting the students to come to blows! However, not to worry—these students were not really engaging in peer editing. I believe that for peer editing to be successful, students must learn to become one another's advocates. In order for students to become each other's advocates in a peer editing setting, they must know and use the social skills involved. Peer editing requires that students assume certain roles and understand their responsibilities within each role. Writers who are having their work evaluated know in advance that they can accept or reject the suggestions provided by peers. The peer editing session often starts with authors reading their work to their peers. After reading it, they may describe the parts of their writing that were most difficult for them, or the parts with which they would like some help. They may even develop some questions for the group. If they want the group to see their written work in order to make some editorial suggestions, they may share their paper, but that is not required. The authors can make notes on suggestions and ideas provided by peers, or ask another student to take notes during conversations about their writing. They leave with the notes and then decide what actions to take (i.e., to take some or all of their peers' editing suggestions).

When students are in the role of peer editors, they need to understand that the job involves being an audience for the author. A teacher I once observed provided peer editors with the following suggestions: First, tell the writer what you liked about the writing; then, ask a question about something that confused you or made you wonder; finally, reread the writing and underline the parts that you liked best.

When training students to be peer editors, this classroom teacher did not even introduce the notion of correcting mechanical errors. I believe that this approach to peer editing allowed her students to become advocates rather than adversaries.

It is important to note that peer editing is not just supposed to provide help for the writer—it should allow students to look at one another's writing in such a way as to realize that other writers encounter the same kinds of problems that they experience. By identifying what they liked about the writing and underlining their favorite parts, students have opportunities to carefully examine and develop appreciation for well-written texts. It stands to reason that careful examination of this kind is likely to lead to improvement of everyone's writing.

In order for students to engage in peer editing as advocates, the teacher has many responsibilities. First, the teacher must help students understand the purposes of peer editing and their roles in the process. An essential aspect of this training is teacher modeling. The teacher must model the role of the writer and share personal writing. The teacher also must model the roles of peer editors.

Brandi has the right idea. I was impressed that she made the attempt to jump in and try peer editing with her students. I suspect that she didn't realize the complexity of peer editing with her students and the teaching and modeling that must precede peer editing. We can't expect students to be able to do what they haven't been taught to do. Brandi's students probably just didn't understand peer editing and their roles in the process. Because they entered the situation with poor peer relationships, it is no surprise that they quickly became adversaries. I think Brandi can solve her problem by helping her students to be advocates.

CASE 7.3: CHALLENGES OF CREATING A BOOK

Kim Anh T. Nguyen

Richards, J., Gipe, J., & Necaise, M. (1994). Find the features and connect them. *The Reading Teacher, 48,* 187–188.

The process of helping students make creative books is harder than I anticipated. Before I discussed the techniques of creating a book with my first-grade students, I used the strategy of find the features and connect them. I chose this strategy to help the students understand the four basic story features of characters, settings, problems, and solutions, and how these features connect to each other. I spent two lessons on this strategy. Then we started the creative books. First, I asked several questions to see if the students could remember the strategy. "What is a character?" I asked.

"It's a man or a woman," Robyn answered.

"Mean people," Charles answered.

"Do they have to be mean to be a character?" I asked.

"No," everyone answered.

I then asked them several other questions, such as: What is a setting? What is a problem? What is a solution? They remembered and answered correctly. Therefore, I assumed that making creative books would be easy because my students seemed to comprehend the components of a story.

The next session, I said, "Class, think of a story that you would like to write about."

Earvin raised his hand. "I don't have a story," he said.

"Well, you can make up a story," I told him.

"I don't know how," he replied.

"Earvin, do you remember the components of a story?" I asked.

"Yeah," he answered.

"Tell me the components in a story," I instructed.

"Characters and solutions," he said.

Because Earvin didn't list the other two components, I went ahead and wrote all four story components on a large sheet of paper. I made four big circles and wrote one component in each of the circles. Then, I went over each component one at a time with Earvin.

"Earvin, we need to fill in all of these circles. Who do you want in your make-up story?"

"I don't know," he answered.

"Do you want to be in the story?"

"Yeah, I want to be in the story," he replied.

"Who else do you want to be in the story besides you?"

"My best friend," he continued.

"What is your best friend's name?"

"Steven," he whispered.

"Okay, now why don't we write Steven's name and your name in this first circle. This is the character circle."

I then moved on to the other children in the group, but they were having just as much trouble as Earvin. They were very confused about how to write a story, so I decided to model the process of creating a story. As I jotted down the characters, settings, problems, and solutions in my story, I could tell that the students were starting to understand the importance of planning their work prior to writing. After that, I drew lines connecting each of my story characters with a particular setting, problem, and solution. When I had finished, I told my story, and all of my students were smiling. Now, they understood what they had to do. This episode helped me realize that I should have modeled how to begin creating a story for my students. I had asked too many useless questions and wasted valuable time. Now I'm wondering exactly how many times I should model this story writing process for them. I also have concluded that teaching the writing process to a group of second graders is not easy.

CASE 7.3: APPLICATIONS AND REFLECTIONS

What do you think is the purpose of this lesson or series of lessons?

_____

_____

_____

_____

How was the original teaching plan interrupted, or what surprised Kim?

_____

_____

_____

What actions did Kim take in response to the interruption/surprise?

_____

_____

_____

Examine the consequences of Kim's actions. What alternative action(s)/procedures would you suggest?

_____

_____

_____

Identify the resources (e.g., outside readings; conversations with peers, teachers, or other professionals) used by Kim in this case. What other specific resources might you suggest (e.g., titles of related articles or books, community agencies, etc.)?

_____

_____

_____

From whose perspective is the case written?

_____

_____

_____

_____

What do you think are these second graders' perspectives?

_____

_____

_____

_____

Who are the players in the case?

_____

_____

_____

_____

What seems to be working well in this case?

_____

_____

_____

_____

What needs to be improved?

_____

_____

_____

_____

Can you distinguish between the symptoms and the problems presented in this case?

_____

_____

_____

_____

Adapted from Morine-Dershimer, 1996; Shulman, 1996; Silverman & Welty, 1996.

COMMENTARY 7.3A: CHALLENGES OF CREATING A BOOK

Terri Austin, Classroom Teacher
Fairbanks, Alaska

I think that Kim made an initial assumption that many new teachers make about helping students' author their own books—focusing solely on the final product rather than the process of writing. I've found that I have to be especially resourceful and focused in teaching the creative writing process to young students. They need time to hear good stories and time to practice telling stories to one another. I find that my students are filled with stories if I structure my introduction to story telling and story writing lessons by tapping into their imaginations and awakening their awareness about what constitutes quality fiction.

I always orally model the type of story I wish them to write. After my students have opportunities to verbally share their own narratives with a partner, I then model actual writing. I consistently model every step of the writing process. I've discovered that I have fewer struggling writers when I break down each step, model it, and then have students try it out.

Kim is correct when she says that teaching creative writing to young learners isn't easy. I've found that I can't assume my students understand story writing just because I've introduced it once. The process of recording a story on paper requires lots of time, many opportunities to talk with peers about stories, lots of examples provided by teachers, and multiple opportunities for students to share their stories.

COMMENTARY 7.3B: CHALLENGES OF CREATING A BOOK

Katherine Perez, Teacher Educator
St. Mary's College, California

Congratulations to Kim. After struggling with these very young writers, she recognized that she had wasted much valuable time asking questions that required trite answers (e.g., What is a character? What is a setting?). After a few of these nonproductive lessons on creative bookmaking, Kim learned that her students caught on very quickly when she modeled how to create a story. Teacher modeling and **scaffolding** are so important, yet I've found that most new teachers forget to model and, instead, talk and question their students too much. I bet that from now on Kim will model for her students how to begin and complete literacy activities. That's a big step in the right direction for a new teacher.

Before students can create their own stories, they need to become thoroughly familiar with some basic elements of fiction—not by memorizing the four main components of a story (i.e., characters, settings, problems, and solutions), but instead by reading and listening to many stories, personally responding to fiction in such activities as literature circles, discussing characters' goals and actions, supplying alternative solutions to problems presented in stories, and so on.

Students also need to become aware of how published authors write and commercial artists illustrate books. For example, Kim might read "Letting Go a Story" by Gauch (1997), and then share the information in this article with her students. The author of this article explores the creative processes and story development used by Eric Carle, the well-known author and illustrator of such wonderful children's books as *The Very Hungry Caterpillar* (1987), *Animals Animals* (1989), *Flora and Tiger* (1997), and *The Very Lonely Firefly* (1995).

I think that Kim really needs to relax and slow down. Kim seems to want to rush through her lessons, going quickly from talking about the parts of a story to having students complete their books. She needs to give her students considerable opportunities to construct knowledge about the writing process. Her students need her to model, model, model the process of making creative books. They need to hear and read many examples of quality children's literature. They need to experiment with writing. They need to learn about and then discuss published authors' writing techniques and artists'

Graves, M., & Graves, B. (1994). *Scaffolding reading experiences: Designs for student success.* Norwood, MA: Gordon.

illustrating techniques. Most of all, they need time to think, create, and enjoy the delights of making books.

SUGGESTED READINGS

Avery, C. (1992). Guide students' choices: Ready to write. *Instructor, 102*(4), 32.
   This short article discusses how teachers can use interventions to help elementary students make thoughtful decisions about selecting writing topics. It also explains how to handle difficult situations associated with students' writing.

Bratcher, S. (1997). *The learning to write process in elementary classrooms.* Mahwah, NJ: Lawrence Erlbaum Associates.
   This innovative text synthesizes what we know about how children learn to write. The text's premise is that how children feel about themselves as writers affects their writing competence. Teachers who are co-learners with their students enhance students' confidence, comfort, and competence.

Daniels, H. (1991). Commentary on chapter 5 (teaching writing to students at-risk for academic failure). In B. Means, C. Chalmers, & M. Knapp (Eds.), *Teaching advanced skills to at-risk students: Views from research and practice* (pp. 168-175). San Francisco: Jossey-Bass.
   At-risk students become better writers when they spend less time on skill/drill activities and more time composing for their own purposes and audiences. These (and all) writers benefit from social interaction and peer collaboration.

Norton, D. (1997). *The effective teaching of language arts* (5th ed.). Columbus, OH: Merrill.
   Chapter 11 discusses several effective ways to teach writing. The text also supplies prewriting, first draft, and revision activities, and describes various methods for evaluating students' writing.

Richards, J. C. (1998b). The reading/writing connection. In J. Gipe (Ed.), *Multiple paths to literacy: Corrective reading techniques for classroom teachers* (4th ed., pp. 142–167). Upper Saddle River, NJ: Prentice Hall.
   This chapter explains how reading and writing are mutually supporting processes; discusses how to implement a writing program; and provides practical teacher-directed, collaborative, and creative writing strategies and activities suitable for all types of learners in any grade.

8

Working With Special Needs Students

Literacy Concepts and Terms

-affective dimensions
-webbing

OVERVIEW

The cases and commentaries in this chapter discuss working with students who have special needs. For various reasons, some students are especially sensitive, emotionally fragile, or easily distracted in teacher-directed situations and in independent learning situations. Others have special literacy learning needs, including the instructional requirements of academically gifted students [see Cases 8.4 and 12.3]. Teachers recognize and appreciate each student's particular literacy learning necessities and **affective dimensions.** Teachers also are deeply concerned when students' actions indicate that literacy lessons and activities are not personally meaningful for them. In addition, teachers worry when some students exhibit emotional and social difficulties that keep them from reaching their fullest potential. Many of these students tend to feel alienated from their peers, and often resist teachers' efforts to involve them in meaningful literacy tasks. When special needs students' accomplishments, particular talents, and successes are acknowledged and highlighted, those students begin to accept responsibility for their actions, develop enhanced self-esteem, and want to contribute to class activities and literacy lessons.

CASE 8.1: DO I HAVE ENOUGH PATIENCE?

Kristen Boyce

For the past month I have been teaching six first-grade students. After the first week I noticed that there was one girl in my group who would not cooperate. As I went over the rules each morning, Kimberly would act up. One thing she did was to repeat the rules in a screaming tone that disturbed the other students, like, "WE LIIIIISTEN WHEN OTHERSSSS SPEEEEEAK!!!" Kimberly always thought it was funny. Kimberly also touched the other kids to annoy them, and she took their pencils and put them in her desk just so the other children would get upset.

After correcting Kimberly time after time about many, many things, the problems would always come back. I am so ashamed to say that I was very intimidated by her aggressive behavior. If something did not go her way she would slam her desk into another student's desk. I tried ignoring her behavior, but she wouldn't stop acting up. I soon realized that I needed to reach her somehow, because she was affecting everything I did with the students.

I searched for an answer by talking to other preservice teachers. Margie told me something that might possibly help, so I followed her advice. This is what I did. The next few classes I made sure to sit right next to Kimberly. Each time I went over her journal entry first. (I always read the students' entries to them and then they dictate to me what they want to write.) I started noticing that Kimberly didn't like to write because she barely could write. She drew shapes or pictures and very seldom wrote even an isolated alphabet letter. It seemed to take a lot of energy for her to write, and I had to sit next to her to get her to put anything down in her journal. After each letter, she would look at me for approval. If I left her side she would go back to acting up and disturbing the other students.

What I did next was to write a lot of questions in Kimberly's journal to keep her busy answering them, but that didn't work because I had to read all of the questions to her and that took me away from the other students. Then, I had another idea. I brought a cuddly teddy bear to class for Kimberly to hold. I thought that this might calm her down. I figured that if I could not be at her side the whole time, at least the teddy bear would be near her. When I came to class I gave her the teddy bear, but while she was holding it she acted up again during journal time so I took it away. I also punished her by not letting her color in her journal although the other students could.

Well, she calmed down after that, so I gave her the teddy bear back to hold while we read our story. Her attitude during story time did change for the better. She listened to the story very well. But she kept humming under her breath, "Hmm, hmm, hmm, hmm."

It seems that she will go to any length to get her way and to get my attention. I wish I could work with her one on one, but I can't [see Commentary 3.1B]. I want to put her under my wing and help her as much as I can. Do you believe miracles can happen? Will I have enough patience to keep on handling Kimberly?

CASE 8.1: APPLICATIONS AND REFLECTIONS

What problems are Kristen and Kimberly experiencing?

What questions did Kristen ask that might help illuminate solutions?

What actions did Kristen take in response to the interruption/surprise?

Examine the consequences of Kristen's actions. What alternative action(s)/procedures would you suggest?

Identify the resources (e.g., outside readings; conversations with peers, teachers, or other professionals) used by Kristen in this case. What other specific resources might you suggest (e.g., titles of related articles or books, community agencies, etc.)?

From whose perspective is the case written?

COMMENTARY 8.1A: DO I HAVE ENOUGH PATIENCE?

Maria Meyerson Teacher Educator
University of Nevada, Las Vegas

Kimberly is a spirited child who needs direction and understanding. My first question to the author of this case is whether Kimberly behaves this way with her regular classroom teacher. Sometimes children do not like an interruption to the routine established by the classroom teacher. If this is the situation, you must enlist the aid of the classroom teacher to help you establish yourself as the teacher when you are in the classroom.

Let's assume that Kimberly's behavior is consistently attention seeking, as described in the case. Kimberly may need to see a specialist to determine if her behavior, including humming, is abnormal. I would contact Kimberly's parents to determine what her behavior is like at home, and I would check her cumulative record to see if any testing results are available. I would also suggest that, after obtaining parental permission, the classroom teacher initiate paperwork for Kimberly to be further tested.

In the meantime, Kimberly's behavior must be channeled in a positive direction. If Kimberly cannot form letters, I suggest letting her use small letter stamps or a computer. She also may do better with crayons and markers than with a pencil. Kimberly may not be ready to write to express her thoughts—she may be better able to give a message by drawing or cutting pictures from magazines.

The positive response to the teddy bear indicates that Kimberly understands rewards. What other kinds of rewards does she like? If she wants your attention, why not read a special story just to her? I also suggest that you keep the rules simple. Involve the other children in demonstrations of appropriate behavior.

COMMENTARY 8.1B: DO I HAVE ENOUGH PATIENCE?

Shirley Howlette, Classroom Teacher
Las Vegas, Nevada

Dear Kristen,

There seem to be two focuses here—behavior and academics. Once the behavior is brought under control, then the academics can move forward. But, before you can focus anywhere, you need to get background information on Kimberly. Is she a young first grader? What is her home life like? Has she been examined by a doctor to determine that her health/hearing/vision is normal? Call her parents in for conferencing. Ask about her behavior at home. What disciplinary tactics are used at home?

Once all of these issues have been addressed, then start moving on the second focus. What does she know? Just because Kimberly is in first grade and the teacher is ready to start journal writing does not mean that Kimberly is ready to journal at that moment.

The trick here is to find logical consequences for her actions. Kimberly likes the teacher's attention. The question is how to make that work for Kimberly and the teacher.

You should heavily use positive examples of what is meant by "Listen when others speak" and positive feedback when Kimberly is behaving appropriately. Even positive comments like, "I'm glad to see you today," are helpful. Children love genuine praise and usually will increase their efforts, behavior, and academics to receive it.

A child with these kinds of behaviors needs very few rules to follow, but these rules must be followed consistently [see Commentary 3.1A]. A method that works for me is to put a time (e.g., 10 minutes) on a child's desk and challenge him or her to work and stay on task for the designated time frame. If this happens, give a reward. Modify this plan to suit individual students.

When the journal difficulty arose, I realized that you wanted Kimberly to respond to questions written in her journal. This was well intended, but Kimberly couldn't write in the journal to answer the questions, let alone read the questions. Hence, this opened the door to negative behavior. A child that age cannot just sit there with no task at hand. Behavior problems and attention-getting techniques increase in direct correlation with children's confusion and frustration level.

CASE 8.2: I DON'T UNDERSTAND

Kathryn Blackwell

I teach reading and language arts to five third-grade students twice a week. Ryan is a quiet child and the most soft spoken in my group. He rarely says a word unless someone asks him a question. My concern is not his shyness, but instead his apparent lack of understanding during our lessons. He frequently needs directions repeated. He stares into space or at others in the room. I call his name to get his attention, and ask him questions such as, "What have you written down so far, Ryan?" to get him to focus on what we are doing. Sometimes he will look at me and point to his paper for me to look at it. Frequently, however, he responds with something unrelated to my question, or he just stares at me as if he does not understand what I said.

I introduced the concept of **webbing** to help my students organize their writing for their *All About Me* book. Ryan included his family members and the sports that he enjoys in his web. However, when he wrote the final copy of his *All About Me* book, he included a report on *Miss Nelson Is Missing* (Allard & Marshall, 1985), a book we had recently read. When Ryan sat in the author's chair to share his *All About Me* book, the other students noticed that he had written a book report. One student said, "Ryan wasn't supposed to write a book report."

Another student responded "Yeah, he wasn't supposed to write a book report in his *All About Me* book."

To try and save Ryan some embarrassment, I smiled and said, "Ryan, did you include the book report in your own book because you liked it and wanted to share this with us?"

Ryan shook his head up and down signaling, "Yes."

The other students said "Oh," almost in unison. I then thanked Ryan for sharing the book with us, and we moved on.

When the students write in their reading logs to record what they read during our lessons, Ryan usually writes about his family. I remind Ryan to write about what we read and to give his opinions about the story, but he usually writes something like, "We like my family and I likee my friends we were talking about cats a poetry," or "I sleep in my bed and we take a pelo and play pelo fight."

Recently, Ryan looked at the other students' reading logs and then his own. With a despondent look, he said, "They have more stickers than I do."

I asked him if he knew why other students had more stickers. Ryan said, "I don't know."

I explained again how he could earn stickers on his folder. I said, "Ryan, you must enter at least one sentence in your reading log telling your opinions about the books we read in order to earn a sticker. Do you understand?"

He nodded yes, and sat down. I am perplexed that he can write a book report at home but he cannot write in school. I asked his teacher if Ryan had any special needs of which I should be aware. She said that he qualified for the corrective reading program and would be placed in that special program as soon as there was an opening. I would like to try teacher dictation to see if he responds positively to that writing strategy. I wonder what would happen if he could dictate sentences to another student in the group—would this help him to process his thoughts more clearly? I do not think that Ryan is learning as much as the others. I want him to enjoy this time, but how can he enjoy it if he does not understand what we are doing? I have asked Jacob, a gifted student in the group, to assist Ryan on several occasions. This approach seems to help, but I would still like to hear more of Ryan's ideas. Today the students were working on writing a readers theatre about the story *Make Way for Ducklings* (McCloskey, 1993), a book that we recently read using the DRTA strategy. I paired Ryan with Jacob again. They seemed to work well together when they were summarizing portions of the story. Ryan would tell Jacob what he thought. Jacob would offer his opinions, and then Jacob would write down what they both agreed on.

I am wondering if Ryan may have a language processing problem. I would like to try a story impressions activity to see how well he can write using that technique. It may be that he knows what he wants to say but has difficulty putting it down on paper.

Richards, J. The reading/writing connection. In J. Gipe, *Multiple pathways to literacy: Corrective reading techniques for the classroom teacher* (4th ed., pp. 142–167). Upper Saddle River, NJ: Prentice Hall.

Wolf, S. (1993). What's in a name? Labels and literacy in readers theatre. *The Reading Teacher, 46*, 540–545.

Stauffer, R. (1975). *Directing the reading-thinking process.* New York: Harper & Row.

McGinley, W., & Denner, P. (1987). Story impressions: A prereading/writing activity. *Journal of Reading, 31*, 248–253.

CASE 8.2: APPLICATIONS AND REFLECTIONS

What problems are Kathryn and Ryan experiencing?

_____

_____

_____

_____

What questions did Kathryn ask that might help illuminate solutions?

_____

_____

_____

_____

What actions did Kathryn take in response to the interruption/surprise?

_____

_____

_____

_____

Examine the consequences of Kathryn's actions. What alternative action(s)/procedures would you suggest?

_____

_____

_____

_____

Identify the resources (e.g., outside readings; conversations with peers, teachers, or other professionals) used by Kathryn in this case. What other specific resources might you suggest (e.g., titles of related articles or books, community agencies, etc.)?

_____

_____

_____

_____

From whose perspective is the case written?

_____

_____

_____

_____

What do you think is Ryan's perspective?

_____

_____

_____

_____

Who are the players in the case?

_____

_____

_____

_____

What seems to be working well in this case?

_____

_____

_____

_____

What needs to be improved?

_____

_____

_____

_____

Can you distinguish between the symptoms and the problems presented in this case?

_____

_____

_____

_____

Adapted from Morine-Dershimer, 1996; Shulman, 1996; Silverman & Welty, 1996.

COMMENTARY 8.2A: I DON'T UNDERSTAND

Jill Lewis, Teacher Educator
Jersey City State College, New Jersey

Dear Kathryn,

Your teaching case tells us a few things about Ryan that may help you in your efforts to work with him. To begin with, you suspect he has a learning disability. The evidence here is that he is quiet, often needs directions repeated, seems unable to focus, and requires lots of coaching and support. He appears to have some ability to read and write, even though his completed products are often not done exactly as assigned.

There are also some things we do not know about Ryan that may have a bearing on his performance. For instance, has Ryan been checked for hearing difficulties in order to rule this out as a complicating factor? What strategies do Ryan's parents use with him that help him to work well at home? You can investigate some of this while working with him. And, rather than worry that Ryan needs special services, let's consider ways in which you might help him directly within the regular classroom.

Because Ryan's main difficulty appears to be with following directions, it is important for you to check his work at various points along the way so as to be sure the directions you have given are being followed. This procedure might help to prevent situations such as the unfortunate one he had in the author's chair. You handled this very well, by the way, and saved him considerable embarrassment. You will want to be sure that your directions to Ryan are particularly clear. Make certain that you have his attention when you give the class directions. Look directly at him and meet with him afterwards to have him restate in his own words what he is to do. For long assignments, Ryan should have a signed contract with you. The assignment could be broken down into smaller units and each unit could be a contract component. Assessment for Ryan might be based on his ability to achieve each of these components. The contract could also provide both of you with checkpoints, so that Ryan does not go too far astray on a large assignment.

It would probably be fun for Ryan to work with a tape recorder, too. You might tape directions to him for doing something fun, such as building a simple model of a boat or an airplane. He would have to attend to each direction and follow it before moving to the next one. Success would be evident from the completed model. He could then audiotape for you a set of directions for something he likes to do. He might begin to appreciate the importance of each step of the process in both listening and speaking situations [see Cases 4.1 and 4.2].

You will also need to encourage Ryan to ask questions when he doesn't think he understands something. Your support for him will be evident as you patiently explain the directions to him again. Finally, and maybe most important, Ryan should receive high praise when he completes an assignment according to directions. Positive response to positive behavior should yield more positive behavior.

COMMENTARY 8.2B: I DON'T UNDERSTAND

Fredda Fischman, Classroom Teacher
Allentown, Pennsylvania

Kathryn may want to ascertain if Ryan's problem is a linguistic problem (i.e., can Ryan understand language), a processing problem (i.e., can Ryan remember important information, such as directions for literacy learning tasks) or a combination of both. One way to assess if Ryan's difficulties are linguistic in origin is to ask him questions beginning with who, what, where, when, and so on, to see if Ryan knows that "who" questions require him to name a person, "where" questions require him to state a location, and so forth. I wonder if Ryan understands what sort of information he is to find. If not, then Kathryn needs to help Ryan develop his vocabulary and understanding of concepts.

The processing aspect of Ryan's development can be addressed through the use of three or four picture cards that require a learner to sequence a story depicted on the cards. Does Ryan know how to arrange stories and events in sequence? Does he see the relationships between cause and effect? If not, then perhaps he needs considerable help in this important area.

It might be beneficial for Ryan to highlight each direction on his worksheets in different colors, using "see-through" markers. Directions for Ryan should be numbered and written on a separate line for each direction stated, rather than in paragraph form, until Ryan increases his abilities to process directions. He also should repeat these directions to Kathryn in his own words (i.e., paraphrase the directions) before beginning his work. Then, Kathryn will know if he understands what he is to do [see Commentary 3.4B].

Have Ryan's hearing abilities been checked? [See Commentary 8.2A.] It seems like he is daydreaming when Kathryn gives verbal assignments, so some auditory problems may play a part in his inability to understand directions. The use of colored cards may help him key into oral directions. For example, Kathryn can hold up a green colored card when the first direction is given, a yellow card for the second direction, and a red for the third direction. The use of these cards will catch the wandering eyes of all of the students, help alert students to what directions are being given, and help students recognize what is expected of them. Initially, it is important that Kathryn gives directions that are simply and briefly stated, with no more than three steps at a time. Having students repeat these verbal directions aloud before they begin working will provide clues about what students did or did not understand. This whole-group activity will not single Ryan out and make him feel that he needs special help.

Asking Ryan's parents to come to school for a conference or having a telephone conversation with them is another suggestion. Kathryn must find out why work Ryan completes at home is done correctly. Is Ryan doing the work himself, or are some other older siblings or an adult helping him? Modeling for his parents how to give Ryan directions may be appropriate. It also would really be helpful if Ryan's parents observed in the classroom so that they could have a context for understanding his work habits and ability levels.

Finding out Ryan's reading comprehension level versus his decoding level may be appropriate as well. Kathryn mentions a semantic map. A semantic map may be too abstract for Ryan at this time. Instead, a numbered listing of ideas may be more helpful to Ryan, because he appears confused. He also might write compositions and creative stories and books by initially numbering and listing his thoughts. Then, he could gradually combine these separate one-line responses into a more cohesive paragraph form as his thinking becomes more organized.

I think that pairing Ryan with another student is a wonderful idea. Students learn so much from interactions with their peers. Finally, I applaud Kathryn for recognizing that Ryan needs special help.

CASE 8.3: BELIEVING IN BILLY

Heather Friloux

I work with six sixth graders every Wednesday. I hope to teach an upper-grade class when I finish my degree, because I think that I really relate well to older students. My lessons so far have been pretty successful, but I do have one student who has been a real challenge to me. His name is Billy.

On the very first day I met with my group, one of my students told me, "Billy is bad. He always gets in trouble."

I was shocked that she so bluntly said that Billy was bad in front of everyone in the group. I thought quickly and remembered learning about how teachers' expectations can either harm or help students. I said, "Well, Billy has been very good in our group, and I know that he is excited to be here with us so that he can learn helpful reading strategies to become a good reader. Right, Billy?" Billy just nodded his head and smiled. I continued to compliment Billy throughout the morning.

When everyone was getting up to leave, I said to him, "Thank you for sharing some excellent suggestions for our theme, Billy. You did a wonderful job today." I personally believe that students will live up to the expectations of the teacher and their peers. Therefore, I wanted Billy to know that I did not think he was a bad person. However, since that first day, I have had a few problems with Billy. For example, Billy was writing his short journal entry and had to stop to ask me how to spell a word. Billy asked me, "How do you spell *communicate?*"

I responded to his question by saying, "Write it like you think it is spelled. I will be able to figure out the word when I read your entry. We can enter the word in our dictionaries when we are all finished writing in our journals."

Billy previously has worked with other preservice teachers and learned that we encourage students to spell words using their own constructions, if necessary. He said to me, "Oh, yeah. You aren't supposed to help us."

Then, rather than spelling *communicate* by using his own spelling constructions, he proceeded to ask Donnie, another boy in the group how to spell the word *communicate.* Donnie could not spell *communicate* either, so Billy finally wrote the word using invented spelling. Later on we did enter the word *communicate* in a meaningful sentence in our dictionaries. After the lesson, I thought to myself, "Do all of these students think that we are not here to help them? Are we really helping our students when we do not tell them how to spell a difficult word?"

I realize that I could have my students enter troublesome words into their dictionaries each time we meet, but Billy always has trouble spelling numerous words. We do not have enough time to enter that many words in our personal dictionaries, and the other students do not have as much difficulty with their spelling. My concern goes beyond Billy's troubles with spelling—I am worried that he does not enjoy writing because he is frustrated with his inability to spell conventionally. Billy is an extremely bright individual. He knows all about various animals that are on cable television's Discovery Channel. He has traveled to many places and has experienced many things.

I would love to see Billy write about animals and the places he has visited, and Billy is very eager to share his experiences and knowledge about these topics. However, the problem is that he likes to talk about things he knows rather than write about them. In fact, the other students in the group get frustrated because Billy goes into such great detail about things he knows. For example, the other day in the middle of our reading lesson, Billy said, "I saw these kinds of monkeys at the zoo. I went to the zoo with my aunt and uncle. The monkeys were swinging on the trees and making funny sounds."

He went on to tell us more about the monkeys. I finally had to say, "Billy, why don't you tell me about your trip to the zoo in your journal next week? Let's see what happens next in the story that we are reading." I do realize that oral communication is an important and vital aspect of learning, but Billy communicates verbally so much that the other students do not get an equal chance to make comments [see Case 4.3].

I also have to remind Billy to raise his hand when he wants to speak to the group. I am afraid to say anything to Billy about his lengthy storytelling, because this seems to help him concentrate on our work in reading and writing. When I don't let Billy speak, he gets restless and doesn't sit in his desk with his feet on the floor—he sits on his knees and leans over the desk. He really has a hard time sitting still. The classroom teacher came up to him and said, "Billy, I am very proud of your behavior lately. This small-group time has helped you. You have improved and it is obvious that you are trying to behave better." She patted him on the shoulder.

He looked up, smiled at her, and said, "Thank you."

I could tell by the look of happiness on his face that he was so proud of himself. This was the clue for which I'd had been waiting. I now realized that Billy was trying to behave and his behavior has improved in comparison to the past. My overall concern is not that I think Billy behaves terribly, because he is making an honest effort to follow the rules and pay attention. Rather, my concern is that he tells lengthy stories, has comments for just about everything, needs more time and help with journaling, and cannot sit still at his desk. The other students get irritated with him. I adore Billy and believe that he has great potential to succeed—he just requires more time and attention. How can I solve these problems with Billy?

CASE 8.3: APPLICATIONS AND REFLECTIONS

What problems are Heather and Billy experiencing?

_____

_____

_____

_____

What questions did Heather ask that might help illuminate solutions?

_____

_____

_____

_____

What actions did Heather take in response to the interruption/surprise?

_____

_____

_____

_____

Examine the consequences of Heather's actions. What alternative action(s)/procedures would you suggest?

_____

_____

_____

_____

Identify the resources (e.g., outside readings; conversations with peers, teachers, or other professionals) used by Heather in this case. What other specific resources might you suggest (e.g., titles of related articles or books, community agencies, etc.)?

_____

_____

_____

_____

From whose perspective is the case written?

_____

_____

_____

_____

What do you think is Billy's perspective?

_____

_____

_____

_____

Who are the players in the case?

_____

_____

_____

_____

What seems to be working well in this case?

_____

_____

_____

_____

What needs to be improved?

_____

_____

_____

_____

Can you distinguish between the symptoms and the problems presented in this case?

_____

_____

_____

_____

Adapted from Morine-Dershimer, 1996; Shulman, 1996; Silverman & Welty, 1996.

Stewart, L. (1997). Reader's theatre and the writing workshop:
Using children's literature to
prompt student writing. *The
Reading Teacher, 51,*
174–175.

COMMENTARY 8.3A BELIEVING IN BILLY

Beverly Bruneau, Teacher Educator
Kent State University, Ohio

There appear to be two concerns in this case—helping Billy develop interpersonal skills that will support his self-esteem, and helping Billy cultivate spelling abilities to support his confidence and fluency as a writer. Both issues are important, and I believe that both will take time to address. There are no quick fixes. However, I think that Vygotsky's zone of proximal development (see Moll, 1993) provides a useful model for how Heather might help Billy.

Billy needs both support and knowledge. It is very difficult and sad to think about cutting off a student's story, especially when the student seems to have a strong need to contribute to the group. In addition, in all likelihood, Billy will act out inappropriately if Heather does not let him tell stories to the group. Heather is caught between letting Billy tell his stories and boring the other students, or ignoring Billy.

If we use ideas from Vygotsky's zone of proximal development, we might find solutions to Heather's dilemmas. Billy needs help in thinking through and putting relevant elements together in his storytelling. Heather might work with him individually, listening to Billy and providing feedback about his stories. Then, when Billy does share his stories with the group, they will be interesting. Heather also could help Billy create a book of stories to place in the school library. Perhaps Heather and Billy could work together, writing a play about Billy's adventures. Drama activities would provide Billy with an outlet for his storytelling proclivities. At the same time, participating in a drama production would provide Billy with lots of admiration and attention from his peers [see Case 9.1].

It is interesting to note that Billy thinks he is not being helped when Heather encourages him to use invented spelling. Using one's own spelling constructions requires confidence and knowledge of some spelling rules in order to write appropriate grapho/phonemic representations. However, to stop writing in order to try to figure out the spelling of complicated words may be too time consuming for an active sixth grader. Here, too, Vygotsky's "zone" may be helpful. For example, if Billy is interested in writing about animals, Heather could provide a keyword dictionary that supplies spelling words he might need for that particular topic. Or, Heather could list words that Billy might need, perhaps as a web or as a listing of animals in alphabetical order. Billy also might use a computer spell check system.

Unfortunately, the two problems discussed in Heather's case are not easy to solve. By sixth grade, many students have been confronted with painful school experiences that affect their learning and affective dimensions. What is promising is that Heather has identified and reflected on two areas of Billy's development that need to be addressed, and she is more than willing to help Billy.

COMMENTARY 8.3B BELIEVING IN BILLY

Mary Gobert, Classroom Teacher
Hancock County, Mississippi

Hello Heather,

Billy sounds like a very bright, frustrated child. I once had a student like Billy in my second-grade classroom. His need for attention was great, but so was the contribution he could make to the class. In order to address both, I recognized that we would have to establish a few out-of-the-ordinary ground rules for our classroom [see Commentary 3.1A].

Whenever we got into a discussion and someone wished to voice an opinion, that person had 1 minute to do it. No one could have another turn until everyone who wished to speak had had the opportunity to do so. I wore an hourglass timer around my neck (it had been part of a board game), so that it was handy when needed. If a student had more to say, even a comment, he or she had to write it down and hand it to me at the end of the day, either as part of his or her dialogue journal or as a note. I kept track of discussion contributors by writing their names on popsicle sticks and handing them out after a student had spoken. When students raised their hands again, they had to hold up their stick. That way I could easily see who had already had a turn. The kids kept track of the sticks and they were sturdy enough to last quite awhile. I gave rewards at the end of the week for those who had followed the rules. I think that this technique helped shy students have more of a chance to participate, made kids like Billy respect others' rights to contribute to our discussions, and created a kind of a buffer zone between my "Billy" and the kids he annoyed. The technique also enhanced my students' informal writing abilities, because they all wrote notes to me every day. It also kept my "Billy" very busy and he became less fidgety.

Journal writing can be torture for poorer spellers, especially for a student in the sixth grade. It doesn't matter how much you encourage invented spelling—students know that they should be conventional spellers by the time they are in sixth grade. Consider word walls to help reinforce students' spelling of words they frequently want to use. When Billy asks for help, instead of telling him to do the best he can, go to him and supply him with some spelling strategies. For example, supply him with some phonetic clues to words he needs to spell. Stay with him when he looks up a word in the dictionary. Help him find the word and compare his invented spelling of the word to the conventional spelling. Try giving Billy a little extra attention.

Wagstaff, J. (1997/1998). Building practical knowledge of letter-sound correspondences: A beginner's word wall and beyond. *The Reading Teacher, 48,* 298–304.

CASE 8.4: TOO SMART FOR HIS OWN GOOD!

Renee Mauffray

Clyzell is a 7-year-old boy in the second grade. He is very intelligent and creative. He likes to distract other students, especially his friend Gerald. From classroom conversations, I found out that Clyzell and Gerald play together after school. Although they are good friends, I think they need to be separated. Sometime Clyzell does more harm than good for Gerald, because Clyzell is always getting Gerald in trouble.

Clyzell likes to disrupt the class by making comments under his breath. Everyone laughs, especially Gerald. Clyzell also laughs and makes fun of other students' work. "That's not a frog. It looks funny," Clyzell said once, criticizing another student's drawing.

It is disturbing for me to watch Clyzell make fun of others. Every time Clyzell starts criticizing other students, I stop him. For example, the other day he told a student, "You are not making your *M*s right." I immediately said that the student was doing the best that he could.

Clyzell is very intelligent. When working on our mural, he asked, "What kind of cloud is this? Oh, I know—it is a stratus cloud. We learned that last year."

I told him what a smart person he was. He always asks questions and answers them for himself. He also answers questions that other students ask.

I think that Clyzell is smarter than many of his classmates, which leads him to bother others. He enjoys being disruptive and this keeps him from being so bored. Now that I know he works faster than the other students, I am prepared for him. I never leave him with nothing to do. Sometimes it works and sometimes it doesn't [see Cases 12.1, 12.2, and 12.3].

When writing in his journal one day, Clyzell kept asking Frederick, "How many pages did you write on? I am writing on the third page. Where are you?"

He is very competitive. He tries to finish his journal first. He tries to write the longest journal entry, and he always wants to finish tasks first. In addition, sometimes Clyzell is very uncooperative. Last week he didn't want to do anything except look at a book about snakes.

The other day he wanted to show me a hand buzzer. I told him, "After class I would be happy to look at your hand buzzer. Right now, we have a lot to do! Let's get started!"

"Miss Renee, I want to show you what I have! Why can't I show you now?" he asked every few minutes.

After I ignored him, he stopped asking. As soon as I was finished with the lesson, he brought me the hand buzzer. I gave him my attention and he was so excited. "Miss Renee, isn't this great? Did you know what is was when I shook your hand? Did it hurt?" he asked me.

Last Wednesday, Clyzell spent a day in ISS (in-school suspension), but I don't know why. At our next class meeting, Clyzell began cracking jokes and disrupting the class. I don't think ISS did him any good [see Commentaries. 11.3A and 11.3B]. He thought it was fun and an easy way to get out of class. When we left the classroom to do our drama presentation, another student told him that he was not following the rules of the hall. He kept asking, "Miss Renee, can I go to the bathroom? I really, really have to go!"

When I told him, "No," he pouted and said, "Ah, man! They get to go," (referring to another class that was using the bathroom). He just wanted to go to the bathroom because another class was going. I told him to ask his teacher when we returned to class.

"We are walking right past the bathroom, why can't I go?" he said. Boy, is he *persistent!* A simple "No" is not acceptable for him.

Clyzell is an excellent reader and is interested in the books I bring each week. However, he doesn't like to do any reviewing. A student missed class one week, so when she returned we reviewed the book that we had read when she was absent. We talked about the characters, settings, problems, and solutions. Clyzell spoke up, "We've done this already. Why are we doing this again?"

I explained to him that we were helping the student who had been absent, but he was not satisfied. He became disruptive and I had to ask him to put his head down on his desk.

I wonder if he lacks attention at home, or what? He could also be so smart that school is not a challenge. His knowledge about the different types of clouds proves that he is an intelligent young man. I think that he needs more challenges in the classroom [see Case 12.3]. Academic challenges might keep him from being disruptive. He also likes to work with his hands. However, I know he doesn't like paper/pencil activities, because he groaned the loudest when we tried the strategy of teacher dictation. Challenging, hands-on activities might be the solution to Clyzell's inappropriate behavior. He also needs a little extra attention, but then doesn't every child deserve a little attention? How do I handle a room full of kids when I have three or four Clyzells in the room?

Richards, J. (1988). The reading/writing connection. In J. Gipe, *Multiple pathways to literacy:Corrective reading techniques for the classroom teacher* (4th ed., pp. 142–167). Upper Saddle River, NJ: Prentice Hall.

CASE 8.4: APPLICATIONS AND REFLECTIONS

What problems are Renee and Clyzell experiencing?

_____

_____

_____

_____

What questions did Renee ask that might help to illuminate solutions?

_____

_____

_____

_____

What actions did Renee take in response to the interruption/surprise?

_____

_____

_____

_____

Examine the consequences of Renee's actions. What alternative action(s)/procedures would you suggest?

_____

_____

_____

_____

Identify the resources (e.g., outside readings; conversations with peers, teachers, or other professionals) used by Renee in this case. What other specific resources might you suggest (e.g., titles of related articles or books, community agencies, etc.)?

_____

_____

_____

_____

From whose perspective is the case written?

_____

_____

_____

_____

What do you think is Clyzell's perspective?

_____

_____

_____

_____

Who are the players in the case?

_____

_____

_____

_____

What seems to be working well in this case?

_____

_____

_____

_____

What needs to be improved?

_____

_____

_____

_____

Can you distinguish between the symptoms and the problems presented in this case?

_____

_____

_____

_____

Adapted from Morine-Dershimer, 1996; Shulman, 1996; Silverman & Welty, 1996.

COMMENTARY 8.4A: TOO SMART FOR HIS OWN GOOD!

Suzanne Gespass, Teacher Educator
Rider College, New Jersey

Hi Renee,

In your case about Clyzell you demonstrate several important strategies that good teachers use. First of all, you show that you are a "kid watcher," a term coined by Yetta Goodman to refer to someone who carefully watches and listens to students in order to determine what learning activities and behavior interventions they need. That you zeroed in on Clyzell's understanding of types of clouds shows that you are listening to your students. You also pay attention to what Clyzell says and does in various situations throughout the day, such as journal writing and drawing. Second, you respond to his disruptive behavior in appropriate ways. You help him see that he cannot make fun of others, and you ignore his attention-getting tactics, like the hand buzzer. You also recognize that he needs plenty of attention, and you give it to him later on in the day.

You attribute Clyzell's disruptive behavior to the fact that he is bored in school. This is a challenge that even very experienced teachers face. The reality is that student populations continue to become more and more diverse, and it is very likely that there will be students at many different levels in all classrooms. The challenge and the joy of teaching lie in that complex orchestration of meeting the needs of individual students [see Cases 8.5, 12.1, 12.2, and 12.3]. At the same time, it is important to set up organizational structures in the classroom that invite students to work together in collaborative and supportive ways.

Your case leads me to identify the following three important issues that I think all teachers need to consider: the building of community in classrooms, including grouping strategies, responsibility, and collaboration rather than competition; the dynamic relationship between assessment and instruction [see Commentary 12.1A]; and high expectations and the need to challenge all students.

You bring up the point that Clyzell distracts his friend Gerald. Friendships and student groupings are important to think about as you work to build a community of learners. You might consider making sure that you utilize different kinds of grouping strategies so that students have the opportunity to work with both their friends from outside the classroom and their friends within the class. One strategy helpful in making sure that students work with a range of their peers is the technique "clock partners." In this technique, all students receive a clock face with the hours on it. They then find a partner for each time on the clock, which means that they have to find 12 different people in the class. This allows the teacher to say, "Today we will work with our 3:00 partners," thus establishing an organizational structure for the classroom that is both efficient and inclusive. Although at times students will get to work with their best friend, other times students will need to reach out and work with someone who wouldn't necessarily be their first choice of a partner. In this way, occasionally Clyzell would get to work with Gerald, but he also would need to work with others in the class.

The second issue has to do with the relationship between assessment and instruction. You have already shown that you are observing Clyzell in an informal way, and jotting down things that strike you about him. These anecdotal records are important for documenting patterns of behavior and learning. You also might consider a more formal approach to observation, to see if there are certain times throughout the day when Clyzell tends to be more disruptive than other times. A way to do this is to record what he is doing at predetermined intervals over the course of a week. If, for example, you decide that every 20 minutes you will jot down what Clyzell is doing, you might be able to see patterns when he is more or less disruptive. If he always is disruptive during journal time, you might want to examine what functions journals are serving in the classroom, and particularly for Clyzell.

If Clyzell is actually bored in school, then you need to find some different ways of challenging him. Interviews or surveys that allow you to find out about his interests and his attitudes toward various aspects of school would be an important place to start. It might be helpful to put him in some kind of leadership role and give him more responsibility in the classroom. If you find out that he is really interested in snakes, for example, then you could have him do a mini-inquiry project about snakes that would allow him to channel that energy in more productive ways. Giving him more to do without ensuring that he is engaged in what he is doing will probably backfire in the long run.

The third issue ties in with the first two. High expectations for all students and challenging all students depend on the climate of the classroom and knowing the students' strengths and needs. Some years you will have more "Clyzells" than others, but if you establish a responsible learning community, use assessment to guide instruction, and maintain high expectations for all children, you will be able to handle the "Clyzells" of the world.

COMMENTARY 8.4B: TOO SMART FOR HIS OWN GOOD!

Karen Guillot, Classroom Teacher
Baton Rouge, Louisiana

Dear Renee,

Clyzell reminds me of the possible politician, lawyer, or salesperson of tomorrow! What great persistence! Renee, your insight is fantastic! You hit the nail on the head when you wrote that, "Clyzell may be so smart that school is not a challenge!" Having taught regular education as well as gifted education, I would say you are probably right—Clyzell needs to be challenged [see Case 12.3].

You seem to have an innate ability to see the possibilities in your students. Thus, you are able to teach and reach students such as Clyzell. You also know that it is important to channel students' detrimental behaviors into constructive and creative endeavors. The only problem I perceive is that you have just begun to work with students, and so it is understandable that you are searching for appropriate ways to channel Clyzell's inappropriate behavior.

I have found students like Clyzell to be wonderful and challenging! When teachers can get past a student's sarcasm and realize that this type of student has marvelous potential, teachers can begin to formulate specific plans about meeting the needs of bright, quick, impatient, sometimes overly verbal students.

Have you thought about allowing students like Clyzell to attend classes with older students to study specific subjects, such as math or reading, depending on students' individual interests and abilities? If no educator at your school has attempted this plan, there are research articles you could find to support this innovative idea. My experience has taught me that most administrators are open to ideas that benefit students as long as these ideas are are backed up by research.

Leland, C., & Fitzpatrick, R. (1994). Cross-age interaction builds enthusiasm for reading-writing. *The Reading Teacher, 47,* 292–301.

There are also many activities that encourage creativity. Here again, there are many research articles that can help you encourage your students' creative thinking and problem-solving abilities. You also can find wonderful journals that offer ideas about teaching gifted students.

Renee, you might also try accelerating and compacting—two workable methods of teaching very bright students. If you give a pretest to Clyzell (or any of your students), you could determine which students possess the knowledge and understanding to skip some particular aspects of your regular instruction (i.e., accelerating). Accelerating instruction for Clyzell may help him become less disruptive in the classroom. Compacting instruction means that you provide opportunities for Clyzell and for your other very bright students to receive instruction on a given topic. However, your instruction is brief and to the point, because Clyzell and other bright students grasp the information so quickly.

Renee, as intuitive as you are concerning Clyzell, you really should consider studying to be a teacher of the gifted. After teaching gifted students for 5 years, I have found that some of the most talkative, disruptive, and annoying students simply needed an outlet for their creativity.

CASE 8.5: FRIGHTENED—BUT WHY?

Marie Turner

The first time I saw Chiquita shyly smile at me from her small desk in the corner of the classroom, I knew that she was different from the other children in this third-grade class. I began my lesson by introducing myself. "I'm studying to be a teacher. My name is Miss Marie and I'll be with you every Tuesday and Thursday morning until December," I said.

Then I began my interest inventory. Everyone joined in—except Chiquita. She would not or could not answer any of the questions like, "What's your favorite TV show?" or "How many people are in your family?" She just sat there at her desk and tried her hardest to smile at me. But I could see right through her—the expression on her face was a mixture of anxiety and embarrassment.

From Day 1 the other children picked on her. One little boy even refused to sit next to her. After knowing Chiquita for 3 months, I still can't figure out why the other children reject her because, in my opinion, she is absolutely the most adorable child in the group.

She is such a sweet and gentle little girl. Physically, she is much smaller than the other children, even though this is her second time in third grade. During class discussions she will raise her hand but, when I call on her, she immediately slides down into her chair and clams up. Usually, she puts her hands over her face to hide from me. When we work on our journals she does the same thing. I usually try to help her read my entry to her, then I encourage her to write back to me. The only thing she will do is copy words from the note I have written to her. When I try to help her she covers her face. Sometime she even looks like she is going to cry. She also covers her journal with her arms so the other children can't see it. She is deathly afraid that the others will try to read what she has written, even though I have told her that I will not let them see her paper.

Recently, while the other children were working on their creative books, a little boy in my group said to Chiquita, "Girl, your picture is ugly. That's not how you draw grass!"

Chiquita's big brown eyes began to fill with tears and I could tell she was fighting to keep from sobbing. I heard her say under her breath in the lowest voice possible, "I ain't gonna cry."

It broke my heart and I made the little boy leave the group for time out. After the episode I found out that Chiquita often cries at school. She is very sensitive and I think that the other children see her as an easy victim.

Chiquita is not a strong student. I could make no sense of her journal for the first 4 weeks of the semester. But, slowly, I have seen improvement in her work. After nearly 3 months of writing, she is trying to write sentences and she usually attempts to write something related to what I have written to her. I have done everything I can to encourage her and build up her confidence, but she still covers her face and clams up.

When I began working with the children on their creative books, Chiquita would not make any attempt to write a story. She literally sat at her desk and did nothing for the entire 1 hour and 15 minutes. Finally, I asked her if she didn't want to make a book. She shook her head no.

In her journal the next day I asked her why she didn't want to make a book, and she wrote, "Becaues I do not care about with a Book and a storyI want to Be behind I do not like t o with a story and a Bok."

She had copied words from what I had written to her, but I got the message. After I read this I was heartbroken. I think she is afraid to try.

The next day I said, "Chiquita, if we go away from the group to write your story, will you tell me what you want to write?" Finally, she agreed! I was so excited that I had made some progress with her! Since then, she has drawn pictures and traced pictures that I have drawn for her, and she has completed her book. However, it was like pulling teeth to get it done.

I can't figure out what the problem is with this sweet little girl. She is really one of the cutest children I have ever known. Her smile is the biggest and brightest I have ever seen. I have done everything I can to build up her confidence, but she is frightened of everything. I don't know what else to do. I feel so helpless. I suspect something is wrong in Chiquita's home. Remember, Dr. Richards, when her parents wouldn't sign her permission slip to go to the museum? And Chiquita is never allowed to attend school parties or go on field trips—it's not a religious thing either. I do know that she is one of eight children and she has a stepmother, but I have no right to speculate or make any assumptions or accusations about something that is none of my business. I know that Chiquita reads pretty well but she is petrified to write. I just wish I knew why she is so afraid. How can I help her with her insecurity and fear? I don't want to see her fail, but I am afraid that she has been beaten down by someone so much that I cannot help her. What can I do to help this precious child?

CASE 8.5: APPLICATIONS AND REFLECTIONS

What problems are Marie and Chiquita experiencing?

_____

_____

_____

_____

What questions did Marie ask that might help illuminate solutions?

_____

_____

_____

_____

What actions did Marie take in response to the interruption/surprise?

_____

_____

_____

_____

Examine the consequences of Marie's actions. What alternative action(s)/procedures would you suggest?

_____

_____

_____

_____

Identify the resources (e.g., outside readings; conversations with peers, teachers, or other professionals) used by Marie in this case. What other specific resources might you suggest (e.g., titles of related articles or books, community agencies, etc.)?

_____

_____

_____

_____

From whose perspective is the case written?

_____

_____

_____

_____

What do you think is Chiquita's perspective?

_____

_____

_____

_____

Who are the players in the case?

_____

_____

_____

_____

What seems to be working well in this case?

_____

_____

_____

_____

What needs to be improved?

_____

_____

_____

_____

Can you distinguish between the symptoms and the problems presented in this case?

_____

_____

_____

_____

Adapted from Morine-Dershimer, 1996; Shulman, 1996; Silverman & Welty, 1996.

COMMENTARY 8.5A: FRIGHTENED—BUT WHY?

Dana Grisham, Teacher Educator
San Diego State University, California

What can you do when a student is constantly fearful in your classroom? I taught third grade for several years (it was my favorite grade), so I can readily visualize this beautiful, frightened girl named Chiquita. I also can vividly imagine how the other students exclude and intimidate her. In my opinion, this situation is one of the most frustrating and saddening that a teacher can encounter.

There are at least two possibilities for Chiquita's fright, both of which require that you get to know this little girl much better. Here's what I would try. First, in order to become more knowledgeable about this girl, it would be worthwhile to spend some extra time—at recess, at lunch, during class if possible—to draw her out and win her confidence. I believe it best to speak to her privately to find out her interests, and to try to find reading materials that match those interests. I also would seat her close to where I spend the most time during the day. I'd spend time looking at her cumulative folder for clues to the original manifestations of this behavior.

Second, I would try to find someone in the class to befriend Chiquita. I'd let them sit together, pair them for activities, and encourage the friendship whenever possible.

Third, I would hold a classroom meeting to talk about how we need to be friendly and helpful to everyone in our classroom. I might encourage role plays where students talk about times that they felt badly when others were mean or hurtful to them. I'd encourage the talk to turn to what it would look like, sound like, and feel like for people to feel included in our classroom.

From the case description, I fear that Chiquita may be a victim of child abuse, or there may be some disruption in her home life, so I would try to find out more about her home situation. I would call Chiquita's parents to tell them about their daughter's achievements. I would follow up by writing complimentary notes to Chiquita's parents about her accomplishments. I would invite the parents to come and visit the class, and then engage them, if possible, in talking about Chiquita's strengths. I would avoid mentioning anything negative, and let them bring up issues if they seem interested. I would check with my principal and school social worker about the advisability of a home visit.

If I did gain Chiquita's confidence, I'd begin to gently inquire about the things she does at home. Students often will open up when they trust their teacher [see Commentary 8.5B]. Should I find out that there is any form of child abuse going on in the home, I would report it immediately in accordance with the requirements of the local jurisdiction.

Hopefully, child abuse is not the issue here. Perhaps there is a divorce or some other familial or neighborhood disruption [see Case 11.2]. In that case, offering information on counseling or other social services could be helpful to Chiquita and her parents. Consistent kindness and encouragement for Chiquita, along with an emphasis on her strengths, should help her to overcome her fears and lead to academic improvement.

COMMENTARY 8.5B: FRIGHTENED—BUT WHY?

Bruce Fischman, Classroom Teacher
Hereford, Pennsylvania

Unfortunately, many reluctant writers and sad students fill our classrooms. As a preservice teacher, Marie has encountered her first reluctant writer and forlorn student. However, as a classroom teacher for over 25 years, I know from experience that Marie will meet many more sad and dejected students in her professional lifetime.

First, I need to caution Marie about losing valuable instructional time. Through coaxing and role modeling, Marie finally reached her goal of helping Chiquita publish a book. However, I think that Marie wasted considerable time waiting for Chiquita to begin writing on her own. When Marie finally took Chiquita aside and worked one on one with her, Chiquita felt more comfortable and less anxious, and she developed some understanding about where to begin her writing project. Therefore, she was able to begin composing.

Second, Marie certainly is correct to feel concerned about Chiquita's social standing in the classroom. Chiquita is made to feel like a social outcast by her peers, and her peers' actions need to be addressed because they influence Chiquita's academic progress. There are some strategies that would help Marie and Chiquita attend to the social welfare of the classroom that must balance the academic considerations. I learned these techniques in a training institute program entitled *The Responsive Classroom,* developed by the Northeast Foundation for Children in Greenfield, Massachusetts (telephone: 1-800-360-6332). One particular activity I learned is called the morning meeting. each morning meeting begins by students saying, "Hello" to each other, using each other's first names. There are many different games and ways to say "Hello," from high fives to rhythm chants. Next, students get to share their current events with each other, with time for questions or comments. An activity that highlights cooperation follows this sharing time. Finally, during news and announcements, the teacher and students talk about the connections between their morning meeting discussions and the academic challenges planned for the day. Marie and Chiquita might find the morning meeting activity a way to build Chiquita's confidence in herself and a way to build peer cooperation and solidarity among her classmates.

Finally, I want to give some suggestions about why Chiquita may refuse to write. A reluctant writer does not trust—but trust touches every part of the writing process. The trust in prewriting is a trust in self that there is a story worth telling. As the writer drafts the story, there must be trust in fluency, just to record ideas without worrying about mistakes. Revising one's writing involves trust in sharing ideas with others and in accepting advice to improve the writing [see Commentaries 7.2A and 7.2B]. Chiquita is reluctant to write because she has learned not to trust. She is the victim of her peers' remarks. Therefore, she retreats to an inner world world and she doesn't trust herself to be able to write or to share her stories for fear that she will receive harsh criticisms from her classmates.

Hopefully, with Marie's help, Chiquita will be able to turn from a reluctant writer and very sad student to a responsible writer and a student who possesses considerable self-esteem and peer acceptance. We need more "Maries" in our schools.

SUGGESTED READINGS

Educational Leadership. (December 1992/January 1993). Themed issue: Students at risk.
This entire issue is worthwhile reading on today's troubled and academically challenged students. "After reading the articles in this issue readers will have a firm understanding of what the term 'at-risk' means"(Gipe, 1998, p. 84).

Morrow, L. (1996). *Motivating reading and writing in diverse classrooms: Social and physical contexts in a literature-based program* (NCTE Research Report No. 28). Urbana, IL: National Council of Teachers of English.
This research monograph begins with an extensive literature review concerning students' motivations for reading. Effects of class size, benefits of using quality children's literature, collaborative literacy experiences, and the importance for developing voluntary readers are explored.

Popp, M. (1996). *Teaching language and literature in elementary classrooms: A resource book for professional development.* Mahwah, NJ: Lawrence Erlbaum Associates.
This text describes classroom practices that can create opportunities for every student to become engaged in integrated language learning. Each chapter of this resource book contains a section geared to help classroom teachers offer lessons that include all students in meaningful literacy activities. The book suggests a variety of student groupings, focusing on students'

interests and cultural experiences, and getting to know students through numerous individual student/teacher conferences.

White, C. (1990). *Jevon doesn't sit in the back anymore.* New York: Scholastic.
  This short monograph is the story of one teacher's efforts to observe and record what happened in her own classroom. She learned that a strong community of learners can be forged when teachers take the time to "understand and respect the strengths, needs, and differences of individual children" (Gipe, 1998, p. 58).

Wigfield, A. (1997, January). Children's reading motivations. *NRRC News: A Newsletter of the National Reading Research Group,* pp. 1–2.
  This article explains the different dimensions of students' motivations for reading, and discusses how student's motivations for reading relate to their intrinsic engagement in all classroom activities. Additionally, students who believe in their competence or efficacy as learners tend to complete class activities. Included is a motivations for reading questionnaire that considers the amount of time students spend reading outside of school and the different types of books they read.

Literacy Instruction and the Arts: Viewing and Visually Representing

Literacy Concepts and Terms

-Caldecott Medal winners
-integrated curriculum
-learning center

OVERVIEW

This chapter presents cases and commentaries that target integrating the visual and performing arts with daily literacy events. According to Tompkins (1998), "Language arts instruction is changing to reflect the greater oral, written, and visual communication needs [of students] as we enter the twenty-first century" (p. 23). As a result, today's teachers know that competent language users must be able to comprehend and integrate visual media, such as films, photographs, commercials, and videos (i.e., viewing) with other literacy knowledge. Competent language users also must be able to create meaning through such activities as drama productions, murals, diagrams, and illustrations for creative books (i.e., visually representing; Tompkins, 1998).

Today's teachers are well aware that they can help meet the individual literacy learning needs of all students—including students from diverse cultural, linguistic, and ethnic backgrounds—by linking daily literacy activities with the arts. Connecting drama, creative book making, music, mural constructions, photography, needlework, and dance with literacy activities also provides opportunities for students with varying learning styles, special learning requirements, and especially well-developed artistic intelligences (e.g., the visual, spatial, and musical intelligences discussed by Gardner, 1983) to portray their feelings and emotions, explore and enhance their understandings, and extend and express their thoughts effectively. Teachers know that artistic and creative endeavors do not take time away from students' learning. Rather, artistic pursuits help all students reach their fullest affective and cognitive potential.

Aschbacher, P. (1996). A FLARE for the arts. *Educational leadership, 53*(8), 40–43.

Cairney, T. (1997). New avenues to literacy. *Educational Leadership, 54*(7), 76–77.

Whitin, P. (1996). Exploring visual response to literature. *Research in the Teaching of English, 30,* 114–140.

CASE 9.1: RICHARD

Heather Stevens

Olshansky, B. (1995, September). Picture this: An arts-based literacy program. *Educational leadership, 54*(7), 76–77.

No one in this first-grade class is as expressive as Richard. He should be an actor some day. For now, he enjoys distracting the class by clowning. When I give Richard a warning, he pretends that he is sobbing as if his heart is breaking. He even convinced me a few times that he was absolutely devastated. He shows wider ranges of expressions than some professional actors I see on television. I was naturally excited when it came time for my students to perform their drama production, because I knew that Richard would do so well.

The group unanimously decided that Richard should play the part of Corduroy, a small, lonely teddy bear portrayed in the story *Corduroy* (Freeman, 1993). When I asked Richard to act like Corduroy, he went limp as a dish rag, just like Corduroy in the story. His head slumped a bit and he looked at me with big, glassy, teddy bear eyes. He pouted just a little to show Corduroy's sadness.

By the next session, I had written two lines for each student to say in our play. Richard's part was not that long or difficult, but he did not want to practice. He shouted, "I don't want to practice it!" and "Do we have to do it again?"

He refused to repeat his lines, and he started a fight with the boy standing next to him. I told him, "We need you. You are a wonderful actor."

But Richard refused to do his part. Why is he against practicing? How can I encourage him to use his creative gifts for constructive purposes? This is such a waste of dramatic talent.

CASE 9.1: APPLICATIONS AND REFLECTIONS

What do you think is the purpose of this lesson or series of lessons?

_____

_____

_____

_____

How was the original teaching plan interrupted, or what surprised Heather?

_____

_____

_____

_____

What actions did Heather take in response to the interruption/surprise?

_____

_____

_____

_____

Examine the consequences of Heather's actions. What alternative action(s)/procedures would you suggest?

_____

_____

_____

_____

Identify the resources (e.g., outside readings; conversations with peers, teachers, or other professionals) used by Heather in this case. What other specific resources might you suggest (e.g., titles of related articles or books, community agencies, etc.)?

_____

_____

_____

_____

From whose perspective is the case written?

_____

_____

_____

_____

What do you think is Richard's perspective?

_____

_____

_____

_____

Who are the players in the case?

_____

_____

_____

_____

What seems to be working well in this case?

_____

_____

_____

_____

What needs to be improved?

_____

_____

_____

_____

Can you distinguish between the symptoms and the problems presented in this case?

_____

_____

_____

_____

Adapted from Morine-Dershimer, 1996; Shulman, 1996; Silverman & Welty, 1996.

COMMENTARY 9.1A: RICHARD

Connie J. Crichton, Reading Recovery Teacher
Long Beach, California

After years of experience as a classroom teacher and having made numerous mistakes, I can completely relate to Heather's frustrations with Richard. I could see myself reacting in the same way and asking the same questions that Heather asks about herself and Richard. The discovery I have made after so many years and numerous discussions with my colleagues is that students desperately need to have opportunities to give input concerning what they are going to read, write, or say.

Providing authentic activities and practice are most important to successful arts lessons. In other words, if Richard understood the essence of the character Corduroy, then he also would know exactly how Corduroy would act and what Corduroy would say. I don't think that Richard had anything against practicing his part for the drama production. I do think that he felt frustrated at having to use someone else's words.

An example comes to mind with Tony, one of my first-grade students. Last week we were making a computer slide show on the animals we had studied during our zoo field trip. I wanted Tony to dictate something that he had learned about the lion. As a hurried grown-up with a time schedule, I hardly had time to let Tony think. When he was slow to give me a sentence, I began giving him ideas. Eventually I ended up writing what I wanted. After I typed it on the computer, Tony's job was to read the two sentences to be recorded on the slide show. Well, surprise, surprise—he simply could not read what I had typed. He substituted words and tried to make this activity work for him. I immediately knew the problem. We changed the sentence to what Tony wanted and he read with fluency, expression, clarity, and pride. He enjoyed what he had written and it was meaningful to him as an author.

COMMENTARY 9.1B: RICHARD

Margaret Olson, Teacher Educator
St. Francis Xavier University, Nova Scotia, Canada

As I read this case, I was immediately reminded of Vivian Paley, who teaches kindergarten in Chicago and writes books about what she learns from and with her students. I thought about how she encourages her students to tell their own stories—sometimes a sentence or a phrase, which she writes down and which they are then encouraged to act out later in the day (Paley, 1990). I thought about Richard and what different scenarios might have had happier endings for Richard, Heather, and the class as a whole. I thought about who was authoring the story, for whom, and for what purpose. I also thought about what it might mean to practice and how practice and performance might be related to each other.

Richard seems to have great talent in the area of self-expression, and he needs the opportunity to develop this gift through practice. Many other students likely have latent talents in this area as well and they, too, need opportunities to develop their talents through practice. Heather was aware of this need and made valiant attempts to provide these opportunities. There is an enormous difference, however, between authentic and nonauthentic practice. Richard, through his clowning, was practicing his expressive talents in ways that were meaningful for him. However, his actions detracted from the shared classroom story Heather was trying to author and have her students enact. Although Heather attempted to include Richard's needs and talents into the classroom story she was creating, she turned the focus away from Richard's need to be an author as well as an actor. Richard resisted when Heather decided to write the scripts herself, denying him (and other students) the opportunity to author their own story versions. Practicing the version created by Heather in order to perform it later on stage was likely a nonauthentic and irrelevant form of practice for Richard and for the other students as well (although they did not show their resistance). Authentic practice emerges from the particular needs of children. Children do this intuitively and passionately. It is difficult to distract students from authentic practice, such as when they are determined to learn how to tie their shoes or when they continue to ask questions about an issue they find personally meaningful. We, as teachers, are often quick to interrupt their practice and replace it with things we believe are more educationally relevant or appropriate and turn it into repetitive practice for a future and impersonal purpose. We then wonder why students seem disinterested or resistant.

We really need to create the opportunity for small groups of students to author and/or dramatize stories of their own choosing on a regular and frequent basis. Then, those who are interested in being authors, actors, or audience members would have the opportunity to do so under less intimidating and more relevant circumstances. Creating their own scripts would enable students to work through and support each other in issues that are personally meaningful. Having the opportunity to be authors, actors, and audience for and with each other would create possibilities for Richard and his classmates to not only practice their dramatic skills, but also to practice living as a community of supportive learners in more authentic ways.

Perhaps Heather would have more success if she allowed Richard to clown a little. He would get the attention he craves and needs, and his clowning would help calm him down so that he could attend to more introspective literacy activities.

CASE 9.2: SHE SANG LIKE AN ANGEL!

Victoria Blackwell

There was one student in my second-grade group named Dominique, who tried to give me a lot of trouble. What Dominique had was an attitude! She was a challenge and I never quite knew what to expect from her.

For example, during our first session, Dominique refused to sit in her seat. I had her read our rules to me. After she read them, I asked her to tell me what they meant. She replied, "Stay in my seat, raise my hand, and be polite."

I said, "That's pretty good, can you do that for me?"

She said, "Yes," and shrugged her shoulders. But then, she began walking around the room.

By our third session, Dominique still had a negative attitude. As I was reading aloud to the group, Dominique laid her head down on the desk. I told her she needed to sit up and pay attention so that we could play a game after the story, but she stuck her tongue out at me. I also noticed that she kept yawning. I told the classroom teacher that I thought Dominique acted as if she had not gotten enough sleep, and the teacher agreed with me.

The next session Dominique was bouncing off the walls so I had her help William, our dictionary person. I gave her a bucket full of plastic letters and had her sit on the floor and spell out the letters to words that we needed to put in our dictionary. This task kept her alert and busy. She was helping William and it also allowed her to be out of her seat.

During the next few sessions Dominique continued displaying an inappropriate, negative attitude. She wouldn't write in her journal and she refused to look at me. In fact, she kept turning her chair around so that all I could see was the back of her head!

Suddenly, something wonderful happened! It was time for us to do our group mural and she absolutely loved working with paint, markers, crayons, and glue. Then, when we began making our creative books, she was no problem at all! She truly loved making her book. Also, we read the story of *The Little Red Hen* (Gayle, 1997) and I was amazed at how she could remember the story. She even wrote out the entire story all by herself!

As it came time to do our play, Dominique kept asking me if we could practice. The play had a song in it. All of the students loved to sing that song, but I noticed that Dominique especially loved singing. I got an idea and asked her, "Dominique, would you like to sing that song alone on the stage?"

Well, she was thrilled! She sang like an angel and the rest of the group decided that Dominique should have a second special song to sing in the play. This whole thing makes me wonder about the place of the arts in elementary classrooms and how the arts extend and complement literacy activities. Not only that—the arts helped Dominique to improve her attitude. So, as classroom teachers, just how much art, music, drama, dancing, creative writing, and similar activities should we do with our students?

Kersten, F. (1996). Enhancing stories through use of musical sound. *The Reading Teacher, 49,* 670–671.

Case 9.2: Applications and Reflections

What do you think is the purpose of this lesson or series of lessons?

_____

_____

_____

How was the original teaching plan interrupted, or what surprised Victoria?

_____

_____

_____

What actions did Victoria take in response to the interruption/surprise?

_____

_____

_____

Examine the consequences of Victoria's actions. What alternative action(s)/procedures would you suggest?

_____

_____

_____

Identify the resources (e.g., outside readings; conversations with peers, teachers, or other professionals) used by Victoria in this case. What other specific resources might you suggest (e.g., titles of related articles or books, community agencies, etc.)?

_____

_____

_____

From whose perspective is the case written?

_____

_____

_____

What do you think is Dominique's perspective?

_____

_____

_____

_____

Who are the players in the case?

_____

_____

_____

_____

What seems to be working well in this case?

_____

_____

_____

_____

What needs to be improved?

_____

_____

_____

_____

Can you distinguish between the symptoms and the problems presented in this case?

_____

_____

_____

_____

Adapted from Morine-Dershimer, 1996; Shulman, 1996; Silverman & Welty, 1996.

COMMENTARY 9.2A: SHE SANG LIKE AN ANGEL!
Kathleen McKenna, Classroom Teacher
Evanston, Illinois

Congratulations, Victoria! You have already begun to do what effective teachers do so well. Through careful observation of students' outward behaviors, use of a variety of different techniques to engage students, and continuous self-questioning about what works for each student, good teachers discover their students' learning styles and strengths. That is critical for helping each individual student achieve success.

You ask, "How much should we incorporate the creative arts into our curriculum?" The answer to that pedagogical question is that it depends on a number of factors. What are your children's learning styles? What interests them? What engages them? What are you capable of doing with them comfortably? And, most important, what are your goals for your students' learning?

I suggest that you first determine the overriding goals for your reading program. In second grade, we generally build on our emerging readers' pleasure in being able to decode a text independently and discover a story for themselves. Therefore, your objectives should include strengthening your students' reading abilities by teaching them comprehension strategies. But you also want to develop students' pleasure in reading and then responding to literature; creative endeavors are the logical choice after a reading lesson. Make costumes and present a play based on the stories your students read. Draw comic strips and make murals about stories. Write a short musical or an opera based on two or three versions of the same story and encourage your students to present productions for others. Help your students discover music that enhances stories the way scary music enhances the scary parts of any Disney movie.

The list of possibilities for incorporating any of the arts into your curriculum is as long and varied as the number of teachers who have tried to engage students over the years. That's where the issue of your comfort level comes in. What do you like to do? What can you do fairly well? Is there anybody in the community who can help you with an artistic endeavor? If you are naturally artistic in some field (and it seems that you love music as much as the children), then use that strength of yours to enliven all the curriculum. Talk about and examine the math concepts within music; listen to the music of various cultures; study the physics of music. Yes, you can do all these things with second graders and create a truly **integrated curriculum.**

Is there an area where a few of your children excel, but where you don't yet feel competent to help them be creative? Look to one of your special teachers or find a parent or other community member who is good in a specific artistic area. The school art teacher (if you are fortunate to have one) is always a wonderful resource for murals, collages, or other visual arts. Maybe your teaching peers love to sew and can work with your children on costumes. Maybe your principal plays the guitar and would love to come and write a song with your kids. Stand up at a faculty meeting, write a note to parents in your school newspaper or newsletter, or speak out at parent/teacher meetings. There are people in your community with artistic gifts who would love to help. And remember your students' ideas—curriculum should start with them. As you did with Dominique, ask and observe what your students would like to do with respect to the visual and performing arts. Then figure out a way to incorporate your students' ideas into the goals and objectives you have for them. Your job as a teacher is to provide a framework to help your students work to their potential. By playing on their natural curiosity and desire to learn while studying the ways they learn best, you develop a variety of teacher tricks, tools, and ideas to inform and enliven that framework.

For the past 2 decades, Howard Gardner at Harvard University has been studying the ways in which people learn. He describes eight different types of intelligences—different combinations of capabilities that all people possess and use to solve problems [see Commentary 9.2B]. Offering students opportunities to engage in art, dance, and music shows that you recognize the importance of developing your students' unique intelligences."

I think Dominique gets an attitude because she is trying to tell you something. It may be that she doesn't feel well that day; it may be that she is tired or simply needs your attention more than anything else; or it may be that she just doesn't learn information the way

Hatch, T. (1997). Getting specific about multiple intelligences. *Educational Leadership,* 55(6), 26–29.

Checkley, K. (1997). The first seven ... and the eighth: A conversation with Howard Gardner. *Educational Leadership,* 55(1), 8–13.

you are presenting it. Any and all of those reasons must be heard. However, that doesn't mean that you have to allow any child to sing all day in class, or that a student with superior visual artistic intelligence should be allowed to draw all day long. Everyone needs to learn to work from their strengths while simultaneously developing better strategies for their weaker areas. It is your job as facilitator of learning to vary the instructional menu so that all of your students can find the ways in which they can achieve success. If you can model the pleasure of learning through reading and discussing great stories enhanced by creating art, music, or dance, you can provide a classroom atmosphere in which all of your students can take pleasure and be productive. You will encourage their creativity, and your students will show you how they learn best.

COMMENTARY 9.2B: SHE SANG LIKE AN ANGEL!

Camille Blachowicz, Teacher Educator
National-Louis University, Illinois

Congratulations to Ms. Blackwell for not initially "strangling" Dominique! Ms. Blackwell also learned a lot as she struggled to find a way to meet Dominique's social and emotional needs. This is the way we grow as teachers, and it is the challenging students who make us think, reflect about our work, and find solutions. I think that this case points out three important things about teaching that Ms. Blackwell learned and that every classroom teacher should know.

The first is that acting-out behavior is often a signal for us to look more closely at a student to see how we can modify the learning context. To do this, we need to look for underlying reasons to students' inappropriate behaviors and then discover solutions. Merely saying, "Sit down *now!*" to students often earns teachers a tongue stuck out when their backs are turned, and doesn't really provide a long-term key to students' behaviors.

The second important issue is that every student wants to do well but often needs a lot of scaffolding and support from the teacher. Really, many students just don't know how to "do school." Giving Dominique an explicit model for her work, such as her journal format, and praise for following the format are what teachers need to do for students who need more support.

Third, and most in line with the questions that Ms. Blackwell asked at the end of her case, is that the arts are not frivolous additions to the school curriculum—they are a powerful motivator and another language for all students. Howard Gardner's writing on multiple intelligences (1983) and work in special education on multiple modalities for learning and learning styles all emphasize that we learn in many different ways, using many different faculties and aptitudes.

Graves, M., Graves, B., & Braaten, S. (1996). Scaffolding reading experiences for inclusive classes. *Educational Leadership, 53*(5), 14–16.

Your descriptions of Dominique's learning from her art involvement with *The Little Red Hen* and her singing with the class are beautiful examples of how children not oriented toward written language can become involved in language through the arts. Primary teachers who do shared and choral reading and language experiences with art activities—as well as teachers of older students who use song lyrics, rap, video, and poetry—all tap into the emotional power of language when it is coupled with rhyme, rhythm, and music. Performance is another way of transforming a literary work and telling it in your own words. In terms of cognitive development and taxonomies of thinking, the ability to take a piece of literature or informational writing and transform it into art, music, performance, video, or hypermedia is a higher-level activity. It also motivates the learner and provides pleasure to many.

In response to how much art teachers should encourage, each teacher needs to look at the balance in his or her own classroom to see that students have multiple ways to respond to reading and writing, and multiple ways to access information. We need a variety of learning materials in each classroom, and a variety of ways students can choose to respond, reflect, and report. This doesn't mean that every arts option is always available every day, but integrating the arts with literacy instruction develops the whole child in the context of the existing curriculum.

CASE 9.3: I CAN'T DRAW

Patricia Suter

Abrahamson, R., & Carter, B. (1997). From author's chair to bookmaker's studio. *Book Links, 7*(3), 16–20.

I thought that making creative books with fifth graders would be easy. Wrong! When I showed my students the book that I had created, they loved it. But when I said, "Now it's time to make your own creative books," Eddie replied, "I can't draw and I can't write."

Another student, Starr, said, "I don't know what to write," and the other students agreed that making creative books was not what they wanted to do. Because we had gone over the find the features and connect them strategy a number of times and we had enjoyed reading quality children's literature the entire semester, I was shocked! Why were my students being so negative about writing and illustrating books?

I continued, "You may write your story based on a book you have read or heard, or you may create your own story. Remember, your story must contain characters, a setting, problems, and solutions."

A. J. said, "I really can't think of anything to write about and I don't want to write or draw."

I ignored A. J. and told the group, "Now close your eyes and clear your minds, and think about being an author until something comes into your mind. When you open your eyes I bet you can start filling in a story features map with your characters, setting, problems, and solutions."

Well, they all really did get started. I circled the table, but I was not sure how much input or help I should give them. We finally got the first draft of the stories completed and we were ready to move on to our illustrations. "This part will be a breeze," I said to myself. Once again, I was *wrong!* My students were so concerned with each drawing being perfect that they started grumbling, "I can't draw," "This looks terrible," and even, "Tell me what to draw." On and on they went!

I explained, "This is just for us and it's supposed to be fun. Please don't make this into a bigger deal than it is. We're not professional artists and we don't need to be. Just do the best that you can."

I went around the table saying, "This looks great," and "That sure is pretty." Their drawings really were fine. They just didn't think so.

Well, I learned a lot that day. When I do this again, I'll repeat the find the features and connect them strategy before we talk about making creative books. I would certainly bring in my own creative book again. But then, I think that I should turn the project into a **learning center.** That way, my students could work at their own pace and perhaps they would not feel so pressured. I think that I was pushing my students too much and making them feel that they had to produce a creative product immediately.

I don't mean to imply that this art experience was a complete disaster, because it was okay. But the biggest problem was that the students wanted to trace their artwork. They didn't trust their own creative talents—and we all have creativity within us. How do I get students to understand that art is unique to each individual artist and, therefore, that artistic efforts should not be compared to others' work? All students' creative endeavors are worthy, aren't they?

CASE 9.3: APPLICATIONS AND REFLECTIONS

What do you think is the purpose of this lesson or series of lessons?

_____

_____

_____

_____

How was the original teaching plan interrupted, or what surprised Patricia?

_____

_____

_____

_____

What actions did Patricia take in response to the interruption/surprise?

_____

_____

_____

_____

Examine the consequences of Patricia's actions. What alternative action(s)/procedures would you suggest?

_____

_____

_____

_____

Identify the resources (e.g., outside readings; conversations with peers, teachers, or other professionals) used by Patricia in this case. What other specific resources might you suggest (e.g., titles of related articles or books, community agencies, etc.)?

_____

_____

_____

_____

From whose perspective is the case written?

_____

_____

_____

_____

What do you think are these fifth graders' perspectives?

_____

_____

_____

_____

Who are the players in the case?

_____

_____

_____

_____

What seems to be working well in this case?

_____

_____

_____

_____

What needs to be improved?

_____

_____

_____

_____

Can you distinguish between the symptoms and the problems presented in this case?

_____

_____

_____

_____

Adapted from Morine-Dershimer, 1996; Shulman, 1996; Silverman & Welty, 1996.

COMMENTARY 9.3A: I CAN'T DRAW

Miriam Jones, Classroom Teacher
Ocean Springs, Mississippi

Upper-grade students often suffer from the "I can'ts." Usually this "disease" stems from their inhibitions that their work may prove inferior. Older students tend to feel that everyone—teachers, parents, and peers—is judging their efforts, and they feel that they just can't measure up. Providing opportunities for student success in a nonjudgmental, supportive atmosphere often cures students' "I can't's."

I agree with Patricia's decision to use the find the features and connect them strategy, using her own creative book as a model. Reading and discussing quality children's literature also serves as a model for reluctant student writers. Another suggestion is to include works from the Kids and Authors Program sponsored by the Teacher Support Foundation and Willowisp Press, 10100 SBF Drive, Pinellas Park, Florida, 34666. These books are written and illustrated by students in elementary and middle schools. The artwork is not as polished as artwork in commercial fiction, and may reflect a more realistic model against which these fifth-grade students can measure their own efforts.

I also suggest working through the process of creating a book as a whole-group activity. This cooperative activity will provide students with the collaborative support of their peers. The process also may highlight students with special skills and talents who can serve as "experts" for future creative projects.

Authors and illustrators need time to develop and perfect their craft, so I agree with Patricia that affording students more time to "cook" their ideas would help them acquire confidence. I am not sure that creating books in a center would prove fruitful. Authors and illustrators need feedback from their audience in order to improve their work. Therefore, students need to continue to share and discuss their attempts.

I like Patricia's idea about having students close their eyes in order to promote their imaginative thinking. Perhaps listening to music would serve as further inspiration. An additional approach is to have students browse through copies of children's literature to discover the different art techniques used by illustrators [see Commentary 7.3B]. They also could research **Caldecott Medal winners**[1] techniques for illustrating books.

As Patricia's students gain confidence in their creative abilities, they will flourish as authors and illustrators. Their "I can'ts" will vanish!

Richards, J., Gipe, J., & Necaise, M. (1994). Find the features and connect them. *The Reading Teacher, 48,* 187–188.

COMMENTARY 9.3B: I CAN'T DRAW

Jill Lewis, Teacher Educator
Jersey City State College, New Jersey

Hi Patricia,

I'm wondering—when you thought "making books with fifth graders would be easy to do," what did you mean by easy? [See Case 7.3.] If learning is to occur, you want to work within your students' ZPD (zone of proximal development; see Moll, 1993). [See also Commentary 8.3A.] Thus, the learning experience should be engaging, challenging, and mutually rewarding. You were right not to give too much input to the children's stories. You also were right when you asserted that trying to do a creative story in one period was not allowing sufficient time. Nevertheless, there were some strategies that could have resulted in a more satisfying lesson for all.

First, it might have been a more successful experience if, after you showed your story, you had asked the students something like, "What do you think I had to do in order to make this creative book?" As students make suggestions, you could write their ideas on the board. After all suggestions have been given, students could try to sequence them.

---

[1]The Caldecott Medal has been awarded annually since 1938 to the illustrator of the most distinguished picture book for children published in the United States during the preceding year.

Then, they might feel sufficiently well informed and committed to the process to start their own books.

In this case you appear to do a lot of the explaining. For instance, you tell the students, "You know what a good story has to have" and proceed to tell them. Why not try to elicit the information from them? This would be an optimal time for review. You might ask students, "Where do ideas for stories come from?" and have them share some experiences that authors have used as bases for stories that were unusual, exciting, mysterious, significant, and so on. Such a discussion can generate considerable creativity and provide story ideas for the children.

Your students show a lot of insecurity about their artwork. Periodically, you might engage children in discussions about the illustrations in stories they read. Some illustrators use very basic drawings, or even collages. Having examples of these simpler illustrations on display would serve as models for the children and may give them confidence in their own artistic endeavors.

Remember, too, that sometimes stories are generated by children from their drawings; sometimes the opposite occurs. Students don't need to write their stories before they draw—stories can first be sketched and a storyboard created [see Commentary 5.2A]. Each story should be created in the way that is most natural for each child. If you keep these ideas in mind, your next creative writing experience with your children can be fun for all of you.

SUGGESTED READINGS

Cecil, M., & Lauritsen, P. (1994). *Literacy and the arts for the integrated classroom: Alternative ways of knowing.* New York: Longman.
   Important features of this book include how to integrate literacy and students' artistic development, including poetry, drama, music, visual art, dance, and writing. A bibliography of children's literature about the arts is included.

Hubbard, R. (1996). *Workshop of the possible: Nurturing children's creative development.* York, ME: Stenhouse.
   This wonderfully motivating and practical book explores the meaning of creativity and suggests that creativity is not the result of special powers or aptitudes—rather, knowledge, expertise, and motivation are the keys to creativity. Ideas include the importance of playfulness and creating classroom environments where students' creative efforts are nurtured and respected.

Pace, N. (1995). *Music as a way of knowing.* Los Angeles: Stenhouse (The Galef Institute).
   This reader-friendly text helps teachers explore and reflect on their teaching in the arts. The text includes reviews of professional literature in the arts, notes from educators who offer different ways of thinking about music in the classroom, and guides for writing and teaching songs.

Tompkins, G. (1998). *Language arts: Content and teaching strategies.* Upper Saddle River, NJ: Prentice Hall.
   This text explains that competent language users are proficient in comprehending and integrating all types of visual media. They also possess ability to create meaning through visual systems, such as computer programs, papier-mache models, murals, drama productions, and illustrations.

10

Linguistic Diversity[1]

Literacy Concepts and Terms

- -code switch
- -communicative competence
- -dialect
- -homonyms
- -language experience approach
- -linguistic patterns
- -linguistic rules

- -miscues
- -pattern books
- -phonological system
- -standard English spelling
- -syntactical
- -vernacular spelling

OVERVIEW

The cases and commentaries in this chapter focus on meeting the literacy learning needs of students who are native speakers of vernacular dialects or other languages. Linguistically informed teachers are able to offer environments and learning approaches that support all students' literacy efforts, including students who are learning English as a second language or standard English as an expanded dialect. Teachers recognize and respect students' first language and heritage. At the same time, they embed students' standard English language learning in rich, meaningful contexts, such as theme explorations, dialogue journaling, authentic social interactions, peer collaborations, and visual and performing arts activities [see Cases 9.1, 9.2, and 9.3]. Knowledgeable, caring teachers also provide reading instruction for students who speak variations of standard English; they accomplish this by using predictable language **pattern books,** language experience stories, and quality literature. Reading instruction also includes purposeful student discussions and writing activities (e.g., pen pal letters, writing and producing a play with a peer partner, brainstorming and listing solutions to a school-based dilemma). Most important, a necessary condition for facilitating students' acquisition of English literacy is for teachers to respect the validity of learners' linguistic and cultural backgrounds.

Wlodkowski, R., & Ginsberg, M. (1995). A framework for culturally responsive teaching. *Educational Leadership, 53*(1), 17–21.

---

[1]The teacher educator commentaries in this section are authored by Dr. John Barnitz, an applied linguist among the literacy/language education faculty at the University of New Orleans, where he also serves as Chair of the Department of Curriculum and Instruction. He is widely published on topics related to language factors in reading comprehension, but is most well known for his numerous publications on linguistic diversity issues in literacy education, especially those related to teaching children who are native speakers of vernacular dialects or languages other than English.

CASE 10.1: ALICIA USES "HER" LANGUAGE

Malinda Cooper

There is one girl in my second-grade group named Alicia, who speaks and writes with a strong dialect. She pronounces words differently from the other students. I think that sometimes she does this on purpose to get attention, but she also has significant problems pronouncing words. One day she wrote the word *sofa* in her spelling log. She showed me how she had spelled the word (*sofer*) and asked, "Is this how you spell *sofer?*"

I said, "That's close," and I wrote the standard spelling next to the word she had written.

Then she looked at how I had spelled *sofa* and said, "That's not how you spell the word *sofer.* My dad told me."

I didn't know how to answer her, so I pointed to what I had written and said emphatically, "This is the **standard English spelling.**"

I don't know anything about Alicia's background, but I want to help her improve her standard English. The other children in the group don't seem to have this problem. They speak standard English. This dilemma with Alicia made me think of the different dialects people have when they speak.

I really didn't know what to do about Alicia's use of dialect, so I told her that when she writes something that is informal, meaning that the writing isn't judged by others, she can choose her own language. However, when she writes something for others to read or something that she is handing in for a grade, she should use standard English spelling. I also told her that when she speaks to others in a formal situation, she should use standard English. I said, "It is okay to talk to friends or relatives the way you choose. Just make sure that they can understand you. If the person doesn't understand what you are saying, you need to use standard English."

I emphasized to her that there is a time and place for different types of language. She has to realize when to use informal speech, like dialect.

I have tried different approaches to help Alicia understand the importance of standard English. I read books that are familiar to her that are written in standard English. She also observes me writing in standard English. Perhaps the whole language philosophy is a good framework for me to follow in order to teach Alicia standard English. Learning in a holistic way would help her engage in meaningful, developmentally appropriate activities. If students are exposed to material that is relevant to them, they will learn standard English while still being able to use their own dialect in appropriate situations. I will not force Alicia to endure endless, noncontextualized phonics lessons to teach her standard English. As you can tell, I am certainly in need of strategies to help Alicia. I haven't been too successful with her, and I certainly need advice.

CASE 10.1: APPLICATIONS AND REFLECTIONS

What do you think is the purpose of this lesson or series of lessons?

_____

_____

_____

_____

How was the original teaching plan interrupted, or what surprised Malinda?

_____

_____

_____

_____

What actions did Malinda take in response to the interruption/surprise?

_____

_____

_____

_____

Examine the consequences of Malinda's actions. What alternative action(s)/procedures would you suggest?

_____

_____

_____

_____

Identify the resources (e.g., outside readings; conversations with peers, teachers, or other professionals) used by Malinda in this case. What other specific resources might you suggest (e.g., titles of related articles or books, community agencies, etc.)?

_____

_____

_____

_____

From whose perspective is the case written?

_____

_____

_____

_____

What do you think is Alicia's perspective?

_____

_____

_____

_____

Who are the players in the case?

_____

_____

_____

_____

What seems to be working well in this case?

_____

_____

_____

_____

What needs to be improved?

_____

_____

_____

_____

Can you distinguish between the symptoms and the problems presented in this case?

_____

_____

_____

Adapted from Morine-Dershimer, 1996; Shulman, 1996; Silverman & Welty, 1996.

COMMENTARY 10.1A: ALICIA USES "HER" LANGUAGE

John Barnitz, Teacher Educator
University of New Orleans, Louisiana

Alicia is a typical second grader who is well on her way to becoming a standard speller [see Commentaries 6.2A and 6.2B]. Many students who are speakers of vernacular dialects will naturally use their native dialect rules in their initial attempts at invented spellings. I agree with Malinda that Alicia does not appear to have any significant problems with pronunciation—a dialect pronunciation is not a pronunciation problem, but instead is a pronunciation that follows specific rules of the speaker's language. Alicia is pronouncing standard words in her own dialect following some of the predictable linguistic patterns (e.g., *r* deletion and its counterpart, *r* insertion, are very common among certain regional and social groups). Of course, these linguistic rules influence students' invented spellings en route to learning standard spelling. Standard spelling is independently neutral to dialects. For example, the spelling of the word *park* is still spelled *p-a-r-k* regardless if the speaker pronounces the word as "pahk," "pawk," or "park." The spellings of the words *them, these,* and *those* are spelled in a standard way irrespective of the oral language of some speakers who may pronounce them as "dem," "dese," and "dose."

Some standard spellings may need to be learned just like **homonyms** in context. I remember learning to spell *Mary, merry,* and *marry* using context because in the native regional dialect of my Chicago neighborhood these words were homonyms. However, these words are not homonyms to speakers of other dialects.

In teaching standard spelling, I recommend providing students with opportunities to learn words within the context of authentic literacy events, such as dialogue journaling or telling and writing language experience stories. I also recommend mini-lessons on selected spelling patterns that may be influenced by dialect. These lessons would allow Alicia and other students to hear and see the systematic contrasts between standard and **vernacular spelling.** However, I would not suggest isolated mini-lessons without having students involved in authentic events. Malinda should keep immersing her students in literacy events with quality literature so they can hear and see models of standard English (i.e., what we now call "the language of wider communication"). Students also can do various choral reading performances through readers theatre, as well as mock radio and video broadcasts—all involving and encouraging standard spelling and pronunciations.

As students learn the various stages of the writing process [see Commentaries 7.2A and 7.2B], they may learn that vernacular dialects will appear most naturally in their rough drafts, but they can learn to revise for standard spellings and syntax in the context of the revision process of writing.

I encourage Malinda and other teachers to continue linguistic studies of children's oral language (dialects, etc.) and how they relate to learning literacy. We teachers must respect whatever dialects students bring from home to school. Their native dialects are starting points to acquiring standard English. We should help kids appreciate that variety in language is an asset, and that there is a time and place for vernacular and dialects. I applaud Malinda for having a positive attitude toward her students' language. This will keep communication going in the classroom with functional contexts for acquiring the richness of language.

COMMENTARY 10.1B: ALICIA USES "HER" LANGUAGE

Jennifer L. Opitz, Classroom Teacher
Land O' Lakes, Florida

Hi Malinda,

It's nice to know that your philosophy of whole language is so prevalent in your teaching. Learners should be the center of teachers' instruction. Your philosophy and style of teaching sound similar to mine.

It looks like you are dealing with a couple of areas of frustration: Alicia and her use of dialect, and figuring out strategies appropriate for helping Alicia achieve competence in oral and written language.

You did not mention reading problems. I am curious about that. Does Alicia have trouble with reading comprehension? How do you deal with her **miscues** if dialect is the cause of her miscues but she is still comprehending? Remember, it is important to not correct everything she says when reading. If you do correct every dialectical miscue she will begin reading word for word instead of reading for meaning. Worse, she will learn to detest reading!

Providing Alicia with quality children's literature that contains standard English text will help spur her motivation to read and, at the same time, she will be exposed to many examples of standard English language.

You also can help Alicia by continuing to model standard spelling. It is important for her to know what is acceptable and unacceptable when writing letters to others, and eventually for filling out resumes and job applications.

When she is writing, it is critical for Alicia to understand that she does not have to focus on standard spelling and English in first drafts of her work. However, in my opinion, by the time she writes a final draft, her language variations should be replaced with standard English. Focus more on process writing and correspond with Alicia in daily journal activities. Also, incorporating the **language experience approach** may be helpful for Alicia to see the relationship between spoken and written standard English.

CASE 10.2: DONNA'S BEV READING AND WRITING CONNECTION

Christal Hammond

On the first day of class, Donna was absent. When she returned to school, she worked very hard and diligently, and completed every assignment. I usually had trouble getting my fifth-grade students to write a significant amount in their journals, but I did not have this trouble with Donna. At the beginning of the semester, as I walked around the class glancing over the students' journals, I thought, "Donna must be one of the more advanced students in the class."

Throughout our session, Donna seemed to know exactly what to do and was always on task. She made entries into her dictionary, prediction log, and literature log without any apparent problems. She did not disrupt the class or cause any discipline problems. Donna actively participated and seemed to have a good understanding of all of the strategies I presented.

That evening when I went over the journals, I was surprised to discover that I had a very hard time reading Donna's entry. Actually, I could not read it at all. I could only make out a few words. Donna seemed to be using the phonics that have been taught at her school coupled with her BEV dialect. So, I thought, "She must be writing words as they sound to her."

Because I am an African American woman who speaks standard English but can also **code switch** to BEV when I wish, I was not concerned. I thought that I could explain the differences between standard English and **dialect** to Donna.

Unfortunately, my attempts to help Donna over the next few weeks didn't work. I think that Donna must not hear the words as they are pronounced in standard English. For example, in one dialogue journal entry, I wrote to Donna about Valentine's Day. In her reply, she wrote, "I have with by my Ante hose in we havd fun in she cavan me a vntni box of cate In athe we with to bena I with bake home in we play with my esn bean."

Using phonics as a guide, I figured out that her letter was about her visit to her aunt's house for the holidays. After reflecting over Donna's writing, I decided I should spend more time helping her with her journal entries. During the next class period, I attempted to spend more time with Donna. However, I was not very successful. There were other students who yelled out for my help—"Ms. Christal, come help me read this."

I said, "I'll come right back to help you, Donna."

Donna said, "That's all right, Ms. Christal, I don't need your help."

It did not bother Donna at all that I had to leave her to assist the other students, because she thought she did not need my help. Again, Donna wrote a significant amount, yet it was not legible. Then I decided I would try letting her read her journal to me. This allowed me to make an important observation. When Donna read her journal entry aloud to me she could hardly figure it out. As she read, she tried to remember the things she had written. Hence, she was reading or saying words that were not on the paper. Occasionally, she stumbled over the words when she didn't remember what she wrote. Using phonics, I was able to figure out some words. Even though she seemed to be writing the same way she speaks, she was not making the appropriate connections among what she writes, speaks, and hears.

During another class period, I allowed Donna to complete her journal entry without any help. Then I attempted to read the entry but I couldn't, so I asked Donna to read it to me. She had the same trouble I described previously. After I had a good understanding of what Donna wanted to say in her entry, I rewrote it for her underneath her entry. I hoped she would notice the differences in what she wrote and what I wrote. She just looked at me with a puzzled face. She could not see that the two letters were very different. She said, "Ms. Christal, what is this for? Why did you write this in my journal?"

"Well, Donna, I just want you to see how to write your entry in standard English," I said.

She did not question me anymore but she did not seem satisfied with my response. I do not know exactly what is missing in my efforts to help Donna. Please offer some assistance.

CASE 10.2: APPLICATIONS AND REFLECTIONS

What do you think is the purpose of this lesson or series of lessons?

_____

_____

_____

_____

How was the original teaching plan interrupted, or what surprised Christal?

_____

_____

_____

_____

What actions did Christal take in response to the interruption/surprise?

_____

_____

_____

_____

Examine the consequences of Christal's actions. What alternative action(s)/procedures would you suggest?

_____

_____

_____

_____

Identify the resources (e.g., outside readings; conversations with peers, teachers, or other professionals) used by Christal in this case. What other specific resources might you suggest (e.g., titles of related articles or books, community agencies, etc.)?

_____

_____

_____

_____

From whose perspective is the case written?

_____

_____

_____

_____

What do you think is Donna's perspective?

_____

_____

_____

_____

Who are the players in the case?

_____

_____

_____

_____

What seems to be working well in this case?

_____

_____

_____

_____

What needs to be improved?

_____

_____

_____

_____

Can you distinguish between the symptoms and the problems presented in this case?

_____

_____

_____

_____

Adapted from Morine-Dershimer, 1996; Shulman, 1996; Silverman & Welty, 1996.

COMMENTARY 10.2A: DONNA'S BEV READING AND WRITING CONNECTION

John Barnitz, Teacher Educator
University of New Orleans, Louisiana

Website: www.cal.org/ebonics.

Donna is well on her way to developing proficiency in literacy events. Influences of her native dialect are natural. As we know, vernacular dialects are not linguistically deficient communications systems, but instead are legitimate communications systems. African American English includes the continuum from African American Vernacular English (AAVE) to the standard English of the community. Previously, the term *Black English* was used to refer to the range between Black English vernacular and standard English. The recent Oakland, California controversy about Ebonics brought to mind a new awareness of our need to study professionally the language communication in African American communities.

Christal, the African American author of this case, acquired the communicative competency to code switch according to the contextual situation. A healthy part of **communicative competence** in any language or dialect is the knowledge of what language forms and functions to use for specific contexts, depending on the nature or the topic of a discourse (e.g., a fishing trip vs. corporate negotiations), the participants in the discourse (e.g., friends vs. superiors), and the social situation (e.g., a football game vs. corporate board room).

It is natural for students of any cultural heritage to use their native language or dialect in their literacy events. This is a natural stage in the acquisition of literacy in general, and the language of wider communication in particular. The acquisition of the more formal, standard, wider communication or style is a gradual process—it just does not happen in a few weeks. Thus, Christal shouldn't be discouraged if few changes in Donna's writing are noted right away.

I applaud Christal's choosing to use dialogue journals. Dialogue journals provide opportunities for vernacular dialect speakers who write their entries with some dialect spellings or syntax to see the same structures modeled in their teacher's entries with standard spellings and structures. However, I think that Donna became confused by the type of response Christal provided. Therefore, she asked, "What is this for? Why did you write this in my journal?"

Regarding Donna's invented spellings: It would be interesting for Christal to sort out what features of invented spellings are due to dialect influences and what features are due to phonological experimentations (a natural component of all students' progressions toward linguistic competency).

Finally, I believe that it is not necessary to change language by corrections of errors. Teachers can design short mini-lessons on standard versus vernacular dialects to help students recognize systematic differences. However, we must remember that new structures and spellings are best learned in context. Motivating students to get things done with language in natural, authentic, interactive contexts facilitates the acquisition of language.

COMMENTARY 10.2B:
DONNA'S BEV READING AND WRITING CONNECTION

Fredda Fischman, Classroom Teacher
Allentown, Pennsylvania

Donna seems like a child who has lots of pride in herself and her accomplishments. Christal needs to be sensitive to Donna's pride, even if it is misplaced (e.g., Donna's negative reaction to Christal's hopes that Donna would notice **syntactical** or spelling differences between Christal's and Donna's work when Christal wrote in Donna's journal). A suggestion is that Donna and Christal might write collaboratively with each other in a separate journal. Writing with Christal in this collaborative journal might help Donna recognize the differences between standard English and the linguistic elements of BEV. I also recommend a program titled *Assured Readiness for Learning* (McInnis, 1996), to help Donna become more familiar with standard English syntax. Among other things, this program focuses on helping writers organize their thoughts before they begin to compose. Although this program contains considerable language intervention ideas for younger students, it also includes a great deal of information about helping students of all ages and grade levels develop proficiencies in using oral and written language.

Christal also should consider using age-appropriate predictable books with Donna, to help her hear and become familiar with standard English **linguistic patterns** of speech. (By *appropriate,* I mean books that suit Donna's developmental stage and interests.) Perhaps Christal and Donna together might compose and print some of their own predictable books to share with the class. In addition, Donna's verbal and written standard English fluency might be positively impacted by using a tape recorder. Donna could use the recorder to retell familiar stories and to tell her own original stories. Then, these stories could be transcribed. She also could listen to taped stories of quality literature as she follows the text silently.

Another enjoyable technique that works for my students is to use a magnetic board with small magnetic letters and recreate a typed short poem, riddle, or rhyme that they use as a reference.

I think that, above all, Donna's age and sensitivity to criticism always must be respected, especially because she seems to be someone who is a hard worker and interested in trying to succeed. Too much correcting and pointing out of language mistakes will discourage her, and turn her off to even trying. She has the advantage of a teacher who understands the linguistic components of BEV and, together, Donna and Christal should make a terrific team of mutual support and learning.

CASE 10.3: WHAT CAN I DO FOR HASA?

Denise Nelon

On my first day of teaching, I attempted to find out about my fourth-grade students' interests through a verbal and informal questioning/sharing activity. All of my six students were a bit hesitant to reply but, to my surprise, one student named Hasa would not speak to me at all. He would only nod or shake his head. When I later gave assignment instructions, Hasa was the only student who would not make eye contact with me. It seemed like he was ignoring me, but I eventually realized that he was waiting to observe the other students' behaviors before he began the assignment.

At first, I assumed that Hasa could not speak or understand English. I tested my assumption by going on a school field trip with my students. On the trip, I observed that Hasa interacted well with his peers, so I decided that my assumption was incorrect—Hasa could understand and communicate in English. However, after a few weeks, it dawned on me that my initial assumption was partially correct.

By listening to some recorded interviews I conducted with Hasa, I learned that he lacked the phonetic ability necessary for expressing himself clearly in English. However, Hasa did have very good English vocabulary knowledge. For example, I asked the group, "What would be an interesting job for you when you are older?"

Hasa's response sounded something like the word *robber*. But, after much probing, one of the other students was able to interpret Hasa's response as "Robo Cop," which is a big difference from a robber.

I also asked the students, "Which famous person would you be interested in meeting?"

This time, no one could understand Hasa's response. But Hasa understood the question and got very frustrated with repeating himself and trying to make himself understood. So he wrote out the person's name: "Banu Bhakta Acharya." From then on, in my lessons I made sure to ask questions that would elicit more than one-word responses from my students, so that I could use the context of Hasa's speech to better understand him. I also noticed that the other students understood Hasa more clearly than I did, and I encouraged them to help me interpret some of Hasa's responses.

One day, when we were doing a language experience story, Hasa surprised me again! Whereas my other students were struggling with writing their thoughts and ideas, Hasa had no trouble at all. In fact, he wrote faster and used more details and expressive language than the other students. This incident solidified my beliefs in the benefits of language experience activities.

Hasa is originally from Nepal, and speaks English as a second language (ESL). He has lived in the United States less than 1 year. Both of his parents are bilingual, so they can communicate with Hasa in English if they choose. Hasa is very intelligent, but his problems with English oral language are causing him to be frustrated. My question is: Should I focus more on verbal interactions with Hasa to help improve his oral communication skills, or should I focus on communicating with Hasa through written interactions? If I focus more on written interactions with Hasa, I think that my other students will become frustrated because their writing abilities are so underdeveloped.

CASE 10.3: APPLICATIONS AND REFLECTIONS

What do you think is the purpose of this lesson or series of lessons?

_____

_____

_____

_____

How was the original teaching plan interrupted, or what surprised Denise?

_____

_____

_____

_____

What actions did Denise take in response to the interruption/surprise?

_____

_____

_____

_____

Examine the consequences of Denise's actions. What alternative action(s)/procedures would you suggest?

_____

_____

_____

_____

Identify the resources (e.g., outside readings; conversations with peers, teachers, or other professionals) used by Denise in this case. What other specific resources might you suggest (e.g., titles of related articles or books, community agencies, etc.)?

_____

_____

_____

_____

From whose perspective is the case written?

_____

_____

_____

_____

What do you think is Hasa's perspective?

_____

_____

_____

_____

Who are the players in the case?

_____

_____

_____

_____

What seems to be working well in this case?

_____

_____

_____

_____

What needs to be improved?

_____

_____

_____

_____

Can you distinguish between the symptoms and the problems presented in this case?

_____

_____

_____

_____

Adapted from Morine-Dershimer, 1996; Shulman, 1996; Silverman & Welty, 1996.

COMMENTARY 10.3A: WHAT CAN I DO FOR HASA?

John Barnitz, Teacher Educator
University of New Orleans, Louisiana

Hasa is one of many nonnative speakers of English whom future teachers will have in classrooms. I frequently receive calls from teachers seeking certification in teaching English as a second language. Some of these teachers have full classes of nonnative speakers of English, whereas others may have only one such student. Denise is doing well, because she does not speak Hasa's native language. She is choosing good techniques, such as helping Hasa with language experience stories, asking him questions that require more than one word responses, and using the context of Hasa's speech to better understand him. Hasa, however, does not lack phonetic ability, but instead is attempting to filter English through the **linguistic rules** of his own **phonological system.** His native language will influence his attempts at English pronunciation and syntax, and emphasis on context as clues to meaningful communication is crucial to his learning to comprehend and produce English. Krashen (1987) argued that comprehensible input is crucial to language acquisition. Using predictable language and good illustrations in quality children's literature is extremely beneficial to Hasa's using and acquiring oral and written English.

Denise should use oral and written interactions with Hasa as much as possible. Written interactions through dialogue journals that are authentic contexts for writing are helpful to both native and nonnative English learners. Oral discourse through role playing, readers theatre, and interactive reading activities (e.g., the experience-text-relationship method; Au, 1979) are most helpful. Many of the authentic activities used for native English-speaking students are compatible with ESL learners. Structural drills can be used in mini-lessons related to the real reading and writing that students do. Many structures can be drilled indirectly through choral speaking activities, using good literature models. With all learners, keep the language arts integrated so that speaking, listening, writing, reading, art, music, sculpture, dance, and so on can all support the many linguistically diverse learners in our schools and wider communities [see Case 9.1, and Commentaries 9.2A and 9.2B]. As we enter the 21st century, all of our schools will reflect the rapidly growing culturally and linguistically diverse communities in which we live.

COMMENTARY 10.3B: WHAT CAN I DO FOR HASA?

Martha Eshelman, Classroom Teacher
Knob Noster, Missouri

In this teaching case, we have not been told how long Hasa has been using some amount of English, only that he has lived in the United States for less than 1 year. When I took an ESL workshop, we were reminded forcefully that we should allow ESL students about 3 to 4 years of getting acquainted with English before they would feel comfortable using it in an instructional work setting, reading and responding to teachers. Put yourself in the shoes of someone studying in a foreign country where texts, board work, and oral lectures are all in an unfamiliar language—how secure would you feel? First, students must feel comfortable using everyday, socially interactive English; thus, Ms. Nelon observed Hasa having a good time with classmates on a field trip.

I think we need to concentrate first on putting Hasa at ease about using what English he does command, all the while helping him to add to his knowledge. We also need to be willing to accept his reticence to make eye contact as normal (not an aberration)—this may be cultural behavior. Of course, Hasa is frustrated at attempting to make himself understood—perhaps that is why he observes the other students before beginning his work.

From my training and experience working with ESL students, I know that patience is a key factor. I believe that Hasa needs time to develop a command of the English language. Denise shouldn't expect too much for some time. She should encourage Hasa to observe the work of his peers, and she should model everything for Hasa.

As to whether Denise should communicate orally or in writing to Hasa, why not use a combination of both approaches? It seems like the consideration of frustrating the other five students because of their underdeveloped writing abilities need not be a serious problem in a small group of only six. In such a small group, one can individualize instruction.

A final consideration to pursue is to refer Hasa to an ESL staff person if one is available in your district. Many school districts have such a resource person to help students like Hasa.

SUGGESTED READINGS

Au, K. (1993). *Literacy instruction in multicultural settings.* Fort Worth, TX: Harcourt Brace Jovanovich.
This text provides a comprehensive discussion about cultural and linguistic considerations for teaching reading and language arts. The role of cultural discourse interactions and using multicultural literature are emphasized.

Barnitz, J. (1998). Developing reading of linguistically diverse students. In J. Gipe, *Multiple paths to literacy instruction: Corrective reading techniques for the classroom teacher* (4th ed., pp. 340–359). Upper Saddle River, NJ: Prentice Hall.
Chapter 13 describes the relationships between communicative competence and students' reading development. This chapter also explains how language characteristics vary across cultural groups. Other important information includes various approaches for supporting the reading development of linguistically diverse students, and implications of language or dialect diversity for assessing students' language and reading abilities.

Kucer, S. (1995). Guiding bilingual students "through" the literacy process. *Language Arts,* 72(1), 20–29.
Helping ESL students develop proficiency in the language arts is one of the biggest challenges educators in the United States face. The article supplies many strategies and techniques for helping ESL students with their reading and writing, including many examples of strategy wall charts, reader response strategies, and spelling strategies.

McCaleb, S. (1994). *Building communities of learners: A collaboration among teachers, students, families, and community.* Hillsdale, NJ: Lawrence Erlbaum Associates.
This book presents a strong case for respect and participation of parents in culturally diverse school settings. The book is enriched by the inclusion of children's and parents' narratives.

Wolfram, W., Adger, C., & Christian, D. (1999). *Dialects in schools and communities.* Mahwah, NJ: Lawrence Erlbaum Associates.
This text offers current trends and issues on language variations that are prevalent in schools and community settings. Information is provided on dialect variations, fostering awareness of dialects in classrooms, and communicative interactions across cultural groups.

11

Social and Educational Factors Affecting Students' Literacy

Concepts and Terms

-class size
-poverty

OVERVIEW

The cases and commentaries in this chapter discuss social and educational factors that affect students' literacy development, sense of well-being, and feelings of security. Sadly, the number of students living in poverty and unstable home and neighborhood environments is increasing (Richards, 1998a). Besides safety concerns, increasing numbers of students suffer physical, emotional, and sexual abuse (Gipe, 1998). In addition, many classrooms remain overcrowded, challenging teachers to find the time and resources to meet the instructional needs of all students [see Cases 8.1, 8.2, 8.3, 8.4, 8.5, 10.1, 10.2, 10.3, 12.1, 12.2, and 12.3]. Establishing an orderly, safe, risk-free learning environment is conducive to all students' success. Research shows that reading curricula for students of **poverty** and unstable home environments should emphasize comprehension and employ a full range of phonemic, contextual, and knowledge-based cues as aids to constructing meaning (Knapp & Turnbull, 1990). Teachers can engage the assistance of educational specialists—such as social workers, counselors, reading resource teachers, speech therapists, and nurses—to provide crucial guidance, direction, and nurturing for students who need additional support.

Leal, D. (1993). The power of literary peer-group discussions: How children collaboratively negotiate meaning. *The Reading Teacher, 47,* 114–120.

CASE 11.1: MY POOR WHITNEY

Alicia Marx

It is now April, and my semester as a preservice teacher in a first-grade classroom is quite rapidly approaching its end. Whitney is one of my students, a very loving child who is, for the moment, trapped in a shell that neither she nor I can seem to break. Since I first met her, Whitney's work has not changed much, but she has become much more vocal. During literature discussions she has quite often made comments, giving her opinions about stories we have read. Unfortunately, part of her increased vocalism has included her often saying, "She hit me," or "He called me stupid."

You see, the other students virtually ignore Whitney, because they see her as different, so Whitney gets upset and tries to get the other kids in trouble. I continuously praise Whitney and try to offer her encouragement, but I have failed in my attempts to help her. Whitney's reading and writing progress has been very minimal, if at all. Due to project deadlines and time constraints, I increasingly took dictation for her in her journal, but that in itself was a tiresome process. As the journals were passed out, Whitney's eyes would sink, knowing it was time to write. She would sit with her head down for awhile, save the once or twice she lifted it for me to quicken my pace reading journals to other students so that I could read hers to her. After reading to her, and going over each word, in my journal entry to her, she would place her index finger in her mouth and look as though she was about to cry. Silently she would sit and suck on her fingers like a baby with a pacifier, and sometimes, even when I'd tell her, "Please try, I'll help you," she'd cry.

She never stopped saying, "I can't do it" or "I don't know how."

"Yes, you can," I always said, "The date, Dear Miss Marx, and Love, are all written there, all you have to do is copy them."

Sometimes she would act on this and begin an attempt to copy at least the date, but more often she sat and did nothing.

Whitney was happiest when she was drawing. She especially loved to use the markers to draw pictures of herself and her brothers. She did surprisingly well with her creative book. Her artwork was wonderful, and it took a lot less work than I had anticipated to get her to pull a story together. Looking at her picture inside the back cover one would think that Whitney never had a sad thought. However, as wide and bright as her smile was that day, her happiness and laughter quickly turned to sadness and silence when, in her journal, I asked her if she liked to have her picture taken. After I had read my entry to her, she mumbled "Yes," but when I repeated the question to clarify her answer she changed it with one shake of her head, "No."

She sank into sadness again after that, and she did not speak anymore to me that day. It is truly amazing how quickly her mood can change because she is not always depressed, even though I may give that impression.

More recently I asked Whitney in her journal entry how she enjoyed Easter. At first she stared at me and said, "I can't do this."

When I offered her encouragement, she proceeded to react to what another student had said. "I didn't go to anybody's house to visit," she whispered.

I replied, "That's okay. Did the Easter bunny visit and bring you something good?"

"Uh-huh, I got candy for Easter," she mumbled.

Those were pretty much the last words I heard from her. Obviously, I can see that Whitney is afraid to write and, more important, afraid to fail. I have tried to address this specifically in her journal and otherwise, but she will not open up to me and her attitude toward reading and writing, as I've stated already, have yet to change.

There have been bright moments when it appeared the ice may be melting and I'd gotten through to Whitney, but I can't help but worry about her. She still is not receiving even a slight percentage of the one-on-one attention she needs for success [see Case 11.3]. I discovered recently, as she wrote her name on our group mural, that she is still unclear as to the exact spelling of her own name. How can this be? Whitney barely knows the alphabet, she cannot associate letters with their sounds, and she is not capable of reading one word. How can she go on to the second grade (which she will probably be passed on to), much less do well in it? Obviously, the school system is not working for her. What Whitney needs is practice, practice, practice at reading and writing, and someone who can help her to believe in herself. She does not believe she is capable. She thinks she is, as the others say, "stupid." The only solution I can see for the problems affecting Whitney and many other students would be to have more teachers and more classrooms so that there can be fewer students per class. Whitney has had to share her classroom teacher's attention with 31 other students. This teacher/student ratio is unacceptable. Until something changes I have little hope for Whitney and her classmates.

Achilles, C., Finn, J., & Bain, H. (1997/1998). Using class size to reduce the equity gap. *Educational Leadership, 55*(4), 40–43.

CASE 11.1: APPLICATIONS AND REFLECTIONS

What do you think is the purpose of this lesson or series of lessons?

_____

_____

_____

_____

How was the original teaching plan interrupted, or what surprised Alicia?

_____

_____

_____

What actions did Alicia take in response to the interruption/surprise?

_____

_____

_____

Examine the consequences of Alicia's actions. What alternative action(s)/procedures would you suggest?

_____

_____

_____

Identify the resources (e.g., outside readings; conversations with peers, teachers, or other professionals) used by Alicia in this case. What other specific resources might you suggest (e.g., titles of related articles or books, community agencies, etc.)?

_____

_____

_____

From whose perspective is the case written?

_____

_____

_____

_____

What do you think is Whitney's perspective?

_____

_____

_____

Who are the players in the case?

_____

_____

_____

What seems to be working well in this case?

_____

_____

_____

What needs to be improved?

_____

_____

_____

Can you distinguish between the symptoms and the problems presented in this case?

_____

_____

_____

Adapted from Morine-Dershimer, 1996; Shulman, 1996; Silverman & Welty, 1996.

COMMENTARY 11.1A: MY POOR WHITNEY

Karen Parker Guillot, Classroom Teacher
Baton Rouge, Louisiana

Dear Alicia,

I sympathize with your sense of despair in facilitating a major, positive change in Whitney's written work. However, your ability to recognize that she has become more verbal during the semester illustrates your capacity for observing strengths in students. I urge you to concentrate on Whitney's verbal strengths and her drawing ability [see Commentary 11.1B].

Because Whitney has become more verbal, why not provide her with a tape recorder so that she can record her journal entries rather than write them? As she becomes more self-assured, she will become more comfortable with her writing. I wonder what makes her reluctant to write. You stated that the other students see her as different. Does she have a specific problem that has not been addressed in your case? Does she reverse words when she writes? Does she know where to begin writing on a page? Does she understand that we read from left to right?

I think you need to consider how free Whitney feels in the classroom. I have a hunch that Whitney is afraid to take risks. By giving her some freedom to feel secure as she writes, she may begin to enjoy journal writing regardless of any reading and writing problems she may possess.

You also stated that, due to time constraints and project deadlines, you have virtually no time to work on Whitney's specific problems. At Brookstown, an inner-city school where I work, we have been using an approach that we find most helpful for students with reading and writing problems. All of the students eligible for this program, first through third grade, are required to read one on one with an individual every day. Initially, we thought that parents would work with their children, but with many parents working or not interested in participating, this plan wasn't feasible. Thus, at our last teacher in-service, we decided to have other students work with those students who needed extra attention. Therefore, students in my class who need extra help in reading and writing now go into another class every morning (a special education class), and read with a student on a one-to-one basis before we begin our class routines. This really works!

At first, I was worried about my students losing valuable class time. However, I soon realized that during this early morning time students walk in late, buses arrive late, and I need to complete paperwork. Therefore, this is the perfect time for my students to read with the other class. I also discovered that during this time I am able to give one-on-one attention to several of my students who are having problems with math, research projects, or reading activities. If your administration will allow this type of interactivity among classes, a student could work with Whitney. They probably would form a bond that would help Whitney develop some needed self-esteem.

Because Whitney seems to possess a talent for drawing, I would focus on her special artistic ability. I would encourage her to respond to my journal entries by drawing pictures. Then, I would help her write a one-word or simple-sentence response to explain her artwork. You also could reward her when she does her best work by providing her with art equipment and free time to draw and paint. Perhaps you could help her create something special for the class, like a class banner, flag, or mural that could be displayed in the classroom. This would allow her classmates to recognize that Whitney has special talent and that you value her artistic ability.

Alicia, you are extremely astute to notice Whitney's verbal and drawing strengths. As you meet other "Whitneys," you will be ready and able to guide them.

Teale, W., & Labbo, L. (1990). Cross-age reading: A strategy for helping poor readers. *The Reading Teacher, 43,* 362–369.

Whitin, P. (1996). Exploring visual response to literature. *Research in the Teaching of English, 30,* 114–140.

COMMENTARY 11.1B: MY POOR WHITNEY

Suzanne Gespass, Teacher Educator
Rider College, New Jersey

Hello Alicia,

Your description of Whitney's behaviors in various contexts is detailed and thorough, but I am left wanting to know more about her. It is clear that you have provided her with important demonstrations of literacy and encouraged her to participate in many ways. What is significant, however, is that she has made little if any progress over the year.

Students start school with many different experiences, and we cannot expect all of them to reach the same level of achievement at the same time. However, what we can expect is progress from where they started. If, as Whitney's teacher, you are not able to document progress, then I think it's time for you to consult other professionals in the school community to make sure that Whitney gets the help she needs. Going to the reading specialist, the learning consultant, and/or the school psychologist might be the next step. Most schools have established procedures for what to do when teachers are concerned about a particular student.

Your possible solution of having fewer students in the class is certainly an important one. Thirty-two students in a first-grade class is just too many students. There have been several recent studies showing quite convincingly that smaller **class size** does make a difference in student achievement, especially in the elementary grades and for disadvantaged youth (Wenglinsky, 1988).

As with all students, it is essential for you to assess and determine what Whitney can do. Try to document what is going on in those moments when you think you've gotten through to Whitney. You've already determined that she is happiest when she is drawing. See if you can use her artwork as a window to see how she is thinking. You mention that you give Whitney a lot of praise. It is important to be positive, but try to make your praise as specific as possible. Instead of saying, "That's great!" when Whitney shows you a picture she has drawn, ask her to tell you more about it. Try to get her to explain the action in the picture and describe her representations. This will help to develop her self-esteem, sense of story, and oral language.

CASE 11.2: SO SAD, SO SAD

Lynne McDonald

When I first met Corey, he seemed to be just like all of the other students in his group. He was happy to see me, and eager to find out what we would be doing together. He seemed determined to get his share of the attention, and so he joked around with the other students in the group. I went over the group rules with the students. "You will receive only one warning if you break a rule," I explained. "After that, you will be asked to leave the group."

Most of the students in the group realized that I meant what I said, especially after the second class meeting, when we started to settle into our routine. But Corey was determined to see just how far he could go. The first day, I put him out of the group five times.

The second day, I realized that I would probably have to put him out for the entire class, and I was right. The third day, he seemed to get the message and was put out of the group only once. Then, he realized that no one was paying any attention to him when he was out of the group and he *really* craved attention [see Commentary 3.1B].

Since then, he has apparently set out to find new ways to get the attention he craves. When he raises his hand and gets to talk I find that he is reluctant to stop. He goes on and on, rushing his words together so that it is difficult to understand him and get him to conclude. That is not even the worst part—it's not so much how much he says, but what he says. He constantly talks about the death and violence he has seen in his 6 years of life. When we were doing our interest inventory, one of the questions was, "How many brothers and sisters do you have?"

When it was Corey's turn to answer, he said, "I had five brothers, but they all died. I have only one sister now."

He went on to describe, in vivid detail, the funerals, his brothers in coffins, and his mom in tears. I was shocked to learn that this boy had lost most of his family to gang violence. No matter what we talked about in the group, he found a way to connect it to his violent life. Once I asked, "Corey, what is your favorite pet?"

He replied, "I want a dog, to protect me and my mom and sister from the gangs."

I asked, "Where would you go if you could go anywhere in the whole world?

He said, "I would never go to school. I'd be home, safe inside my house with my mom where I belong."

He talks a lot about death and guns and fear. He has eyes that are old and tired, and he is only 6 years old! How do I comfort this child? How do I teach him? So far, I've just been listening. I keep thinking that perhaps this is what he really needs—someone who will listen to his problems, even when there is no way to fix them. So I listen. I read to him and try to bring in pictures from home that will give him and his peers more background knowledge about happy people and pretty places. I bring in Bach's *Brandenburg Concertos* to lift his spirits and mine. From my bag of treats, I pull out scraps of velvet and satin for Corey and his peers to touch and enjoy, and cinnamon sticks for them to smell. I have pictures of mountains and beaches and boats that I share. But is there more I should be doing? Am I allowed to hug him? One of the preservice teachers who taught here last semester said I should be very careful about touching the students. Her classroom teacher told her that hugging students was definitely not allowed. Please tell me that's not true, because students like Corey could use a hug. I know I can't make his life outside school any different, but I would very much like to make every second I have with him count. What should I do?

Kersten, F. (1996). Enhancing stories through use of musical sound. *The Reading Teacher, 49,* 670–671.

CASE 11.2: APPLICATIONS AND REFLECTIONS

What do you think is the purpose of this lesson or series of lessons?

_____

_____

_____

How was the original teaching plan interrupted, or what surprised Lynne?

_____

_____

_____

What actions did Lynne take in response to the interruption/surprise?

_____

_____

_____

Examine the consequences of Lynne's actions. What alternative action(s)/procedures would you suggest?

_____

_____

_____

Identify the resources (e.g., outside readings; conversations with peers, teachers, or other professionals) used by Lynne in this case. What other specific resources might you suggest (e.g., titles of related articles or books, community agencies, etc.)?

_____

_____

_____

From whose perspective is the case written?

_____

_____

_____

_____

What do you think is Corey's perspective?

_____

_____

_____

_____

Who are the players in the case?

_____

_____

_____

_____

What seems to be working well in this case?

_____

_____

_____

_____

What needs to be improved?

_____

_____

_____

_____

Can you distinguish between the symptoms and the problems presented in this case?

_____

_____

_____

_____

Adapted from Morine-Dershimer, 1996; Shulman, 1996; Silverman & Welty, 1996.

COMMENTARY 11.2A: SO SAD, SO SAD

Fredda Fischman, Classroom Teacher
Allentown, Pennsylvania

This teacher's concern to make school a safe haven for her students is well founded, especially for today's troubled youngsters. As well, her awareness that students act out because they desire attention and recognition is insightful and sensitive. However, has anyone ever verified Corey's stories of family death and violence? Has his mother been in contact with the school? Has the guidance counselor or school psychologist been involved? Are the city's social services for children and families aiding what could truly be a severely distressed family in need of family as well as individual counseling? Does this teacher know what type of movies Corey sees, or what television shows he watches, or the music he is exposed to at home? All of these cultural/media influences, especially if they are unchecked by adults, could upset and distress any young child.

Does the teacher know anything about Corey's home life and the adults or other neighbors or children in his immediate environment? If Corey's life story is one of such drama and terrible tragedy, this teacher needs to work with the school guidance counselor and art therapy personnel to provide Corey with other outlets besides verbal expression to describe and work out his anxieties and fears. He also might want to work in clay, or with Legos, to portray and come to grips with the "monsters" and the anger in his life.

The issue of teachers touching or hugging students is especially sensitive in our current political and social climate. A student can always sit next to the teacher for personal contact if hugging is forbidden. The teacher also might bring in her own favorite stuffed animal for Corey to hug and protect; Corey may even have his own best silent stuffed friend that he could bring to school.

Dramatic role playing may be another avenue to explore with Corey. This teacher might involve other students in role playing their perceptions of life and learning.

No content can be taught or learned when the student is so personally consumed by either real or imagined scary events. The best thing this teacher can do is to try to help Corey sort the real from the imagined, using all the support personnel and help available. Corey needs to be heard and attended to. He also needs to get on with his life and his schooling, especially because he is so young.

COMMENTARY 11.2B: SO SAD, SO SAD

Margaret Genesio, Teacher Educator
University of Wisconsin

Dear Lynne,

You are a caring teacher with so much to give to your students. Corey is lucky to be with you. My first and most important teaching position was in a neighborhood like Corey's, in the southeast Anacostia area of Washington, DC, at Ketcham Elementary School, just two blocks down from the dilapidated Frederick Douglass Home. I, too, thought that if I could only hold my students to sooth their burdens, they would be saved! I was 20, and these thoughts soon faded to reality—I had to be proactive and an advocate for learning and living in this community. My students were all latchkey kids. The keys they had actually hung around their necks on strings. This didn't signify much, because sometimes when they went home some families actually had moved to another apartment somewhere!

I once saw Gloria Talbert, age eight, come to school on a January morning wearing open-toed, sling-backed, high-healed pumps, without socks because that was all she could find in her house to put on her feet. She tramped three blocks in ice and sleet to get to school. Ice was embedded between her toes! She wanted a hug and she also wanted to be with a community of learners—the community we had established in our classroom.

I found that in order to really help my students, I had to get close to their community. I worked in ways that positioned me to give something back to the Ketcham School neighborhood so that I had an authentic stance from which to work. I worked with developing groups that targeted the Frederick Douglass Home, Neighborhood Watch, the Police Athletic League (PAL). I also wrote several grants, one of which targeted use of part of the nearby high school gym as an after school homework/arts/sports center for Ketcham students.

My advice for you is to continue to see brilliance within Corey. Facilitate that brilliance; help it become reality by working with Corey to aid him in taking the risks necessary to be comfortable outside of his apartment and away from his mother and sister—with you and his allies at school. I suggest that you become an advocate for Corey's neighborhood and those neighborhoods from which your other students come. I can tell that you are a caring and wise teacher, and I know that you will refrain from pitying your students, thinking that they will fail, and viewing yourself as a savior—one who will infuse new knowledge into a decaying place.

A wonderful way to engage Corey's determination to survive is to capture his determination at school. Cooperative learning and collaborative experiences will help Corey become part of his classroom family. Pair your students with each other as they experience book making, buddy reading, readers theatre, and mural constructions of the stories they have heard or read together. Encourage interaction, the formation of strong peer relationships, and the use of cross-grade activities. Cross-grade activities that aim to develop bonding of an older child with a younger child from the same neighborhood also lay the foundation for these partnerships to continue outside of the school boundaries. Try some of the following cross-grade activities: letter exchanges, art exchanges, readers theatre, and recreational reading. Help to develop a mentoring system at your school so that younger students like Corey know that older students are looking out for them at school and on the way home. Discuss the possibility of having this mentoring continue during lunchtime.

Involving parents was terribly hard for me at Ketcham School. I wrote a grant that dovetailed onto the Title I program already in place. This small grant, totaling $10,000, was awarded and funded the startup of a parent liaison program. We hired several part-time liaison/parents whose job it was to communicate directly with neighbors to let them know what was going on at school; that report cards were coming home; or that there would be an open house, a potluck supper, a talent show, an after-school program in the gym, or a meeting with the District of Columbia Park District to talk about the Frederick Douglass Home. You can look into these same kinds of activities and become an active participant in the neighborhood in which you teach. Ask your School Board Grants Office about the possibility of funding availability for a parent/liaison program. Be part of a committee that hires parents who will be liaisons. They must be from the neighborhood in which Cory lives or a similar one, because these are the neighborhoods with the strongest need! Even if the liaisons do not own cars, if they reside in Corey's neighborhood they can walk to visit their neighbors, just like they do now!

Let me compliment you on your desire to provide a good learning environment for Corey. Your fervor and your pain are apparent to me. I commend you on your sensitive concern for Cory. He is ready to venture outside of his home into the safe, collaborative, giving, exciting, and stimulating environment of his classroom. You are genuinely a part of the learning experience with your students. Corey will flourish by your side with his new family, his newfound freedom, and his love of life and learning.

Johnson, D., Johnson, R., Stevahn, L., & Hodne, P. (1997). The three C's of safe schools. *Educational Leadership, 55*(2), 6–13.

CASE 11.3: NARDARIUS

Rebecca Clemens

There is a little boy in my second-grade group named Nardarius. At first, I thought he was a typical boy—curious and into everything. But, as time went on, Nardarius began to miss quite a few of our sessions because he was in ISS (in-school suspension). I asked him why he got sent to ISS and he answered, "I don't know because I don't do anything bad."

Now, he is considered the problem child in the classroom. He will not do anything and he does not listen to anyone. The thing that I can't figure out is what is wrong with Nardarius. Every time I meet my group of students I try to talk to him first to give him extra attention. For example, I always ask him, "How are you today, Nardarius?"

He rarely answers me, and he often stares off into space. Last week we had special adult readers come to class and he didn't pay any attention to them. He made noises and "cut up." He strummed on a rubber band. I told him, "Please pay attention!" I knew that if he acted badly it would reflect on the classroom teacher, because the reader was an administrator from the school board.

When we created our mural, Nardarius' behavior was intolerable. He did not want to participate in any way. At first I thought that he was afraid to draw but, after thinking about his behavior, I realize that Nardarius always acts inappropriately, regardless of the activity. I cannot believe that he acts this way because he is lazy. I do know that he makes my life very hard. I want to include him in our group but no matter what I try, it fails. After we have finished reading our story for the day and we have completed our literature and prediction logs, we sometimes read the story aloud as a choral reading activity. Most students really enjoy this, but not Nardarius. I always ask him, "Do you want to read or tell us about your favorite part of the story?"

Nardarius always answers, "I don't want to do anything."

Then he acts up and disturbs us. I have grown so tired of sending him out of the group. It doesn't work, anyway.

Our drama presentation is coming up soon. We have discussed it and Nardarius says that he isn't interested. I am completely at a loss! I have never met a student like him.

He finally was back in the group last week after being in ISS the two previous meetings. I noticed that he had a new haircut. I complimented him and said, "Ooh, I like your new haircut. It looks very nice."

His answer was, "It looks stupid and I hate it."

The problem is that I don't know what to do about Nardarius. I'm sure that over the years I will teach other students like him. I do know that ISS isn't the answer. What else can a teacher do to help students like Nardarius?

CASE 11.3: APPLICATIONS AND REFLECTIONS

What do you think is the purpose of this lesson or series of lessons?

_____

_____

_____

_____

How was the original teaching plan interrupted, or what surprised Rebecca?

_____

_____

_____

What actions did Rebecca take in response to the interruption/surprise?

_____

_____

_____

Examine the consequences of Rebecca's actions. What alternative action(s)/procedures would you suggest?

_____

_____

_____

Identify the resources (e.g., outside readings; conversations with peers, teachers, or other professionals) used by Rebecca in this case. What other specific resources might you suggest (e.g., titles of related articles or books, community agencies, etc.)?

_____

_____

_____

From whose perspective is the case written?

_____

_____

_____

_____

What do you think is Nardarius' perspective?

_____

_____

_____

_____

Who are the players in the case?

_____

_____

_____

_____

What seems to be working well in this case?

_____

_____

_____

_____

What needs to be improved?

_____

_____

_____

_____

Can you distinguish between the symptoms and the problems presented in this case?

_____

_____

_____

_____

Adapted from Morine-Dershimer, 1996; Shulman, 1996; Silverman & Welty, 1996.

COMMENTARY 11.3A: NARDARIUS

David Clarke, Classroom Teacher
New Orleans, Louisiana

In my 9 years of teaching in an alternative, urban school, I've taught many students like Nardarius. This past year I worked with a student named Kevin who, in many ways, reminds me of Nardarius. Kevin was an extremely bright student, but he never wanted to do any work. All he wanted to do was play with his friends, hang out, and tell jokes. His efforts in class were always disappointing to me. So, Rebecca, I can empathize with your feelings of frustration.

Early in the school year, I discovered that Kevin loved to draw [see chap. 9 and Case 11.1]. I do a lot of process writing with my students (prewriting, first draft, editing, etc.), and instead of participating in our writing activities, all Kevin did was draw beautiful, intricate pictures. Unfortunately, his artwork often did not correspond to our writing assignments. I also noticed that Kevin loved to entertain his peers by telling funny stories and acting out his drawings in great detail.

Gardner, H., & Hatch, T. (1989). Multiple intelligences go to school: Educational implications of the theory of multiple intelligences. *Educational Researcher, 18*(8), 4–8.

Following Howard Gardner's conceptions about learners' multiple intelligences (1983), I encouraged Kevin to illustrate his ideas about our writing topics. I also allowed him to perform his work for his peers' enjoyment and information. Then, I began to urge Kevin to jot down some of his ideas so that he could polish and improve his dramatic performances. As the school year progressed, Kevin became more motivated to complete at least some of our assignments. He never did produce a large quantity of writing; however, over the course of the school year, his writing abilities and his motivation to write improved tremendously. In addition, he began to participate in other learning activities as long as I allowed him to decide how he would handle an assignment. For example, instead of writing a 2-page paper, he would choose to write a 1-page paper and then illustrate his writing on a second sheet of paper.

As you know, Rebecca, every student has special interests and talents. I suggest that you discover those of Nardarius. At the same time, it would be helpful if you gave Nardarius some leeway as to how he will complete assignments. For example, after Nardarius told you that he hated his new haircut, you could have asked him to write about what type of haircut he would have preferred. In addition, he might draw a comic strip depicting his trip to the barber shop, or he could create a mural illustrating his emotions about having to cut his hair.

I am concerned that Nardarius may be experiencing difficulties at home. Check with your school guidance counselor or social worker. Call Nardarius' parents to try to discover what's going on. Make a home visit [see Commentary 3.2B]. Home visits are so valuable. Telephone Nardarius weekly—not to complain about his lack of motivation, but to compliment him on the work he has accomplished during the week. In addition, check to make sure that Nardarius does not have a health, learning, or emotional problem. Above all, don't give up on Nardarius—keep trying to figure out how to motivate him.

In closing, I must tell you that I believe placing students in ISS produces what I call "decreasing results." Some students enjoy ISS because they become the focus of peers' attention and they can get out of class for the day or longer. Other students become angry at their teacher if they are sent to ISS. They carry this anger around with them and then become increasingly more difficult to handle in the classroom. Be fair, firm, and consistent. Have high expectations for all of your students, and always try to handle your own discipline problems. Your students will appreciate your care and concern, and they will want to try to please you.

COMMENTARY 11.3B: NARDARIUS

Nancy Masztal, Teacher Educator
University of Southern Mississippi

After reading this case, I have many questions. Have Nardarius' hearing, vision, and overall physical health been checked? I'd start there in trying to put together this puzzle, because I've found that students who appear negative and hostile may often have some physical problem that is causing distress. I also wonder if the classroom teacher has administered an informal reading inventory to determine Nardarius' approximate reading level [see Commentary 5.3B]. Can he read? Perhaps Nardarius has a learning disability that impacts his literacy performance. Does he refuse to contribute to literacy learning activities because he can't read or write? Rebecca needs to determine Nardarius' reading and writing proficiencies as a precursor to understanding why Nardarius avoids schoolwork.

Rebecca also needs to get to know Nardarius. What is he interested in? I've never met a second-grade boy who wasn't interested in something (e.g., bikes, football, snakes, Nintendo, pizza, etc.). What are his favorite pastimes? In addition, I suggest that Rebecca make a home visit for a parent conference. Are Nardarius' parents aware of his unwillingness to participate in discussions, art activities, drama productions, and reading and writing lessons? Is his negativity about schoolwork of recent origin, or has Nardarius always resisted participating in learning? Is there some home or neighborhood situation affecting Nardarius (e.g., an abusive parent, drug or alcohol abuse, a stressful environment)? I also question the classroom climate. Has the classroom teacher set up a democratic, student-centered classroom where every student knows he or she is a valuable, valued, and productive member of the class? It's a sad fact that students may act hostile and negative because they are treated unfairly in classrooms.

I do have some suggestions. I think that Rebecca might consider putting Nardarius in charge of some "important" class activity or event [see Commentary 4.2B]. For example, she might choose Nardarius as the stage manager of their upcoming drama production. He also could be the person to select a committee to work on the next group mural. He might choose a book for his learning group to read, or perhaps he could choose the next field trip destination from a listing of approved excursions. These types of "important" jobs would get Nardarius into the habit of doing rather than not doing.

Finally, I question the value of in-school suspension [see Commentary 11.3A]. Sitting in ISS obviously hasn't helped Nardarius become a productive member of the class. In fact, I think that ISS is contributing to Nardarius' negative and hostile feelings. There are no good role models in ISS, only pessimistic students who have learned that school is not always a fair place.

Brookhart, S., & Rusnak, T. (1993). A pedagogy of enrichment, not poverty: Successful lessons of exemplary urban teachers. *Journal of Teacher Education, 44*(1), 17–26.

SUGGESTED READINGS

Jacobs, M., Beane, A., & Malone, B. (1996). Addressing security needs of students. *Educational Horizons, 74*(3), 120–123.

This article is based on legal principles that define "safe place" as an obligation of school personnel to provide a place for students in which all reasonable danger has been removed. In safe classrooms there are fair discipline policies, and students are helped to understand their thinking and feeling processes.

Johnston, J. (1989). *Class size and life in second grade classrooms: A Project Star progress report.* Nashville: Tennessee State Department of Education (ERIC Reproduction Document NO ED 312 079).

Teachers' perceptions of their experiences in small classes are discussed as part of a 4-year longitudinal study. Teacher interviews clearly reveal that fewer students in the classroom contributed to significant improvements in student learning.

Knapp, M., & Turnbull, B. (1990). *Better schooling for the children of poverty: Alternatives to conventional wisdom. Study of academic instruction for disadvantaged students* (Volume I). Washington, DC: Department of Education, Office of Planning, Budget, and Evaluation.

This document summarizes a 3-year study of curriculum and instruction in elementary schools serving high concentrations of students who live in poverty. Implications are that teachers should provide teacher-directed and learner-directed instruction, vary grouping arrangements, and offer adjustments to classroom management according to the academic work being done [see the overview to chap. 3]. Furthermore, teachers should emphasize the knowledge that students bring to school, and accentuate meaning and understanding in all academic work.

12

Providing for Students' Varying Literacy Abilities

Literacy Concepts and Terms

-differential reading instruction
-informal assessment
-integrated curriculum
-literature-based curriculum
-trade books

OVERVIEW

The cases and commentaries in this chapter highlight meeting the instructional needs of students with varied literacy abilities. Beginning teachers are challenged to find ways to differentiate reading and writing lessons. Teachers can maximize student involvement and enhance students' reading achievements through such methods as pairing a proficient and a struggling reader together, and creating opportunities for students to interact with older students and adults through cross-grade and community partner book buddy experiences [see Commentaries 2.1A and 2.1B]. Teachers also can provide ample opportunities for all students to engage in artistic expression so that they can respond to text ideas and events in their preferred modes of learning and through their special aptitudes [see Commentary 5.2A and Cases 9.1 and 9.2]. In addition, teachers can tape reading materials and form literacy discussion groups so that all students can share their ideas and opinions in a risk-free environment.

Teale, W., & Labbo, L. (1990). Cross-age reading: A strategy for helping poor readers. *The Reading Teacher, 43,* 362–369.

CASE 12.1: ADAPTING TO MEET ALL STUDENTS' NEEDS

Karyn Pennison

I am working in a first-grade classroom with a group of five boys and three girls. When I first started meeting with the kids, I thought that they had similar abilities in reading and writing. However, as I have continued to work with them, it has become clear that I was wrong. I have two (Jesse and Jordan) who are very good readers, writers, and spellers; one (Elaina) who is in the middle; and two (Taylore and Lisa) who have difficulty reading, writing, and spelling. Once I realized that the students had different abilities, I also realized that my lessons were either frustrating the students who have difficulty or boring the two more advanced students. A dilemma surfaced: How do I create lessons that meet the needs of all five students without frustrating the two who have difficulty, boring the two more advanced students, or neglecting the student in the middle?

One recent lesson illustrates the differences in my students' abilities. I read the book *Trains* by Gail Gibbons (1987), and then I gave the students precut sentence parts to put together to make sentences. I told them that the sentences did not have to be the same ones that were in the book, but that the capital letter pieces had to start the sentence and the pieces with a period at the end had to be at the end of the sentence.

Jesse immediately constructed sentences that made sense, but he would not follow the rule of having the piece with the capital letter at the beginning of the sentence. Jordan took awhile to make sentences because he was helping Lisa and Taylore find the pieces they wanted. He followed the rules and created sentences that made sense. Taylore made two sentences after receiving some help with finding pieces, but she kept asking me, "Does this make sense?"

I told her to write her sentence on the board and the group would decide if it made sense. Her sentences were strange. For example, one of her sentences was, "Freight trains carry food that moves on again." Elaina seemed to have difficulty and took a long time, but I think it was because she wanted to make sure her sentence was right. This is typical behavior for her. She also kept asking me, "Miss Karyn, does this make sense?"

Lisa had the most trouble. After the other students had started, she was just sitting there staring at the pieces. She told me, "I don't understand how to do this."

I explained it to her again. Then she made up sentences in her head and tried to find the pieces to go with that sentence. She said, "I need the piece that says, 'The train' on it."

When she could not find the pieces to match her sentence, she became frustrated. Jordan helped her find some pieces, but her final sentence did not make sense. While Lisa and Elaina were taking a long time to make their sentences, the other students became bored and started playing and talking loudly. The lesson ran smoother after we started looking at the sentences the group had made. This lesson made me realize that I needed to adapt my lessons to accommodate my students' varying abilities.

I did present one lesson in which I was able to take advantage of my students' differing abilities. I read a book and then, after some activities, had my students write words on a dry erase board. Jordan and Jesse began to help the students who were having trouble spelling, and Lisa and Taylore made progress in their spelling during the course of the lesson. This lesson went very well. Jesse and Jordan wanted to help the other three students. Each kept asking me to let him be the one to help. The three girls are used to asking Jesse and Jordan for spelling help, so they welcomed it. I realize from my experience that letting students help each other is a good idea for dealing with students' varying abilities, but how can I incorporate this into more lessons? Not every lesson lends itself to having the students help each other. How can I create lessons that help students who have more difficulty but don't bore the more advanced students?

I have found several possible ideas for dealing with this dilemma. One suggestion is to pair students, but I have five of them. Would this work with a group of three and a group of two? Another idea is to offer thematic units on topics that interest my students. The last suggestion is to integrate music with reading and writing [see Case 9.2]. I have learned about this in another class, but I never thought about using it in this class. Will any of these ideas work? Are there other ideas out there for handling this situation? I also

MacGillvray, L., & Hawes, S. (1994). "I don't know what I'm doing—they all start with B." First graders negotiate peer reading interactions. *The Reading Teacher, 48,* 210–217.

have found out that there is an ERIC document titled *How to Differentiate Instruction in Mixed-Ability Classrooms* by Carol Ann Tomlinson (1995). I need to find it. (Note: This work is discussed in the suggested readings at the end of this chapter.) The abstract made it sound very helpful. Will all these ideas be enough to help me meet students' varied abilities? How other teachers handle their students' varying abilities?

Dickinson, D., & diGisi, L. (1998). The many rewards of a literacy-rich classroom. *Educational Leadership, 55*(6), 23–26.

CASE 12.1: APPLICATIONS AND REFLECTIONS

What do you think is the purpose of this lesson or series of lessons?

_____

_____

_____

How was the original teaching plan interrupted, or what surprised Karyn?

_____

_____

_____

What actions did Karyn take in response to the interruption/surprise?

_____

_____

_____

Examine the consequences of Karyn's actions. What alternative action(s)/procedures would you suggest?

_____

_____

_____

_____

Identify the resources (e.g., outside readings; conversations with peers, teachers, or other professionals) used by Karyn in this case. What other specific resources might you suggest (e.g., titles of related articles or books, community agencies, etc.)?

_____

_____

_____

_____

From whose perspective is the case written?

_____

_____

_____

_____

What do you think are these first graders' perspectives?

_____

_____

_____

_____

Who are the players in the case?

_____

_____

_____

_____

What seems to be working well in this case?

_____

_____

_____

_____

What needs to be improved?

_____

_____

_____

_____

Can you distinguish between the symptoms and the problems presented in this case?

_____

_____

_____

_____

Adapted from Morine-Dershimer, 1996; Shulman, 1996; Silverman & Welty, 1996.

COMMENTARY 12.1A: ADAPTING TO MEET ALL STUDENTS' NEEDS

Marilyn McKinney, Teacher Educator
University of Nevada, Las Vegas

Dear Karyn,

The challenge of meeting the needs of all students is a situation that every teacher faces on a daily basis. I am curious about how this group of students was originally organized. Was it interest in the book topic? What assessments were used to determine students' variations in reading abilities? Did you use **informal assessments,** such as observations or a developmental spelling inventory? After assessing what students actually can do, you might be more prepared to meet their individual literacy learning needs.

I'm also curious about the purpose of the lesson—putting sentences together from words in the Gail Gibbons story you read to them. Perhaps part of the problem may have been that your students didn't understand why they were required to perform this task. Was it to practice and build sight vocabulary? Was it to reinforce sense-making when creating sentences? Was it to practice language conventions, such as starting sentences with capital letters? Although you were attempting to reinforce the idea that capital letters go at the beginning of sentences and periods go at the end of sentences, perhaps that direction was too confining for your students. For example, some students wanted to create sentences that weren't in the book. Other students found it too difficult to put several words together that made sense. I assume this was because many of the words were not in their sight word or reading vocabulary. Perhaps you could have supplied extra capital letters and periods on cards to assist your students in creating their own original sentences. I also suggest having blank cards available so that your students can use them to write and add words of their own to their sentences.

I suggest varying the way this activity is carried out. Students love to write on the board, as you discovered in your lesson. They could write their sentences on the board, create their own books with illustrations, or add words from their own word banks to words from the story. Students could tape record their sentences for other students to listen to and reconstruct.

You mentioned that the situation became easier when your group began to look at their sentences and analyze them. To me, this suggests that they found this task engaging, partly because they were involved in a meaningful activity. Thus, as you noted, the trick is to keep kids involved. This happens best when authentic literacy activities are offered and when students understand the purposes for lessons. In fact, there could have been multiple purposes for the lesson, depending on each of your individual student's abilities and learning needs. Those who were easily able to put words together into sentences could have been encouraged to compose other stories and then examine Gail Gibbons' sentence structures in relation to their own. For students needing different kinds of practice, you could plan different, equally engaging activities.

The fact that your students learned from talking and helping each other suggests that you created a safe learning environment. I encourage you to continue finding ways for students to work together according to their interests.

COMMENTARY 12.1B: ADAPTING TO MEET ALL STUDENTS' NEEDS

Mary Gobert, classroom teacher
Hancock County, Mississippi

Dear Karyn,

You have touched my heart with a first-grade story, because I taught first grade for 12 years. At all grade levels there are students with varied literacy abilities. However, I believe that first graders are especially receptive to teachers' suggestions, so be sure to use that to your advantage!

The peer tutoring that goes on in your class is a great idea. Regardless of your students' variances in literacy abilities, do you try to find things in which each student can excel, and do you have them share that knowledge with peers? Look hard for students' special talents [see Cases 9.1 and 9.2]. They're there, and it's so good for students' self-esteem when they can display their knowledge and share their special understanding. Your students need to believe that Jesse and Jordan are not the only "smart ones" in the group, nor do they have all the answers. For example, I've had kids who were barely able to read but could find a word in the dictionary faster than anyone. Some had beautiful handwriting. Others excelled in artistic talent [see Cases 9.1 and 9.2].

You can break up your small group into even smaller groups through pairing, but make sure you know the specific purpose you have in mind. Mix the three/two combination of student grouping in different ways to capitalize on the strengths of each student. Group according to students' interests, temperament, needs, abilities, and so on [see the Overview to chap. 3]. Give your students free choice sometimes, if it suits your purpose and doesn't become a popularity contest. Avoid feelings of competition, but encourage a spirit of cooperation.

You ask if thematic units will work. The answer is—always! Using thematic units allows you to modify all activities from remediation to enrichment, and include all disciplines of learning, such as the music aspect you mentioned. Themes should be very diverse and address the interests of your students. Your high achievers will go where their needs take them if you provide an adequate base from which they can choose. While they are off exploring independently, you can be guiding your less able little ones to competency in their underdeveloped areas through the discovery learning process. Go for it big time!

Now I am going to give some unsolicited advice. Drop that sentence construction activity as it is, or do a lot of modeling before attempting it again! What was your purpose? There were too many rules, too much confusion, and there was too much pressure on some of your students!

The best advice I can give is to love those little ones. They'll do cartwheels for you.

See *Book Links* (a magazine that connects books and classroom activities). July issues are cumulative index issues. *Book Links* is published bimonthly by Booklist Publications, an imprint of the American Library Association.

Altwerger, B., & Flores, B. (1994). Theme cycles: Creating communities of learners. *Primary Voices K–6, 2*(1), 2–6. (Entire issue is on theme cycles.)

CASE 12.2: TOO SMART FOR ME

Colleen Vizzini

Anderson, V., & Bereiter, C. (1975). Sentence tic-tac-toe. In *Thinking games, book 1, ages 5–9* (p. 5). Toronto: The Ontario Institute for Studies in Education.

After 8 weeks of working with my four third graders, I've learned that one of my students catches on quicker and finishes written work ahead of the other students. Josh definitely needs more challenges in reading and language arts.

My students have participated in a **literature-based curriculum,** and I think that they have learned a lot. But Josh isn't getting as much out of our time together as the other students are. For instance, Josh won the game every time In the sentence tic-tac-toe activity. While he was spelling sentences that made sense, my other students were still struggling with the meanings of the words. I didn't know what to do with Josh after that. Should I have given him a book to read while the other students were still trying to create meaningful sentences? I almost feel that giving Josh another activity to do is more of a punishment than a prize. Josh asked, "Can I write on the board?" So I asked him to write some ways that we could keep peace in the classroom, because this involved the theme of a book that we had recently read.

In another lesson, I reread a story so that my students could point out words that were unfamiliar to them and their respective context clues. Each student except Josh found at least two words they didn't know. Josh knew all of the words, so he didn't learn anything in this activity and I wasted his time. I'm certain he knew all of the words and their meanings, because all I could think of to do was to ask him to define the meanings of the words, which he easily accomplished. Should I have done that?

Ever since I noticed Josh's capabilities I've been thinking of ways to challenge him without hampering the entire group. How do I present literacy lessons so that eveyone is challenged? Is it okay to have different explanations for different students? What will the other students think if Josh does work that's more challenging than theirs? How will Josh feel if I ask him to do something that's not expected of the other students?

CASE 12.2: APPLICATIONS AND REFLECTIONS

What do you think is the purpose of this lesson or series of lessons?

_____

_____

_____

_____

How was the original teaching plan interrupted, or what surprised Colleen?

_____

_____

_____

_____

What actions did Colleen take in response to the interruption/surprise?

_____

_____

_____

_____

Examine the consequences of Colleen's actions. What alternative action(s)/procedures would you suggest?

_____

_____

_____

_____

Identify the resources (e.g., outside readings; conversations with peers, teachers, or other professionals) used by Colleen in this case. What other specific resources might you suggest (e.g., titles of related articles or books, community agencies, etc.)?

_____

_____

_____

_____

From whose perspective is the case written?

_____

_____

_____

_____

What do you think are these first graders' and Josh's perspectives?

_____

_____

_____

_____

Who are the players in the case?

_____

_____

_____

_____

What seems to be working well in this case?

_____

_____

_____

_____

What needs to be improved?

_____

_____

_____

_____

Can you distinguish between the symptoms and the problems presented in this case?

_____

_____

_____

_____

Adapted from Morine-Dershimer, 1996; Shulman, 1996; Silverman & Welty, 1996.

COMMENTARY 12.2A: TOO SMART FOR ME

Jill Lewis, Teacher Educator
New Jersey State University

Dear Colleen,

Josh is fortunate that he has you as his teacher. You recognize that he is advanced, and you are willing to make instructional modifications for him. Many classrooms are heterogeneously grouped. Therefore, the situation you describe is very common. But rest assured, there are some things you can do so that Josh's needs are met without making him feel that he is being penalized for being ahead of the other students in language arts literacy.

To begin with, you will want to spend some time closely observing other students in your classroom. You may find that there are a few more as talented as Josh in language arts, but who have found ways to avoid looking "smart." (Sometimes kids do this so as not to intimidate their friends.) See whether you have a student who seems to be working extremely slowly, but who makes few mistakes and doesn't appear to be struggling with the work. Also, look for students who might be doing work on their own (such as reading a book, drawing, writing extra sentences, etc.) but who haven't asked for other work as Josh did when he asked to write on the board. If you find one or two other very bright students, they can be grouped for classwork that is identical in activity to what the rest of the class is doing, but with more challenging material.

There are other possible solutions. You need to recognize that Josh is aware of his "difference." He doesn't know what to do about it, but he knows he is bored and would like to be learning new material or at least doing an activity that is more interesting to him. The other students also are aware of his "difference." They will not be surprised at all if you give Josh an alternative assignment.

Students like Josh are capable of working independently for long periods of time. They often have unique and multiple interests, and you can capitalize on these interests to create new learning experiences for Josh. You were on the right track when you gave Josh a special assignment to write some ways that everyone could keep peace in the classroom. However, this might not have been the best assignment for him to do, as it could be construed as putting him in the position of being a "know it all."

So let's talk about what you could do that might help Josh learn without causing psychological distance from his classmates. The first order of business is to contact Josh's parents to let them know that you are aware of Josh's special needs and that you would like to provide for them by planning some special projects with Josh. Assuming they agree, you next need to meet with Josh to discuss your concerns and develop an action plan with him. He can assist you in designing a project he would like to do during those instances when you feel he'd be wasting his time on a class activity. You can reach an agreement with him that during those times he can either work quietly in the classroom on his project or he can go to the library. The project can be an extension of something being studied in class, or something for which he is using more advanced skills related to ones for which the rest of the class is getting additional practice, such as honing research skills or writing adventure stories or letters.

Josh will need to be accountable for completing assignments within the time limits you set, performing up to his ability, asking for assistance as needed, and reporting to you periodically about his progress. If his work is related to areas the class has studied, he would probably benefit from sharing his project with his classmates. They might enjoy the new information he has researched and would be learning, too!

This kind of approach to the dilemma of students like Josh has several benefits. It enables them to work at their ability, utilizes their interests, builds their independence, develops their self-esteem, and keeps them interested in school and learning. Additionally, you will feel that you are meeting the needs of all of your students, including those who already know the material you are expected to teach.

COMMENTARY 12.2B: TOO SMART FOR ME

Tom Nass, Classroom Teacher
Waterloo, Iowa

Dear Colleen,

Every classroom has students who are exactly like Josh, and it's these students who make teaching challenging. To recognize that Josh needs more of a challenge in the classroom is a true sign of an effective teacher. One of the many joys of teaching involves meeting the individual literacy learning needs of every student in the classroom.

It's obvious that Josh is academically ahead of the other students in his group of four. The gap is quite wide. Who is benefiting from this gap? I would rearrange the groups so that Josh can work with other students on the same level. However, be flexible—Josh needs to interact with all of the students in the class, not just the brighter ones.

Clearly define what students are expected to do in the group. Consider using cooperative learning strategies. Assign a role to each student and give clear, concise directions that promote group cooperation. This model does not happen instantly. Time, guidance, and teacher modeling must be provided for your students.

When Josh asked, "Can I write on the board?" he demonstrated interest in learning. Be thankful that he chooses to be involved instead of acting out with inappropriate behavior [see Cases 3.1, 3.2, and 3.3].

I am wondering if Josh is a gifted student. If so, is a gifted education teacher available for Josh? Additionally, making contact with Josh's parents is a good idea. They would appreciate knowing that you have recognized his abilities and are willing to address his academic needs.

You can help meet Josh's learning needs. First, have a mini-conference with him and let him know that you have high expectations for his literacy achievements. Then, determine his particular strengths and learning needs and go from there. Enrich and expand Josh's literacy lessons by incorporating higher-order skills based on Bloom's taxonomy (1984) [see Commentary 12.3A], and Gardner's multiple intelligences (1983). Incorporate **trade books** that expand Josh's vocabulary and comprehension. Integrate technology and the visual and performing arts into his lessons [see Commentary 5.2A and Case 9.2]. As you start to see success with Josh, you will want to begin enriching and extending all of your lessons so that all of your students will be challenged.

CASE 12.3: A CHALLENGE WHEN THE WORK IS LESS CHALLENGING

Karyn Pennison

I work in a first-grade classroom with six students: three girls and three boys. I sure had an idealistic view of teaching when I started. As a preservice teacher with no teaching experience, I knew that problems would arise. But I was not prepared for Jesse!

Early on, Jesse showed me that he would be a challenge. During our second session, I read a book to the group and asked them to write about their favorite parts. Jesse refused and said, "I don't like that book."

Dr. Gipe suggested that he write about why he didn't like the book. Jesse took her suggestion and wrote a beautifully crafted opinion piece. Thus, I decided that the problem was solved—give Jesse choices and he would participate in our lessons. For example, after reading a book about pets to the group, I asked them to write about pets and Jesse immediately wrote about a Black Widow spider that he wanted to buy.

As the semester has progressed I have discovered that Jesse is more of a challenge when the work is less challenging. For example, I asked the students to create their own story, using a wordless picture book as inspiration. Jesse said, "I'm not doing that." Instead, he wrote a story about Beavis and Butthead.

At the next session, I had the students design *All About Me* books. Again, Jesse did not follow directions. Instead, he wrote a book about a movie he recently had seen. Furthermore, even though the other students were still writing, he deliberately began to disturb them by reading his completed story aloud in a very shrill voice.

I do notice that when the assignments are more of a challenge, Jesse wants to participate. One day I read a book and we did word sorting, using some words in the book. After the students did some simple categorical word-sorting activities, I asked them to pick out the nouns in the group of words. Jesse immediately volunteered to do that activity and he did a great job.

I know that Jesse is bright and talented, because he has very well-developed writing and drawing abilities. The problem is that I do not know how to design activities that will interest and challenge Jesse. I also need to keep in mind the abilities of the other students in the group. What is the best way to handle this? How can I develop reading and language arts activities that suit the needs of all of the students? In the past, I had always assumed that students with academic difficulties would be more of a challenge for me. Jesse has proven me wrong!

Fresch, M., & Wheaton, A. (1997). Sort, search, and discover: Spelling in the child-centered classroom. *The Reading Teacher, 51,* 20–31.

CASE 12.3: APPLICATIONS AND REFLECTIONS

What do you think is the purpose of this lesson or series of lessons?

_____

_____

_____

_____

How was the original teaching plan interrupted, or what surprised Karyn?

_____

_____

_____

_____

What actions did Karyn take in response to the interruption/surprise?

_____

_____

_____

_____

Examine the consequences of Karyn's actions. What alternative action(s)/procedures would you suggest?

_____

_____

_____

_____

Identify the resources (e.g., outside readings, conversations with peers, teachers, or other professionals) used by Karyn in this case. What other specific resources might you suggest (e.g., titles of related articles or books, community agencies, etc.)?

_____

_____

_____

_____

From whose perspective is the case written?

_____

_____

_____

_____

What do you think is Jesse's perspective?

_____

_____

_____

_____

Who are the players in the case?

_____

_____

_____

_____

What seems to be working well in this case?

_____

_____

_____

_____

What needs to be improved?

_____

_____

_____

_____

Can you distinguish between the symptoms and the problems presented in this case?

_____

_____

_____

_____

Adapted from Morine-Dershimer, 1996; Shulman, 1996; Silverman & Welty, 1996.

COMMENTARY 12.3A:
A CHALLENGE WHEN THE WORK IS LESS CHALLENGING

Kathryn Carr, Teacher Educator
Central Missouri State University

Hi Karyn,

It is not surprising that a bright and independent student like Jesse would pose a problem. You are to be congratulated on your observations that led you to identify the fact that Jesse works best when he is challenged and given choices.

Your school's gifted program is an obvious source of help for you and Jesse. But regardless of whether Jesse is receiving services from a gifted program, there are many exciting learning activities that exceptional students can do within a regular classroom setting. These types of activities also can enrich the learning environment of all students in your group. Multilevel instruction is important for meeting the wide range of student abilities in any classroom. Following are some suggestions for planning and implementing multilevel activities that will challenge some students to higher-level thinking and allow others to work at their own level on the same topic.

Differentiated reading instruction begins by carefully considering your objectives for students' learning (i.e., what you want students to gain from the experience). I find that Bloom's taxonomy of the cognitive domain (1984) is useful for planning multilevel objectives and instructional activities. When you form the habit of asking yourself, "What would students do at the analysis level, the synthesis level, and the evaluation level?" it becomes easier to design multilevel lessons that foster critical and creative thinking—which is just what Jesse needs.

Language arts activities are more purposeful to students when they are integrated with literature and/or content subjects. For a literature example, listening to several different trade books on a theme or listening to different versions of a folk tale gives students opportunities to compare and contrast in group discussions and through writing.

Implementing an **integrated curriculum** by teaching through broad thematic units is an excellent way to individualize instruction; incorporate higher-level thinking in the curriculum; and integrate reading, writing, and literature with social studies and science. The resulting hands-on projects give students real reasons to read and write, and help them see the connections across subjects.

For example, first graders might have a unit on birds that would incorporate many objectives for language arts and science. A teacher might begin the unit with a K-W-L lesson on birds [see Case 4.3 and Commentaries 4.3A and 4.3B]. The teacher uses a chart to jot down students' collective knowledge about birds. Then, students could list their questions about birds. Pairs of students would then choose to research the answers to one or two questions listed. Ultimately, after listing and categorizing what they have learned, students might create a book about birds with illustrations of pictures cut from magazines. Advanced students might write a paragraph or two. Jesse might decide to include the migratory routes of certain birds, or he might classify certain birds by genus and phylum. When he shares this information, all students would benefit.

I doubt that Jesse will continue to be openly defiant if you give him choices and appropriately challenging activities. But, if so, you might have a private discussion with him. Tell him that you have important reasons for assignments and although you will make every effort to accommodate him, there will be times when you need and expect his cooperation [see Commentary 12.3B]. Perhaps you could work out a secret code as a way for Jesse to let you know that he would like to negotiate a different activity.

COMMENTARY 12.3B:
A CHALLENGE WHEN THE WORK IS LESS CHALLENGING

Elizabeth Pickell, Classroom Teacher
Warrensburg, Missouri

Hello Karyn,

Jesse sounds like the kind of bright and interesting student whom you will someday see as the sunshine of your life. Each year I hope for at least one student who will challenge me to be the best teacher I can be. However, the bright free-thinker is often the one whom teachers consider a problem, because there are few resources and little research to provide teachers with support and guidance for dealing with this type of student. I would first ask myself how important conformity of writing assignments is to the objective of the lesson. Usually, lesson objectives can be met in more than one way. For example, the assignment to design *All About Me* books might have been of great interest to Jesse if grade-level-appropriate books on anatomy had been available to use as a resource. Jesse certainly would have designed a different book than the other students, but his book would have been well within the objective of the lesson and probably would have greatly interested the other students. By offering some choices and giving students some control, Jesse might have completed at least part of the intended assignment, and other students might have gone way beyond your expectations.

How to make assignments more challenging for Jesse seems to be the major focus of your dilemma. When writing your lesson plans, try to think of ways to extend, enhance, or involve aspects of the arts with writing; for example, as music, dance, creative dramatics, visual art, oral interpretations, or choral reading before your students begin a writing activity [see chap. 9]. Then, vary the types of writing assignments and allow students a choice in how the assignments will be completed, such as extending a story, writing a skit, or providing a personal opinion. Limit the number of choices for each assignment, because some students will get bogged down making decisions about what to do and they may not get to the assignment.

I also would spend some instructional time teaching Jesse and your other students how to use semantic maps, and how to engage in K-W-L activities [see Case 4.3, and Commentaries 4.3A and 4.3B]. Semantic webs and K-W-L activities provide opportunities for students to list what they know about a given topic, and also to discern what they might need to find out.

I would demand that Jesse not disturb and interfere with the learning of other students. Providing Jesse with a tape recorder so that he can practice reading and then listening to his completed stories might keep him busy when he finishes his work before the other students.

If Jesse continues to resist conforming to assignments, I suggest that you have a discussion with him regarding your need for his cooperation. I would then develop a contract that lays out the frequency of assignments to which Jesse must conform. I also might initiate dialogue journaling with Jesse so that he could communicate his feelings privately to me [see Commentary 3.1B].

I think that Jesse is a bright, talented young man who will blossom into a skilled writer. Continue to provide him with many resources and opportunities for developing his interests, and count your lucky stars that you have Jesse in your classroom.

Ogle, D. (1986). K-W-L: A teaching model that develops active reading of expository text. *The Reading Teacher, 39,* 564–570.

Weissman, K. (1996). Using paragraph frames to complete a K-W-L. *The Reading Teacher, 50,* 271–272.

Bryan, J. (1998). K-W-W-L: Questioning the known. *The Reading Teacher, 51,* 618–620.

Sippola, A. (1995). K-W-L-S. *The Reading Teacher, 48,* 542–543.

SUGGESTED READINGS

Conway, A., & Coyle, D. (1993). *Differentiation—taking the initiative.* Bedfordbury, England: Center for Information on Language Teaching and Research.
This easy-to-read manual provides an overview of some of the major, complex issues associated with providing differentiated language learning instruction. The authors explain that differentiation places emphasis on the requirements of individual learners. Explicit suggestions for differentiating instruction in reading, speaking, and listening skills are offered.

Elbaum, B., Bayta, E., Shay, J., & Vaugn, S. (1997). Urban middle-elementary students' perceptions of grouping formats for reading instruction. *Elementary School Journal, 97*(5), 475–500.

This survey investigates third-, fourth-, and fifth-grade urban, minority students' perceptions of reading groups. Whole-class instruction and working alone were used more frequently than group or pair instruction. Students at all levels of reading ability, regardless of grade or gender, liked mixed-ability groups and mixed-ability pairs, followed by whole-class instruction.

Popp, M. (1996). *Teaching language and literature in elementary classrooms: A resource book for professional development.* Mahwah, NJ: Lawrence Erlbaum Associates.

Throughout, the text supplies innovative ideas and resources for meeting the needs of students with varying reading and language arts abilities, including those with learning disabilities, limited English proficiencies, hearing problems, and wide ranges in reading comprehension and interests.

Tomlinson, C. (1995). *How to differentiate instruction in mixed-ability classrooms.* Alexandria, VA: Association for Supervision and Curriculum. (ERIC Reproduction Document Service No. ED 386 301)

This 11-chapter booklet provides teachers with ideas for creating learning environments that address typical classroom diversities in students' learning styles and abilities. The booklet defines differentiated instruction, explains why differentiated instruction is appropriate for all learners, discusses how to plan and manage differentiated instruction, and shows how to assess students' progress.

References

Allard, H., & Marshall, J. (1985). *Miss Nelson is missing.* Boston: Houghton Mifflin.

Anderson, H. (1985). *The princess and the pea.* New York: North-South.

Atwell, N. (1998). *In the middle: New understandings about writing, reading, and learning* (2nd ed.). Portsmouth, NH: Heinemann.

Au, K. (1979). Using the experience-text-relationship with minority children. *The Reading Teacher, 32,* 677–679.

Au, K. (1993). *Literacy instruction in multicultural settings.* Ft. Worth, TX: Harcourt Brace Jovanovich.

Avery, C. (1992). Guide students' choices. Ready to write. *Instructor, 102*(4), 32.

Banks, K. (1988). *Alphabet soup.* New York: Knopf.

Barnitz, J. (1998). Literacy instruction in linguistically diverse classrooms. In J. Gipe, *Multiple paths to literacy: Corrective reading techniques for classroom teachers* (4th ed., pp. 340–359). Upper Saddle River, NJ: Prentice Hall.

Barton, B. (1991). *The three bears.* New York: HarperCollins.

Bloom, B. S. (Ed.). (1984). *Taxonomy of educational objectives, Book I: Cognitive domain.* White Plains, NY: Longman.

Bolton, F., & Snowball, D. (1996). *Teaching spelling: A practical resource.* Portsmouth, NH: Heinemann.

Braithwaite, E. (1990), *To sir, with love.* New York: Jove.

Bratcher, S. (1997). *The learning to write process in elementary classrooms.* Mahwah, NJ: Lawrence Erlbaum Associates.

Brett, J. (1987). *Goldilocks and the three bears.* New York: Dodd Mead.

Brock, B., & Grady, M. (1996, August). *Beginning teacher induction programs.* Paper presented at the National Council of Professors in Educational Administration, Corpus Christi, TX. (ERIC Document No. ED 399 631)

Carle, E. (1987). *The very hungry caterpillar.* New York: Philomel.

Carle, E. (1989). *Animals animals.* New York: Scholastic.

Carle, E. (1995). *The very lonely firefly.* New York: Philomel.

Carle, E. (1997). *Flora and tiger (19 very short stories from my life).* New York: Philomel.

Cecil, M., & Lauritsen, P. (1994). *Literacy and the arts for the integrated classroom: Alternative ways of knowing.* New York: Longman.

Cohen, E. (1994). *Designing group work.* New York: Teachers College Press.

Collins, J. (1994). *Dialogue and resistance in small group reading-writing instruction.* (ERIC Document reproductive Service No. ED371 306)

Conway, A., & Coyle, D. (1993). *Differentiation—taking the initiative.* Bedfordbury, England: Center for Information on Language Teaching and Research.

Cullinan, B. (1993). *Children's voices: Talk in the classroom.* Newark, DE: International Reading Association.

Cunningham, P. (1994a). *Making big words: Multilevel hands on spelling and phonics activities.* Columbus, OH: Good Apple.

Cunningham, P. (1994b). *Making words: Multilevel hands on developmentally appropriate spelling and phonics activities.* Columbus, OH: Good Apple.

Cunningham, P. (1995). *Phonics they use* (2nd ed.). New York: HarperCollins.

Daniel, P. (1996). A celebration of literacy: Nine reluctant students and one determined teacher. *Language Arts, 73,* 420–428.

Daniels, H. (1991). Commentary on chapter 5 (teaching writing to students at-risk for academic failure). In B. Means, C. Chalmers, & M. Knapp (Eds.), *Teaching advanced skills to at-risk students: Views from research and practice* (pp. 168–175). San Francisco: Jossey-Bass.

Educational Leadership. (December, 1992/January, 1993). Themed issue: Students at risk.

Eggleston, E. (1984). *The Hoosier schoolmaster.* Bloomington: Indiana University Press.

Elbaum, B., Bayta, E., Shay, J., & Vaugn, S. (1997). Urban middle-elementary students' perceptions of grouping formats for reading instruction. *Elementary School Journal, 97*(2), 475–500.

Five, C. (1992). *Special voices.* Portsmouth, NH: Heinemann.

Flemming, D. (1993). *In the small, small pond.* New York: Holt.

Freeman, D. (1993). *Corduroy.* New York: Puffin.

Gardner, H. (1983). *Frames of mind: The theory of multiple intelligences.* New York: Basic.

Gauch, P. (1997). Letting go to a story: A study based on Eric Carle's Flora and Tiger. *Book Links, 1*(2), 16–19. (EJ 554 175)

Gayle, S. (1997). *The little red hen.* New York: GT.

Gestwicki, C. (1995). *Developmentally appropriate practice: Curriculum and development in early childhood education,* Boston: Delmar.

Gibbons, G. (1987). *Trains.* New York: Holiday House.

Gibbs, J. (1987). *Tribes: A process for social development and cooperative learning.* Santa Rosa, CA: Center Source.

Gilbert, S. (1996). *Hawk hill.* San Francisco: Chronicle.

Gill, C., & Scharer, P. (1996). Why do they get it on Friday and misspell it in Monday?: Teachers inquiring about their students as spellers. *Language Arts, 73*(2), 89–96.

Gipe, J. (1998). *Multiple paths to literacy: Corrective reading techniques for the classroom teacher* (4th ed.). Upper Saddle River, NJ: Prentice Hall.

Goodman, Y., Altwerger, B., & Marek, A. (1991). *Print awareness in preschool children..* Tucson: University of Arizona.

Harrington, H., & Hodson, L. (1993, April). *Cases and teacher development.* Paper presented at the annual meeting of the American Educational Research Association, Atlanta.

Harris, T. L., & Hodges, R. E. (Eds.). (1995). *The literacy dictionary: The vocabulary of reading and writing.* Newark, DE: International Reading Association.

Heath, S. B. (1983). *Ways with words: Language, life, and work in communities and classrooms.* Cambridge, UK: Cambridge University Press.

Hilton, J. (1986). *Goodbye Mr. Chips.* New York: Bantam.

Hubbard, R. (1996). *Workshop of the possible: Nurturing children's creative development.* York, ME: Stenhouse.

Hunter, E. (1994). *The blackboard jungle.* Cutchogue, NY: Buccaneer.

Jacobs, M., Beane, A., & Malone, B. (1996). Addressing security needs of students. *Educational Horizons, 74*(3), 120–123.

Jalongo, M. (1995). Promoting active listening in the classroom. *Childhood Education, 72,* 13–18.

Johnston, J. (1989). *Class size and life in second grade classrooms: A Project Star project report.* Nashville: Tennessee State Department of Education. (ERIC Reproduction Document Service No. ED 312 079)

Katz, W. (1996). *Out of the dark.* Old Tappan, NJ: Simon & Schuster.

Kiley, M., & Thomas, B. (1994, February). *Concerns of beginning, middle, and secondary school teachers.* Paper presented at the annual meeting of the Eastern Educational Research Association, Sarasota, FL.

Kincaid, L. (1983). *The three little pigs.* Windermere, FL: Rourke.

Knapp, M., & Turnbull, B. (1990). *Better schooling for the children of poverty: Alternatives to conventional wisdom. Study of academic instruction for Disadvantaged Students* (Volume I). Washington, DC: Department of Education, Office of Planning, Budget, and Evaluation.

Krashen, S. (1987). *Principles and practice in second language acquisition.* Englewood Cliffs, NJ: Prentice Hall.

Kucer, S. (1995). Guiding bilingual students "through" the literacy process. *Language Arts, 72*(1), 20–29.

Laminack, L., & Wood, K. (1996). *Spelling in use: Looking closely at spelling in whole language classrooms.* Urbana, IL: National Council of Teachers of English.

McCaleb, S. (1994). *Building communities of learners: A collaboration among teachers, students, families, and community.* Mahwah, NJ: Lawrence Erlbaum Associates.

McCloskey, R. (1993). *Make way for ducklings.* New York: Puffin.

McInnis, P. (1996). *A guide to readiness and reading: Language processing and blending.* Penn Yan, NY: Tillman.

Merseth, K. (1991). The early history of case-based instruction: Insights for teacher education. *Journal of Teacher Education, 42*(4), 243–249.

Mitchell, M. (1993). *Uncle Jed's barber shop.* New York: Simon and Schuster.

Moll, L. (1993). *Vygotsky and education: Instructional implications and applications of sociohistorical psychology.* New York: Cambridge University Press.

Morine-Dershimer, G. (1996). What's in a case ... and what comes out? In J. Colbert, K. Trimble, & P. Desberg (Eds.), *The case for education* (pp. 99–123). Boston: Allyn & Bacon.

Morris, D. (1982). Word sort: A categorization strategy for improving word recognition ability. *Reading Psychology, 3,* 247–259.

Morrow, L. (1996). *Motivating reading and writing in diverse classrooms: Social and physical contexts in a literature-based program* (NCTE Research Report No. 28). Urbana, IL: National Council of Teachers of English.

Munro, J. (1997). *The case in teacher education: Guidelines for writing cases and using them to train teachers* [on-line]. Available: http://www.abacon.com/customcase/.

National Council of Teachers of English and Whole Language Umbrella. (Eds.). (1997). *Teacher inquiry: Reading matters* (elementary section). Urbana, IL: Authors.

Ng, M., Guthrie, J., McCann, A., Van Meter, P., & Solomon, A. (1996, Summer). *How do classroom characteristics influence intrinsic motivations for literacy?* (Reading Research Report No. 56). Athens, GA: National Reading Research Center, Universities of Georgia and Maryland.

Norton, D. (1997). *The effective teaching of language arts* (5th ed.). Upper Saddle River, NJ: Prentice Hall.

Noyce, R. M., & Christie, J. F. (1989). *Integrating reading and writing instruction in grades K–8.* Boston: Allyn & Bacon.

Pace, N. (1995). *Music as a way of knowing.* Los Angeles: Stenhouse (The Galef Institute).

Padgett, R. (1997). *Creative reading: What it is, how to do it, and why.* Urbana, IL: National Council of Teachers of English.

Paley, V. (1990). *The boy who would be a helicopter: The uses of storytelling in the classroom.* Cambridge, MA: Harvard University Press.

Paratore, J., & McCormick, R. (1998). *Peer talk in the classroom.* Newark, DE: International Reading Association.

Patton, F. (1954). *Good morning, Miss Dove.* New York: Dodd, Mead.

Polacco, P. (1996). *I can hear the sun.* New York: Philomel.

Popp, M. (1996). *Teaching language and literature in elementary classrooms: A resource book for professional development.* Mahwah, NJ: Lawrence Erlbaum Associates.

Rhodes, L., & Dudley-Marling, C. (1996). *Readers and writers with a difference: A holistic approach to teaching struggling readers and writers* (2nd ed.). Portsmouth, NH: Heinemann.

Richards, J. C. (1998a). The analytic teacher. In J. Gipe, *Multiple paths to literacy: Corrective reading techniques for classroom teachers* (4th ed., pp. 42–58). Upper Saddle River, NJ: Prentice Hall.

Richards, J. C. (1998b). The reading/writing connection. In J. Gipe, *Multiple paths to literacy: Corrective reading techniques for classroom teachers* (4th ed., pp. 142–167). Upper Saddle River, NJ: Prentice Hall.

Robeck, M., & Wallace, R. (1990). *The psychology of reading: An interdisciplinary approach* (2nd ed.). Hillsdale, NJ: Lawrence Erlbaum Associates.

San Souci, R. (1996) *Young Guinevere.* New York: Dell.

Scieszka, J. (1989). *The true story of the three little pigs.* New York: Viking Kestrel.

Sendak, M. (1988). *Where the wild things are.* New York: HarperCollins.

Shulman, J. (Ed.). (1992). *Case methods in teacher education.* New York: Teachers College Press.

Shulman, J. (1993). *Tips on writing cases.* San Francisco: Far West Laboratory for Educational Research and Development.

Shulman, J. (1996). Tender feelings, hidden thoughts: Confronting bias, innocence, and racism through case discussions. In J. Colbert, K. Trimble, & P. Desberg (Eds.), *The case for education* (pp. 137–158). Boston: Allyn & Bacon.

Shulman, L. (1992). Toward a pedagogy of cases. In J. Shulman (Ed.), *Case methods in teacher education* (pp. 1–30). New York: Teachers College Press.

Sierra, J. (1992). *The elephant's wrestling match.* New York: Dutton Child Books.

Silverman, R., & Welty, W. (1996). Teaching without a net: Using cases in teacher education. In J. Colbert, K. Trimble, & P. Desberg (Eds.), *The case for education* (pp. 159–171). Boston: Allyn & Bacon.

Spark, M. (1989). *The prime of Miss Jean Brodie.* New York: NAL-Dutton.

Stevens, J. (1995). *The three billy goats gruff.* San Diego: Harcourt Brace.

Strickland, D., & Morrow, L. (1989). *Emerging literacy: Young children learn to read and write.* Newark, DE: International Reading Association.

Sykes, G. (1992). Foreword. In J. Shulman (Ed.), *Case methods in teacher education* (pp. vii–ix). New York: Teachers College Press.

Sykes, G., & Bird, T. (1992). Teacher education and the case idea. In G. Grant (Ed.), *Review of research in education, 18,* 457–521.

Tomlinson, M. (1995). *How to differentiate instruction in mixed-ability classrooms.* Alexandria, VA: Association for Supervision and Curriculum. (ERIC Reproduction Document Service No. ED 386 301)

Tompkins, G. (1998). *Language arts: Content and teaching strategies.* Upper Saddle River, NJ: Prentice Hall.

Wassermann, S. (1994). Using cases to study teaching. *Phi Delta Kappan, 75*(8), 602–611.

Wenglinsky, H. (1988). *A policy information memorandum: The effect of class size on achievement: What the research says* [on-line]. Available: www.ets.org/research/pic/memorandum.htl.

White, C. (1990). *Jevon doesn't sit in the back anymore.* New York: Scholastic.

Wigfield, A. (1997, January). Children's reading motivations. *NRRC News: A Newsletter of the National Reading Research Group,* pp. 1–2.

Wilde, S. (1992). *You kan red this!* Portsmouth, NH: Heinemann.

Wildsmith, B. (1975). *Squirrels.* New York: Watts.

Wolfram, W., Adger, C., & Christian, D. (1999). *Dialects in schools and communities.* Mahwah, NJ: Lawrence Erlbaum Associates.

Zeichner, K. (1983). Alternative paradigms of teacher education. *Journal of Teacher Education, 34*(3), 3–9.

Index